A Collection of Canadian Plays
Volume 3

Bastet Books. Toronto. 1973

With the completion of "A Collection of Canadian Plays — Volume III", the first phase of our publishing program comes to an end. This set of three volumes represents the works of 15 Canadian authors, 21 plays in all. In selecting the plays we have attempted to give as broad as possible a representation, both geographical and in terms of the different approaches.

We have used in many instances actual stage photographs to illustrate these works, but whenever the character of the play required it, we used art illustrations as well as art photography. By this method we have succeeded in introducing, along with our authors, some artists whom we consider to be an equally important part of a series of this nature.

We do not claim, and we have never claimed this set to be an anthology. Our intention from the beginning was to create the basis for a Canadian theatrical library which then, with our future volumes as well as the many very valuable books distributed by other publishers, will create and indeed already does create, an impressive documentation of our national theatrical achievements.

Many vitally important areas, however, are still not adequately covered, and as we plan the next set — again consisting of three books — we will attempt to cover some of them. One volume will contain plays written for children and young people. Since this kind of play is seldom full length, we will probably have an opportunity to introduce more than the usual 5 authors to our readers. It is our intention to use children's illustrations as much as possible.

A very significant contribution made by our authors whose mother tongue is French is as yet not adequately represented in English translation or adaptation. One volume of the next set will consist of the works of some of these authors. The third book of the set will be the reverse, where a selected group of English-speaking authors will be translated into French to make their work available to the many million French-speaking Canadians and their theatrical organizations.

We will continue to follow our established practice whereby all authors' works will be available in single soft-cover editions simultaneously, just as they have been in the past.

R. K.

Bastet Books are published and distributed by Simon & Pierre, Publishers, P.O. Box 280, Adelaide Street Postal Station, Toronto M5C 1J0, Ontario.

Publishing Editor	Rolf Kalman
Assistant to the Publishing Editor	Catherine P. Wilson
Associate Editor	Marian M. Wilson
Staff Writer	Jean Stewart Hannant
Designed by	Design Workshop
Cover Artist	Nancy De Boni

Printed and bound in Canada by T. H. Best Printing Company Limited

ISBN 0-88924-000-0

Marsh Hay

Merrill Denison

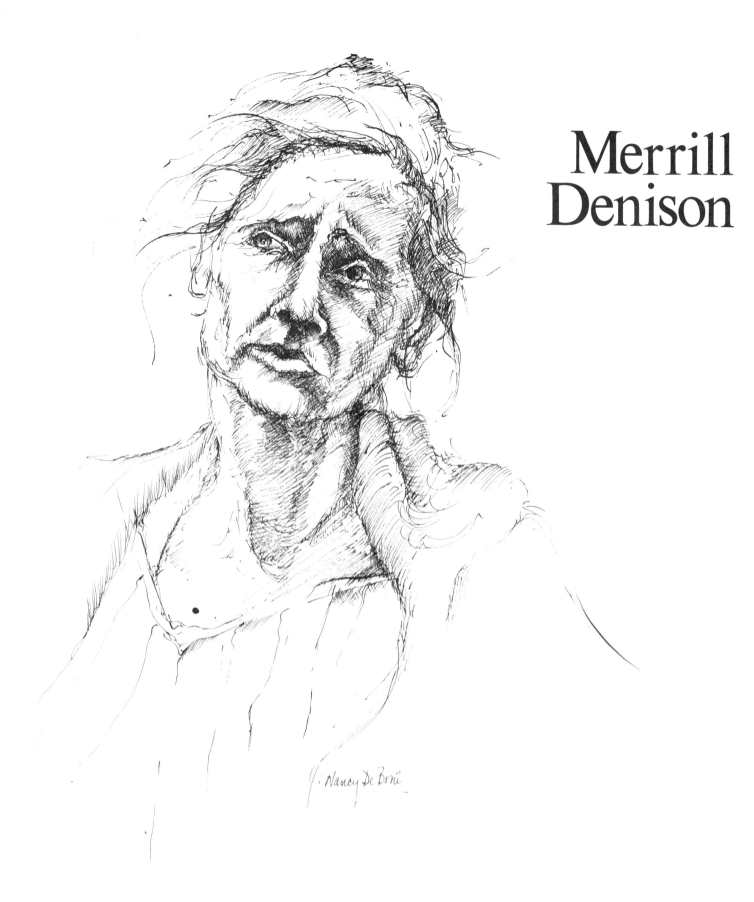

Nancy De Boni

Portrait by Joseph Oppenheimer
Courtesy of The Arts & Letters Club
Photograph by Bishop

Protest is a popular activity in these times and we tend to forget that we did not invent it. Some people are rebels before they are born, and writer Merrill Denison is one of them. His very birthplace was decided by protest when his suffragette mother went to Detroit for her confinement so that her child would not be born under the Crown. He carried on this tradition when at the age of eight he was sent home from school for refusing to say the Lord's Prayer, in protest against the merger of Church and State. This was followed a few years later when he published a rebel paper — "Little Vesuvius" — at Jarvis Collegiate Institute in Toronto in protest (again) against the school's decree that boys and girls could not walk to and from school together. (He won his point). In fact, it may fairly be said that practically everything Merrill Denison has accomplished in a long and fruitful life has been done out of some form of protest. Let no one make the mistake, however, of thinking that he was just another angry young radical protesting against *everything*. As intelligent and well educated as he was, Merrill Denison had a special target: he fought, and is still fighting, against the injustice and misery which inevitably obtains when the rosy wash of romanticism is laid over the practical and often grim realities of life. Small wonder that his literary heroes were H. L. Mencken and George Bernard Shaw.

To say that Merrill Denison is the grand old man of Canadian theatrical literature admittedly is to employ a time-worn chiche; yet, like all such cliches, it contains a hard core of truth. Furthermore, in his case, it is not time-worn but time-honoured: Merrill Denison *is* a grand old man, and his contribution to the wealth of Canadian dramatic literature is not only legendary but also incalculably valuable.

The special quality of Merrill Denison's kind of protest lies in his inherent sense of fair play, and his refusal either to deplore or condone. He has little use for "folk heroes"; to him, the truly heroic were the honest hard-working men and women who, though beaten down by nature and circumstance, nevertheless fought to stay on their land and work it. He was the champion of integrity and the enemy of hypocrisy. His best-known plays are pungent commentaries on the inter-relationships between country and city folk, particularly in rural Ontario; but the playwright never fails to make it clear that he holds no brief for either group and that prejudices and other grave faults — as well as much that is admirable and good — lie on both sides.

"Brothers in Arms" — possibly his most famous play — and "Marsh Hay" were both written in the early twenties and are especially expressive of the double-edged satire at which Merrill

sequential confusion: tours de force of well-nigh insupportable boredom . . .". He therefore put his own monumental talents to work and produced "The Romance of Canada", a series of twenty-six radio plays directed by none other than Tyrone Guthrie. He later acquired a solid reputation as a corporation historian by chronicling the histories of such prestigious companies as Massey-Harris, Molson, Robert Simpson and CCM.

Needless to say, a man of such stature must have had unusual family influences. In the case of Merrill Denison, there is no doubt that he owes a great deal to his redoubtable mother who, if not necessarily the fore-runner of Women's Lib, was certainly in the vanguard of women's rights. She campaigned tirelessly for such things as equal pay for equal work, and enthusiastically championed the cause of birth control as a realistic means of combatting poverty, lack of education and criminal abortion. While she did nothing to discourage her son in his literary efforts, he is the first to admit that she influenced him enormously in human terms, and that much of his dramatic characterization was based on her indomitable personality. She was herself a writer, and an ardent conservationist. The family bought a huge tract of land around Bon Echo in 1911, and the people of Canada can now be grateful to Merrill Denison not only for his impressive literary gifts but also for the fact that Bon Echo is now a provincial park.

A vast collection of published and unpublished manuscripts, histories, scripts, letters and articles now known as the Merrill Denison papers were acquired in 1969 by Queen's University at Kingston, Ontario — an encouraging sign that perhaps things are changing in the literary climate of this country. It is surely inescapably significant that the very protests which inspired most of Merrill Denison's work were the instrument of his neglect by the Canadian public at large. It is only now that we are beginning to realize that this great writer's vision is as true today as it was many years ago, and that all that "Marsh Hay" says to us is as valid and current now as it was when it was written.

Denison excels. Yet, while the former has been given approximately fifteen hundred productions, and is still being produced, "Marsh Hay" has never been performed. This play, written in seventeen hours, sprang from the author's deepest feelings about certain aspects of Ontario rural life. It takes a long, hard look at the socio-economic climate of the times, which created an atmosphere of grim hopelessness from which few people ever managed — or in fact tried — to escape; it struck, perhaps, too close to home for the comfort of any potential audience. An extremely interesting, though unfounded, rumour has it, however, that the play found its way to Kiev in the late twenties, where certainly no such sensitivity could have existed. However, as far as Canada was concerned, if it was not performed, it was most definitely read, and in its printed form had considerable influence on the temper of the times.

In yet another area of protest — the lamentable lack of truly inspiring Canadian historical texts — Merrill Denison's own words best express his feelings: " . . . veritable masterpieces of incon-

In this, Merrill Denison's eightieth year, we are proud to present "Marsh Hay" in this volume on the fiftieth anniversary of its first publication.

With the beautiful drawings used to illustrate "Marsh Hay", we introduce the work of Nancy De Boni, a 29-year-old Toronto artist who was educated at Jarvis Collegiate Institute and the Ontario College of Art. She had the distinction of having a one-man show at Toronto's Gallery 76 immediately following her graduation from O.C.A.

An unusual feature of this young artist's work is her ability to portray worn-out middle age and grinding poverty with a deep and delicate feeling far beyond her years or personal experience. On the subject of her own drawings, Nancy speaks of "capturing life through the subjects' faces and gestures." That she succeeds most admirably is well proven through the series of drawings she has created for "Marsh Hay".

Cast of characters is omitted since the author introduces them in order of appearance.

An August day at dusk.

The kitchen living-room of a backwoods farm-house. Squalid and dirty. A twisted lithograph, hanging on the side wall, gives a hint of the indifference, the tragic futility of the lives lived here. At the back are two windows, one on either side of the door. Many of the lights are covered with newspaper. Beneath the window to the right is a bench with a tin wash basin on it. A string of towelling hangs from a nail in the door jamb. To the left, a door leads into the other downstairs room and opposite it a staircase debouches three or four steps into the room. In the corner between the doors is a stove. Loose pieces of cordwood lie scattered on the floor near it. In the center of the room is a table, its near end loaded with the refuse of a half eaten meal, its head near the rear door.

At the left side of the table are seated Tessie, a girl of twenty and her younger sister Sarilin, four years younger in age but much less in development. Jo, the youngest boy, is seated at the opposite side of the table. All three are eating hurriedly and silently. Lena, the wife, bends over the stove. She is a woman of forty-two, tired, crushed and worn out. She puts a stick of wood in the stove, turns and watches the children for an instant, hopelessly, and goes to the rear door, which she opens. The children pay no attention to her.

Lena: Pete! Pete! Peter! *(She waits and calls again)* Peter!

Sarilin: What's she want Pete for?

Jo: He went to see if paw was over at Andy Barnood's.

Sarilin: What's she want paw for?

Jo: His supper, I guess.

Tessie: *(Rising and going to the tea pot on the stove)* I'd let him starve. *(She pours a cup of tea)* Wasn't he looking for hay, to-day?

Jo: He says there ain't much this year.

Tessie: *(Sitting down)* What there is someone gets before him. It's his own fault. Maw!

Lena: *(Turning from the doorway)* I don't know what's keepin Pete or where your paw is. He's late.

Tessie: Sit down, Maw, and have your supper. They'll come when they're hungry.

Lena: Everythin will be cold.

Tessie: What if it is? It won't kill him if he has to eat a cold meal. Sit down, Maw. *(Lena turns to the door and looks out again.)*

Jo: He mightn't come back to-night at all.

Sarilin: I wished he wouldn't.

Tessie: So's you could stay out all night, I suppose?

Sarilin: *(Doggedly)* Well if you can . . .

Tessie: *(In an angry whisper)* You keep your little mouth shut about what I do or I'll . . . *(Lena turns)*

Lena: Jo, I wish you'd go and see where Pete is and perhaps you might see your paw comin.

(Jo pushes his chair back, rises and slouches out the door.)

Sarilin: You go out every night whenever you want to. I ain't let do a thing. It ain't fair.

Lena: You're too young to be runnin around nights. Your paw don't like it.

Tessie: *(Scornfully)* Paw? He don't care what we do.

Sarilin: You'd find out if he cared if he knew you was out with Tom Roche every night.

Lena: You know your paw don't hold with the Roches, Tessie. He ain't spoke to old Hank for fifteen years.

Tessie: That ain't my fault.

Lena: He'll be awful angry when he finds out. You're only makin trouble for yourself and all of us to get your paw angry. I don't know what he'll do when he finds out.

Tessie: I don't care what he'll do. He's got you to slave for him. He ain't goin to have me, too. You'd do better to look after that young one than bother about me.

(Tessie rises, throws back her chair defiantly and marches into the other room. Lena watches her go and turns aimlessly to the stove.)

Sarilin: Everybody does what they want but me.

Lena: (Wearily) You're too young . . .

Sarilin: I'm almost sixteen.

Lena: Your paw don't like you to run round.

Sarilin: Paw don't like us to do nothin. It don't make no difference to him but he won't let nobody have no fun. He never has done hisself and he don't know what it is.

(Pete, a year younger than Saralin, a cheerless boy, comes in.)

Lena: Did you see your paw?

Pete: I seen him crossin the back fields. (He throws his hat into a corner and drops into a seat.)

Lena: Where've you been?

Pete: I was talkin to Tom Roche and Walt. (Sarilin gets up and goes to the window.)

Lena: Get up outa your paw's chair. Saralin!

Saralin: (Turning slowly) What is it, maw?

Lena: Clear your paw's place there.

(Saralin listlessly clears a space at the end of the table simply by shoving dirty dishes away. Lena hurriedly examines the pot on the stove and puts in another piece of wood. The door opens and John Serang comes in. He is about forty-five, a powerful, loosely knit man. He closes the door, hangs his hat behind it and turns to the wash-basin. The atmosphere is noticeably more heavy. The others are silent while he turns from the towel. He has a characteristic, half twisted smile. An unwholesome smile, because it is so viciously discerning.)

Lena: (Awkwardly) You're late.

John: (Savagely) I'm late, am I?

Lena: (Soothingly) It's almost dark.

John: You might be late too if you'd walked twenty miles lookin for hay and not find a damned marsh that had enough on it to winter a cat.

Lena: Did you try in there back of Mink Lake? (John walks over to the chair at the head of the table.)

John: Yes. And Duck Lake and Little Mud Lake. Every marsh in the township. Where they ain't dried up, they've been drowned by the beavers. There ain't enough marsh hay in the country to bother cuttin; let alone haulin out. (He sits down and tilts his chair back, long arms bracing him. Sarilin and Pete have retreated as far from their father as possible.)

Lena: You'd best have somethun to eat, anyways. What'll we do for the cattle if there's no marsh hay?

John: We'll let them starve or get rid of 'em. What else can we do? Buy hay at thirty dollars a ton?

Lena: (Placing a plate in front of him, soothingly) If you'd just take your food and get finished. You're late now.

John: (Dropping his chair to the floor and pushing the plate from him) Food?

Lena: (Still quietly) It's what we've all had.

John: And it's all there is, I suppose. Ast a man to eat that after walkin twenty miles through the bush. It ain't a fit meal for a man. Sarilin! Get me some tea. (Sarilin obeys and Jo slips in the door.)

Lena: It's just what we've always had, John. I can't see why . . .

John: Just what we've always had. The same rotten victuals, year in and year out.

Lena: *(Doing her best to avoid trouble)* You must've had a hard walk.

John: *(Angrily)* And this is what I come back to. Rotten . . .

Lena: *(With suppressed anger)* Rotten, are they? Who gets them . . . eh? Why can't we have any better . . . eh? Livin from hand to mouth on fifty acres of grey stone and fifty acres of cedar swamp. Who keeps us here . . . eh?

John: Who keeps us here? I suppose you mean I do.

Lena: And who is it, if it ain't you?

John: And if it is who saddled me with a farm that's too poor to raise a good crop of weeds? How did I get it?

Lena: *(Defensively)* You wouldn't've had a thing if it wasn't for the farm. We got a house here at least and a barn. The land's worth somethun.

John: It's worse than nothin and I got it with you. Your father gave it to us for a weddin present. Bah! He'd done better to give us each a shot of cold lead. *(Jo opens the rear door.)* Here. Where're you goin?

Jo: No place, paw. Just out in the yard. To play.

John: You stay in here.

Jo: It's Pete's night to do the chores.

John: You heard me.

Jo: Aw, paw . . .

John: *(Rising)* Stop that whinin. I ain't goin to have you young ones doin whatever you want round here all hours of the night.

Jo: It ain't hardly dark yet, paw.

Lena: *(Stepping between them)* Let the lad go. You'd almost think we was to blame because the marshes is drowned out. Go on, Jo.

Jo: *(Edging out the door)* Can I go, paw?

Lena: Go on and play if you want to.

Jo: Paw?

John: Oh, go on. Stay out all night if you want to. *(He turns to his chair and Jo goes out.)* Sarilin, get away from that window and clear these dishes.

Lena: *(Resuming her work)* First you tell him to stay in like it was a prison he was livin in, then you say for him to stay out all night. You don't care what they do. If it wasn't for me your children'd run wild for all you care.

John: They might as well as stay around this hole. *(Looking around the room, contemptuously)* Pig sty. That's what is is . . . a pig sty.

Lena: You'd think I made it to hear you talk. You've been glad enough to live here these twenty years. Just because there's no marsh hay . . . *(Flaring)* I'm not keepin you. Why didn't you go west and get free land, like I wanted you to.

John: Free land? West? You wouldn't go west. You heard they was no trees there. Besides, how could I go west? It takes money to go west . . . where'd I get it. *(His face twists into a malevolent smile.)* Raisin marsh hay, I suppose?

Lena: You could've walked.

John: And left you starve on this place? You'd had a fine time scratchin a livin off'n these fifty acres of grey stone.

Lena: It couldn't've been much worse than what it is now. Sarilin, you help with them dishes. What do you see outside there, anyways?

Sarilin: *(Sulkily)* I done the last dishes. I ain't goin to do all the work.

Pete: *(Hoping to forestall an oft repeated altercation)* Aw, go on and do them, Sarilin. You'll have to anyways and there'll only be another row.

Sarilin: I won't do them.

John: You'll do what you're told and you'll do it without any back talk.

Sarilin: Tessie . . .

John: Get on there . . . you little rat. Another word out of you and you'll come out to the barn. (Saralin rises, whimpering, and starts to pile the dishes.)

Sarilin: It ain't fair. I got to do everythin and Tessie don't do a thing. She does what she pleases.

Pete: Maw, can I have some more tea?

Lena: You've had a cup, ain't you?

Sarilin: Tessie says she's made up her mind to do what she likes. She says Tom . . .

Lena: (Hurriedly) She was just talkin.

Sarilin: She says Tom'll . . .

John: Tom? Tom who? Tom Roche? Is Tessie hangin round with him?

Sarilin: (Nodding her head) And Tom says . . .

Lena: I told you she was, John. More than oncet. You wouldn't listen. You wouldn't do nothin to stop him and you wouldn't say nothin to her.

John: (Rising slowly to his feet) Where is she?

Lena: She's gone out.

Sarilin: She's in there, gettin fixed up. (She goes to the door and calls) Tessie! Paw wants you.

John: What did you say she'd gone out for?

Lena: I . . . she . . .

John: You said she'd gone out.

Lena: (Her control breaking) She goes out with him every night. I've warned you. I told you one of your girls'd been hangin around with one of the Roches. You never listened. You done

nothin. You was afraid to. You was afraid to do anythin. You was afraid to go west. You done nothin but cut marsh hay and grumble at me when the marshes is dry. At me! Me, that's slaved for you twenty years.

John: (Angrily) Slaved! Slaved, have you! What have I done? Hoed the rocks on your father's damned farm. Gone into the bush and cut marsh hay every summer and hauled it out on the ice in winter. Twenty years of a man's life gone into workin fifty acres of grey stone and cuttin marsh hay. You've slaved?

Lena: Ain't I been a good wife to you all these years?

John: A good wife? Do you call havin another young one every year . . . bein a good wife? Bringin another mouth to feed, year by year, on fifty acres of grey stone? Twelve! Do you call that bein a good wife? Wife? More like a damned sow.

(Tessie has opened the door at the left and has slipped behind Lena and John. She has put on her hat and carries a small bundle in one hand. Lena comes slowly to John, vehemence and heat forgotten and nothing but cold, bitter rage left her.)

John: (To Tessie) Come back here.

Lena: (Bitterly, and very, very slowly) It's a wonder I ain't killed you before this John. Callin me . . . look at me! Look at me! Worn out before my time . . . bearin your children. And you call me that. It's a wonder I ain't killed you.

John: (Indifferently) I wish you had. (Tessie has her hand on the door) Where are you goin? Out with a Roche?

Sarilin: I seen Tom down by the gate.

Tessie: Yes, I am. Tom's waitin.

John: (Incredulously) You'd go out with that scum? A girl of mine? His father and me ain't spoke since we shantied on the Mippinaw fifteen years ago this winter. You know that and you'd go out with one of his. Get in there and take that hat off'n your head.

Tessie: *(Defiantly)* I won't. Tom's waitin for me. I'm goin to him. *(She opens the door)*

Lena: *(Frantically)* Don't let her go, John.

John: You can't go. Not with that scum.

Tessie: He's no more scum than we are and Hank Roche is just as good, every bit as good, as you've ever been.

John: If you go, you go for good.

Tessie: Why shouldn't I go for good? What've I got here? Dirt . . . and half starved. And your beatins. Why shouldn't I go for good?

Lena: It's not fair. We're your paw and your maw. You've a home here. This is your home. You can't leave us this way. You can't.

Tessie: Why can't I? What've you ever done for me? You had me because you couldn't help yourself. What've I been? One more mouth for fifty acres of grey stone to feed. He said so . . .

Sarilin: Tessie! You're talkin awful. God'll . . .

Tessie: *(With a hint of hysteria)* God? God! He made it. Fifty acres of grey stone . . . and me. Only another mouth to feed. Goin? Goin? I'd go anyways . . . *(A whistle is heard outside)* even if Tom wasn't waitin.

(Lena rushes toward her but John stops her. Tessie opens the door and goes out quickly.)

John: Let her go.

Lena: *(Trying to pass him)* It's your fault. You'd never let any of the young ones have a bit of play or fun. You'd never let nobody come to the house. Mary went the same way . . . next Saralin'll go. One by one they've all gone . . . boys and girls. And they never come back. *(She breaks down and weeps)*

John: It shows their good sense.

Lena: It's all your fault, I tell you.

John: Oh, shut up. What if she has gone? If she can get Tom Roche or anybody else to feed her,

we're better off. She's gone and that's the end of it. Quit blubbering about it.

(Lena is wiping her eyes on the hem of her apron and, as she moves away from John, Sarilin tries to comfort her.)

Sarilin: Don't take on so, Maw. Tessie talks all the time but she don't mean nothin. She'll be back. You see. Tom can't take her yet, anyways. She'll be back.

Lena: They've all gone the same way. First Mary. Then little John . . . and Charlotte . . . now Tessie. All of them gone.

(Lena goes into the room on the left, wiping her eyes and quietly sobbing. Sarilin turns to the dishpan.)

Sarilin: Pete. Lift this dish pan over on the wood box.

Pete: Lift it yourself. You're as strong as me.

Sarilin: I'm tired, Pete.

Pete: So'm I. You ain't walked eight miles to school and back.

Sarilin: Aw, Pete. Please.

John: *(Over his shoulder)* Lift it yourself. *(Lena appears at the side, her hat on)* Give Sarilin a hand with that dishpan. *(While Lena automatically obeys, John puts his foot on the wash bench, cuts the heel of a plug of tobacco into his hand and looks out the window)* Twenty years of a man's life gone into workin fifty acres of grey stone . . . cuttin marsh hay to keep a couple of cows and a half dead horse alive. Cuttin marsh hay because the land won't raise enough fodder to winter a rat. A dozen scrawny chickens . . . twelve children. Five dead, thank God. Twenty years of a man's life. Free land in the west. And walk to get there. If we'd lived in England they'd a paid our fare. *(Lena is at the door)* Where're you goin?

Lena: I'm goin to get her.

John: Oh, let her go. We're better off without her. She'll only be a surly bother if you brung her back now. Besides, I told her she couldn't come back.

Lena: Ain't you any pride, even? Lettin your girl go off with the son of a man you ain't spoke to in fifteen years. If you ain't I have. I'm goin to bring her back.

John: Bring her back then. If you had any sense you'd leave her go. *(Lena opens the door)* You'll never find her. *(Lena goes out)* How do you know where she's went?

(John follows Lena out, talking as he goes. As soon as they have gone the attitude of the two children changes. They become more valiant. Sarilin stops her work.)

Sarilin: I ain't goin to do these dishes. I'm sick of doin all the work. They can wait till mornin, anyways. *(She wipes her hands on her skirt)*

Pete: I do twice what you do and go to school besides.

Sarilin: I can't see no sense walkin eight miles to school. I quit as soon as they let me.

Pete: Perhaps you don't see no sense in it. I want to get some learnin so's I can get out a this back country and go out front. I ain't goin to spend my life workin this farm.

Sarilin: What good'll learnin do you? The school teacher's got more learnin'n you'll ever get and she don't make but three hundred and fifty dollars a year and has to board out . . .

Pete: I don't care. A feller'd stand a better chancet if he knowed how to read and write . . . *(Sarilin goes toward the other room)* You ain't goin to leave them dishes?

Sarilin: Ain't got time to do them now.

Pete: *(Rising)* Where're you goin?

Sarilin: *(With a hint of coquetry)* Goin out.

Pete: You ain't hangin around with . . .

Sarilin: What if I am? You and Jo play with them half the time. A girl has a right to some fun.

Pete: Paw won't let you go.

Sarilin: I'll crawl out'n a window.

Pete: You'll be gettin yourself into trouble if you ain't careful. They been talkin about you and Walt Roche down at Bronton already.

Sarilin: What if they is? Think I'm goin to stick in this hole all my life washin dishes? I ain't.

(Jo slouches in the rear door.)

Jo: All the dish washin you do'll never strain you. I seen Walt Roche just now.

(Sarilin turns quickly and goes into the other room.)

Pete: What's he doin?

Jo: Waitin for Sarilin, I guess.

Pete: Paw'll beat her awful if he finds out. Tessie run away with Tom to-night.

Jo: She'll be back.

Pete: She might. It's hard to say. Maw and paw's gone after her. He and maw had a fight. He's gettin worse. He says there ain't a ton of hay in the marshes . . . drowned out by the beavers.

Jo: He'll have to let the stock go.

Pete: Maw says it was a wonder she ain't killed him before this.

Jo: He's outside talkin to old man Barnood about the elections. What's Sarilin doin?

Pete: Slicking up, I guess.

Jo: If I was her I'd be kinda scared till I seen how Tessie made out. She ain't hangin around with Walt, is she?

Pete: I guess she's hangin around with anyone that'll have her. She don't get no fun here she says, with paw and maw fightin and paw never lettin her go out. I wonder why paw don't try to get a job out front. It'd be better than this farm.

Jo: I heard maw say he tried one winter but he couldn't find no work.

(John and Andrew Barnood enter. Barnood is an older man than John; better kept and more placid, a man of some education.)

Barnood: *(Continuing his conversation)* You're wrong, John. I tell you what the country needs is a change in government. There's never been a party in power worse than the present one. They've done nothing or what they have done has been wrong. We need a change . . . *(The two men seat themselves)*

John: What good would a change do us back here? What the hell difference will it make to you or me or this farm of mine if the Tories or the Grits are in at Ottawa or Toronto. All the laws in God's wide world wouldn't make a blade of grass grow in that back field of mine.

Barnood: I tell you we ought to have a change. It's time, John.

John: And I tell you, Andy, that it don't make no difference to you or me what party is in . . . or whether we're part of the States or Canada. We'd still cut marsh hay to winter our half starved cattle, that we have to drive forty miles to a railroad to sell . . . raise a few chickens . . . kill a deer when we got the chancet. Andy, the only thing a change in government ever changes, Andy, is the government. *(To Jo and Pete)* You two go to bed.

Barnood: This ain't a bad country, John. A man's away freer back here than what he is in the city. It's not a bad country. Especially for a single man. If they wouldn't raise such large families . . .

John: *(Cynically)* What chancet has a lad of stayin single? What chancet, Andy? Look at my girl Tessie and young Tom Roche. They've went away together. He'll have to marry her. They'll make him. Lena . . . his maw . . . the church . . . both churches . . .

Barnood: He should marry her, John.

John: He will, anyways. You two go to bed, do you hear me? *(The boys shift their positions)* And once he's married to her he might as well have a loggin chain around his neck and the other end buried a thousand feet deep in this country. What chancet has he? *(He rises and smiles)* Not a damn one, Andy. *(Vehemently)* While he's young enough to go, she won't move. She'll want to stay near her people . . . or they won't be trees in the west . . . or she'll be scared of the trip. When she's ready to go, he'll be sour, sour like milk after a thunder storm. And there'll be young ones . . . one a year . . . and then he won't give a damn. *(Scornfully)* Change of government? Bah! *(The two boys are still in the room and John suddenly realizing that they have not gone to bed, walks over to them and grabs Pete by the arm)* Ain't I told you two to go to bed? Well, get then.

Pete: Aw, Paw. It ain't late.

John: Get up there, both of you. Jo!

(He drags Pete to the staircase and nods to Jo. They both go cringing past him. While John is looking up the staircase Sarilin backs into the room and tip-toes rapidly and furtively across to the other door. She has her hand on the doorknob and is about to open it when Barnood speaks.)

Barnood: Goin out, Sarilin?

Sarilin: Oh!

(John wheels around, sees her, takes four long steps toward her, catches her arm and pulls her back into the room.)

John: Where're you goin?

Sarilin: *(Wincing)* Just down the road aways. I ain't goin anywheres, Paw.

John: *(Tightening his hold on her arm)* You're right. Take off that hat. *(As the child squirms a long whistle is heard outside)* You're up to Tessie's tricks, eh? You little scut. Get in there to bed. *(The whistle is heard again)* You'll do no scalavantin round the country with him. Get that out'n your head.

Sarilin: We never had no fun. You won't let us do nothin . . . but work. I'll run away like Tessie did. I'll run away . . . oh! You're hurtin . . .

A16

John: *(Leading her toward the other room)* Get in there.

Sarilin: It ain't fair.

Barnood: *(Placidly)* Startin her sparkin pretty young, ain't she, John.

John: Hurry up or I'll . . .

(The rear door opens and Lena bustles in followed by Mrs. Clantch, a neighbor. Mrs. Clantch is backwoods, about Lena's age but more ample. She sits down, stiff as a ramrod, and nods to John and Barnood.)

Lena: Come right in, Mrs. Clantch. John, leave Sarilin alone. What's she done, anyways? Have a chair, Mrs. Clantch. Sarilin, come here. *(John lets her go)* There's someone hangin round down by the barn.

John: Waitin for her. Look at her. All dressed up.

Barnood: Got a ribbon in her hair, too.

Mrs. Clantch: And pinned a flower on herself. Was she goin to a dance?

Sarilin: I ain't goin no place. Can't I get dressed up, sometimes? I was only goin down the road aways, maw.

John: Admirin the scenery, I suppose?

Lena: John, you keep out of this. You done enough harm for one night.

Barnood: Seems to me like she's got dressed up for some feller.

Lena: Is that so, Sarilin? Don't lie now. Is there someone waitin for you, outside there? *(The whistle is heard again)*

Sarilin: No there ain't.

Lena: *(Listening)* You're lying. Who is it?

Sarilin: I won't tell you.

Lena: You'll come to harm if you don't watch out. Ain't you got no sense at all? Hangin round

nights like this? Ain't it enough that you've got a home without gaddin round? Walkin out? You'd best get to bed and get these ideas outa your head.

Mrs. Clantch: *(Approvingly)* The best place for her, I'd say.

John: Get on. You know what'll happen to you if I ever catch you again. *(Sarilin goes into the room at the left, followed by Lena. When they have closed the door, John turns to Barnood resuming his conversation as if nothing at all had happened)* No, Andy. It won't make no difference what party comes in. They'll still pass fool huntin laws and you'll still think we need a change.

Barnood: But it's time for a change, John. Look what the war's cost us.

Mrs. Clantch: What a terrible waste it all was. All the boys that went from back here alone.

(Lena returns.)

John: We was better off while the war was on than we ever was in our lives.

Lena: You was better off? You that lost two sons fightin for their country.

Barnood: And fine strappin lads, they were.

Mrs. Clantch: They were nice boys, both of them.

John: Fighting for their country? These folks know how they got killed. Why don't you stick to the truth when you're sure people'll know you're lying? They never got a chance to fight for their country. Hank died at Valcartier with the flu and Sam . . . Sam got killed by a car in London. Fightin for their country?

Barnood: But that wasn't their fault, John. They enlisted . . .

Lena: Oh, he don't care.

Barnood: You're too hard on him, Mrs. Serang, John's not feelin up to the mark to-night. What with all the hay drowned out in the marshes, it'll be pretty hard to winter any stock. He's been stonin that back field, too.

John: It's enough to keep a man from feelin up to the mark. Stonin this place. It's nothin but stones.

Lena: That's no reason for you to treat those children the way you do. If it wasn't for Mrs. Clantch here being a good neighbor and takin her in, Tessie'd have no place to sleep to-night. She says she won't come back. Not while you're here, she says.

John: She could sleep out. It wouldn't kill her. *(To Mrs. Clantch)* Did she come to you?

Mrs. Clantch: No, she didn't. Young Mina Roche come down and said they was full up at their place and would I let Tessie stay all night with us.

John: You took her in?

Mrs. Clantch: *(Rising)* And why shouldn't I take her in? After her bein thrown out of her own home by her father. You ought to be ashamed of yourself, John Serang, that's what you ought.

John: She wasn't thrown out. She left.

Lena: You forced her to go and you says she could never come back. It's no wonder they call you Black John.

Barnood: *(Soothingly)* Oh, Mrs. Serang, he's no worse than the rest of us. No worse. It's a wonder sometimes we're half as good as we are. *(He rises)* I'll be sayin good night to you. Good night, John.

John: Good night, Andy. I'll be round to get the loan of that hand stone in the mornin. *(He walks to the door with Barnood and stands there for a moment, talking to him)*

Lena: *(Anxiously)* You'll do your best now, won't you, to get her to come back?

Mrs. Clantch: If talkin'll do any good . . . I will. I must be goin.

Lena: Good night, then. I'll be over the first thing in the mornin.

Mrs. Clantch: Good night. And don't worry. Perhaps it's all for the best. *(As she passes John)* Good night.

(Mrs. Clantch goes out and John walks over to the table and picks up the lamp.)

Lena: John. *(He puts the lamp back on the table)* John. One by one they've gone. There's only Sarilin left and she'll come to harm the way you're treatin her.

John: How'll I treat her? Let her run wild? The way you let Tessie?

Lena: *(Weakly)* She'll come to some harm . . .

John: Well, that's your look-out. You're her mother. If I can work sixteen hours a day feedin them surely to God you can see she keeps straight.

Lena: *(Ineffectually)* It's hard. There's no place to go. Nothin for them to do . . .

(She picks up the lamp and walks to the door of Sarilin's room. She opens it and peers in. John waits impatiently at the foot of the stairs.)

John: Well . . . are you goin to stay up all night?

Lena: *(Listlessly)* No, I'll come now. She's sleepin.
(They go upstairs, taking the lamp with them. The room is left in darkness except for the little light that comes in through the windows. A moment elapses and there is a tap on the window. The silhouette of a man's head appears. There is another tap on the window. The door into Sarilin's room is opened very carefully. Sarilin creeps on tip toe across to the outer door, watching the staircase nervously. She opens the door with an admonitory "sh!" A man steps into the frame of the doorway.)

The man: *(In an intense whisper)* What kept you?
Sarilin: Sh! They ain't asleep. Maw and paw sent me to bed.

The man: I been waitin an hour. Come on.

Sarilin: All right.
(He takes her arms and swings her to him viciously and kisses her, her head bent far back.)

Curtain.

A December morning.

The interior of a general store. A long counter occupies the rear of the store and behind it are shelves with bolts of cloth on them. At one end of the counter is the post office wicket, next to it an open space for the serving of customers, scales and a show case. Harness, shanty boots, pans, the tools of human existence in the north country, hang in cluttered strings from the ceiling. The entrance from the street is at the left, that into the house at the right. Beyond the street door is a large window. The space in front of the counter is taken up by a large box stove and scattered around it are up-ended boxes, which serve as seats.

Tad Nosse, the storekeeper, a small, fair man with drooping moustaches, is leaning over the counter talking to William Thompson, an elderly man with the city stamp upon him. A prospector, horse trader, a lawyer, an amateur backwoodsman, whom ambition and economic necessity forced to the city . . . which never liked him and which he never liked. Barnood is seated on a box near the stove, lighting his pipe. After a long contemplative draw, he speaks to Thompson.

Barnood: *(Deliberately)* Yes, Mr. Thompson, it's my opinion that the country needs a new party in power. You'd see a change then.

Thompson: *(Turning from Nosse)* That isn't the trouble, Andy. We haven't the men we used to have in Canada. We don't seem to breed them any more. Look at old Sir John A. and Laurier. They were men! This was a great country back here in those days.

Barnood: It was a great country. The pine was still here. Millions of acres of it. *(Reminiscently)* Ah, it was a fine sight.

Thompson: I remember it slightly. My father brought me back here from Belleville when I was a lad. It must be forty years ago.

Barnood: *(Enthusiastically)* I can remember when a man could drive a team through a stand of white pine for days . . . but the lumber companies and the fire gouged her clean. Turned it into so much bare rock and scrub popple. Just like that farm of John Serang's next to mine.

Nosse: They was governments when the lumber companies gouged her clean, Andy. Grits or Tories, it ain't made much difference. A Grit gets the layin out of the road grants when the Grits is in and a Tory gets it when the Tories is in. And whichever spends the money, the first rain washes her clean.

(Mrs. Clantch comes in, nods to the men present, walks over to the counter and sits down as if the entire phenomena of life were a personal insult.)

Mrs. Clantch: A pound of tea and ten cents worth of salt, please.

Nosse: They's some at fifty and some at sixty.

Mrs. Clantch: That seems awful dear.

Nosse: They ain't none cheaper.

Mrs. Clantch: *(With a deep sigh)* I'll take a pound of the fifty, then. *(Nosse gets it for her)*

Thompson: Driving up yesterday I was wondering how men like Serang ever make a living, Andy. Lazy, shiftless . . .

Barnood: I don't know as you call a man that works fourteen or sixteen hours a day, lazy. They don't make much of a livin, Mr. Thompson. Pick up a few dollars from the city people that summers on the lakes back here . . . do a little trappin . . . kill a deer or two . . . raise a few potatoes between the rocks and cut marsh hay.

Nosse: 'Ll that be all, Mrs. Clantch.

Mrs. Clantch: That'll be all, thank you. I don't suppose you heard how the trial come out yet?

Nosse: Ain't heard nothin yet but they ought to be comin back pretty soon.

Mrs. Clantch: It's likely to go hard with young Walt, ain't it?

Barnood: *(Rising)* He could be sent down for twenty years, I've heard, but I don't see how that'd do anybody any good. Serang would do better to take fifty or a hundred dollars and forget about it.

Mrs. Clantch: It'd be better all round if he was to marry Sarilin. It don't seem right to send a lad like Walt to jail for the best part of his life.

Nosse: If Sarilin was a young one of mine there wouldn't be no trial. Young Roche wouldn't have got away with no twenty years neither. I'd a shot him like I'd shoot a dog. If it'd happened in the States they'd a lynched him.

Barnood: *(Sharply)* It didn't happen in the States, Tad. It happened right back here and for some reason or other lynchin's never been very popular in Canada. Besides, she was as much to blame as he was, to my way of thinkin.

Mrs. Clantch: It was her paw that was to blame. He never let the young ones do nothin. Lena tried to stand up for them but she couldn't do much. You can't hardly blame Sarilin or young Walt. It seems a shame for her to come that way and her only a child.

Nosse: By God, if I was John Serang I'd shoot him and give myself up. There ain't a jury in the country'd convict. Why, that girl ain't sixteen. Black John ain't got the courage of a louse. He'd never had Walt arrested if it hadn't been for his woman. She made him.

Mrs. Clantch: She told Mrs. Roche she'd scauld her eyes out if she ever come near the house. Mrs. Roche was only tryin to be what help she could when they found out it was Walt. Lena didn't used to be like that.

Barnood: She seems to've got some queer notion in her head about Sarilin. I can't make it out.

Nosse: You mean the way she's lookin after the house and buyin all kinds of fripperies for it? Curtains and table cloths and the like? She even ast me for the calendar, there. Says it was pretty and it'ld brighten Sarilin's room up. Perhaps she's got religion.

Barnood: Not by the way she talked the minister, she ain't.

Mrs. Clantch: I don't think she done right. He was only bringin her what comfort and blessin he could to her in her trouble. She was in sore need, too, and she told him to get and never set foot in her house again.

Thompson: (Who has been following the discussion with great interest) Why was that?

Nosse: Because they's heathen, the lot of them. There ain't a decent Christian in the house. If they had been Walt Roche wouldn't be livin to-day. He'd a had a bullet in him.

Barnood: (To Thompson) The minister done the best he knowed how. He consoled her for havin a daughter steeped in sin and says it was God's will and that she'd have to bear it as best she could.

Thompson: (Understandingly) And she told him to get, eh?

Mrs. Clantch: Run him out'n the house. I told her she done wrong to talk to him the way she did. She said she wouldn't have no more to do with them if they talked that way about Sarilin. (Sighing) It's a sad thing anyways you look at it, Sarilin havin a baby before she's sixteen and Walt arrested and all, but it's queer the way she's carryin on. She's changed altogether. You wouldn't know it was the same house to go in it.

(Mrs. Clantch picks up her parcels and rises, shaking her head sadly.)

Nosse: Ought've been shot. I told John so.

Mrs. Clantch: (Turning at the door) If Lena comes in, tell her I went over to the Hazard's. She drove down with me. I'll leave these parcels here in the window.

(Mrs. Clantch goes out.)

Thompson: What's all this about a trial, Andy. Young Walt Roche get that girl of Serang's into trouble?

Barnood: They're tryin him down at Hendale to-day.

Nosse: If it'd been me, there'd been no trial.

Thompson: I gathered as much. (To Barnood) But what's all the stir about, Andy? Isn't that sort of thing fairly common back here?

Barnood: (Doubtfully) Yes . . . but it seems a bit different this time.

Thompson: What are they tryin him for? Won't he marry the girl?

Barnood: No, he won't. That's the trouble. (Pete Serang comes in the door and goes to the post office wicket. There is a tangible difference in the boy's bearing, perhaps a new sense of self-respect, perhaps a defensive reaction to the talk he hears. Whatever it is and subtle as it is, it is noticeable.) Nothin might've come of it if he hadn't gone round braggin he wasn't the only one and that he'd be damned if he'd marry her. (Nodding toward Pete) That's Pete.

Thompson: Serang?

Pete: Any mail for us to-day? (Nosse looks behind the counter)

Barnood: I'll call him over.

Nosse: Nothin but one of them catalogues. Your paw ain't back from Hendale yet, is he?

Pete: I ain't seen him. I'm waiting for maw. She ain't come in, has she? We left the house with no one but Jo to look after Sarilin.

Nosse: (With a sneer) Can't she look after herself?

Pete: We don't let her do any work now and maw don't like to leave her alone for long. Is that all the mail there is?

Nosse: That's more'n usual, ain't it?

(Pete turns toward the door and Nosse leaves the wicket.)

Barnood: Pete:

Pete: (Stopping) Yes?

Barnood: Come here. You know Lawyer Thompson, don't you?

Pete: You and paw had a hunt a couple of years ago, didn't you?

Thompson: Yes. Up to Little Mud Lake, beyond the big marsh. What's this I hear about the trouble up at your place, Pete?

Pete: *(With remarkable dignity)* There's no trouble that I know of. *(He turns and goes slowly to the door.)* You might tell maw if she comes in, I've gone to fetch the buggy.

(He opens the door and goes out.)

Nosse: Did you hear the way he talked Mr. Thompson? Won't let her do no work. The whole nest of them are like that now. You'd think they was harbourin a saint instead of Sarilin.

(Thompson nods his head and turns to Barnood as if silently requesting him to resume his story.)

Barnood: As I was sayin, there wouldn't have been nothin done if young Roche'd kept his face closed. John wouldn't've done nothin but Roche talked round so much his woman got him to get Roche arrested. They're tryin him down to Hendale to-day. Most everyone in the village is down there.

Thompson: A pretty serious charge, too, if the girl is under sixteen. Next to murder. How'll he plead?

Barnood: Not guilty, I guess. He claims there are four or five other lads as much to blame as he is.

Thompson: But it wouldn't make any difference if there were a thousand. They'd simply be guilty of the same offense.

Nosse: There should've been no trial at all. Fellows like young Roche is no good in the country anyways. Been better if John'd took his gun and waited for him on the road. It'd teach some others a fear of the law.

Barnood: *(His patience at an end, rises and walks over to the counter)* Look here, Tad. Fellows like young Roche and the rest you hint at are just as good in the country as a cowardly blood sucker that charges five prices for everythin and stands behind a counter shrieking for some other man to go out and do murder.

Nosse: *(Cringing)* If it was anybody but you that said that to me Andy, he'd never come in my store again. I'd . . .

Barnood: Sit down, Mr. Thompson, he won't do nothin.

Thompson: I'd be a bit careful if I were you, Nosse, how I advised murder as a cure-all.

Nosse: I didn't mean no harm, Mr. Thompson. It's just the way the thing struck me.

Thompson: I'd forget all about it if I were you. Sit down, Andy, and tell me more of this.

Barnood: Just like a damn ling, Nosse is.

(The street door opens and Lena comes in. She is very quiet, very preoccupied. The same dignity which characterized Pete is noticeable. She goes directly to the counter where Nosse is waiting, very surly after his calling down.)

Lena: Good morning, Mr. Nosse.

Nosse: Want somethun?

Lena: I want some more of that cleanin powder like I had last time and a broom. And have you got any more of that white muslin left? And I'd like some tea.

Nosse: It's sixty and seventy five a pound.

Lena: I'll take a couple of pounds of the best. And I'd like half a dozen eggs and some corn starch and some of the jelly that comes in a powder and . . .

Nosse: See here! Who's goin to pay for all this? I ain't goin to have you runnin a big bill here. You owe over twenty dollars now.

Lena: Well I . . . John'll . . . I've got to have it, Mr. Nosse. It's for Sarilin.

Nosse: It ain't like you was buyin food you had to have . . .

Thompson: Don't worry about that, Nosse.

Barnood: Let her have what she wants, Tad.

Lena: Oh, thank you. And three cans of peaches and this medicine the doctor told me to get.

(She looks wistfully at the calendar to which Nosse has referred. Barnood walks over to it, takes it down, rolls it up and gives it to her.)

Lena: Oh, thank you, Mr. Barnood. It'll help brighten Sarilin's room up.

Barnood: How is she?

Lena: Simply fine and the boys are so good to her.

Barnood: I suppose you're kinda anxious to hear how the trial come out.

Lena: No, I can't say I am. It don't seem to make much difference what happens to him as long as Sarilin keeps well and strong.

(Pete comes in.)

Pete: It's most time we was gettin back, Maw. Mrs. Clantch is waitin.

Nosse: She left them parcels over there.

Barnood: Your maw has some here, too.

(Pete takes the parcels and goes out.)

Lena: Come in and see us, Mr. Barnood.

Barnood: Thank you.

(Lena goes out.)

Nosse: Canned peaches . . . jelly powders . . . seventy five cents a pound tea . . .

Barnood: Tad! When you're makin out that bill put that tea down at fifty. I saw where you got it.

Thompson: (With amazement) Was that really John Serang's woman Lena?

Barnood: Yes, that was her. She seems to've gone half crazy in a way. Did you hear the things she bought? Soap and brooms and jelly? Did you see her when I give her that calendar? Did you notice the way she talked and looked?

(Nosse is standing with one foot on the broad window ledge, looking out.)

Thompson: I never saw such an amazing change in a person in my life. What's come over her?

Barnood: It's this trouble of Sarilin's that's done it.

Thompson: There's a kind of religious intensity about the woman. And you say she kicked the minister out of the house.

Barnood: Yes, she did. Most people would count what's happened somethun of a disgrace but she goes around as if she was nursin a saint. You ought to see the house, the changes in it and the way the boys do all the work.

(Nosse has become very excited over something he sees down the street. He peers out with both hands on the sill and then goes to the door and opens it.)

Nosse: They're back. Here's young Walt and Tom comin up the road with some of the other lads.

Barnood: Seems kinda queer that he should be let out.

Thompson: Bail? (Barnood shrugs his shoulders)

Nosse: Harye, Walt. Didn't send you down, eh? Come on in and tell us all about it and have a cigar. Where's the rest of them? Where's Black John? What happened?

(Walt Roche comes in the door in the middle of Nosse's speech. There is nothing of the villain about him. He is a light, good looking lad of medium height and carries himself with a distinct swagger. He is followed by his brother Tom. Three other youths, the ever present tail to any kite of excitement, drift in after them. Walt is very sure of himself for he goes directly to Thompson, with whom he shakes hands.)

Walt: Harye, Mr. Thompson? Back again for a hunt?

Thompson: Hello, Walt. How are the deer this year? Lots of them, eh? Hello, Tom. How's everything with you? Hear you've been married since I was back last. How do you like it?

Tom: (*A rather shy chap*) It ain't too bad. I got me a good woman. Tessie Serang.

Nosse: Have a cigar, Walt?

Walt: I don't mind if I do.

(*He saunters over to the show case and takes the cigar offered to him by Nosse, who even goes to the extent of lighting it for him.*)

Nosse: Tom?

(*Tom shakes his head and Nosse hurriedly puts the box away as one of the other boys step up. The three unnamed boys distribute themselves on boxes while Walt takes the centre of the stage before the stove, very much in the limelight.*)

Walt: (*Critically*) It ain't a bad cigar.

Nosse: (*Impatiently*) Old man Spenton let you off, eh? Was it old man Spenton tried you? (*Walt bides his time*)

Tom: Yes, it was Spenton.

Barnood: (*To Thompson*) Old man Spenton, down to Hendale.

Thompson: That isn't the old chap that used to keep the hotel across from the Methodist Church?

Nosse: That's him. Give it up when they took away the bars.

Thompson: But I thought he was only a justice of the peace.

Barnood: That's all old Sam is.

Walt: He's a good man, old Sam. He seen right away he couldn't hold me for nothin. Oncet I told him how it was and told him there was four other lads willin to swear I wasn't the only one he seen he couldn't hold me. Old John was rarin mad but it didn't do him no good.

Barnood: (*Severely*) It seems to me you was pretty lucky to get off. Not only you, but the whole pack of you, if what you say is true.

Nosse: Was there many down to it?

Tom: It was pretty well packed till old Sam sent everybody out but Walt and John and some witnesses.

Thompson: Wasn't the girl there?

Walt: Sarilin? Her maw wouldn't let her come, would she, Tom? (*Tom shakes his head*) It was this way . . .

Thompson: This is a strange business, Andy. The most material witness not present and the case tried before a justice of the peace. The thing's absurd.

Walt: Nothin strange about it that I can see. First of all when we went in Sam ast Black John to tell what he had to say and he says how Sarilin said I was the one that got her into trouble.

Nosse: What did you say?

Walt: I spoke right up, didn't I Tom? And I says, if she says that, she's lyin and I can prove she's lyin. She don't know who done it and she can't prove who done it. Sam asts me what I meant and the lads there (*Pointing to the three boys*) says they was willin to swear. Didn't you? (*The three nod their heads*)

One of them: Sure, I'm willin to swear.

Another: Me, too.

Walt: You see. He couldn't find nothin agin me. I says so before they had me arrested.

Thompson: Did Spenton dismiss the case entirely?

Walt: He says the only thing for John to do was to try and settle in a friendly sort of way between ourselves and if we couldn't he says somethun about a trial at Belleville or somewheres if John wanted to go on with it. But I ain't afraid of goin to Belleville or anywheres else.

Barnood: Told you to settle it out of court, did he? Are you goin to do the right thing and marry her?

Walt: *(Indignantly)* No. What the hell would I want to be tied to her for the rest of my life for? I ain't goin to stick in the backcountry all my life, cuttin marsh hay and raisin kids. No, I won't marry no one.

Thompson: You should pay her doctor bills anyway. That's the least you can do, Walt.

Walt: I ain't goin to pay a cent, Mr. Thompson. Why should I? Her old woman's gettin more fun out'n this'n she ever got in her life before. Ain't you heard how they're all actin? Won't let Sari-lin raise her hand to do a thing. They wait on her like they was slaves.

Barnood: It's my opinion that John'll make you pay.

Walt: How'll he make me? *(Unseen by everyone but Thompson and Barnood, John Serang comes in the door)* He wouldn't've had me arrested even if it hadn't been for his old woman. She made him do it. He was afraid to do anythin to me. He's afraid of paw. *(John has walked to a position immediately behind Walt and has been seen by everyone except the boy. With the exception of the two older men, Thompson and Barnood, all cringe away from him. His hand is above Walt's shoulder. Walt goes on talking)* He's been afraid of paw ever since they shantied together on the Mipin . . .

John: *(His hand closing on Walt's shoulder)* Afraid of your paw?

Walt: *(Thoroughly frightened)* Let me go. Damn it, let me go. Let me go, I tell you.

John: Afraid of your paw? Bah! I licked him at Cemetery Shoots and I licked him at Ragged Rapids.

Walt: Let me go.

Barnood: Let the youngster go, John. You'll do no good that way. Come over here and sit down.

John: Afraid? I'll lick him to-day, too.

(Serang lets Walt go and comes over to where Barnood and Thompson are.)

John: Is that you, Lawyer Thompson?

Thompson: Hello, John. Been having quite a time of it, eh?

John: Been doin some teamin. Had to pay all the bills that's comin in.

Barnood: Look here, John. Why don't you two settle this thing between yourselves right here? The lads say that's what Spenton told you. Settle it between yourselves.

John: *(Menacingly, taking a step forward)* I'm willing to settle it.

Barnood: How about you, Walt? Will you listen to reason?

Walt: *(Considering the chances of escape)* Sure I'll listen. Though there ain't nothin to listen to.

Thompson: You ought to do something, that's certain. John, what is the least you'll take to drop the whole business?

John: By rights, he ought to marry her. She's his now.

Walt: She ain't neither. And I ain't goin to marry her. What'd I marry her for? Settle down like you and try to scrape a livin off'n your place?

John: I'll make you . . .

Thompson: You can't make him marry her, John. You might in some communities. The people might make it too hot for him.

Barnood: There's no chancet of that back here, now. Not with the way John's woman has been actin and the way she treated the minister.

John: Well, he ought to pay the doctor's bills anyways and pay me somethun a week while I got to feed 'em.

Barnood: Suppose he gave you a couple of hundred dollars?

Walt: Where'd I get a couple of hundred dollars?

John: You'll have to pay somethun.

Walt: I won't pay a damn cent. I don't have to and I won't. And you daren't touch me, neither.

(Barnood places himself between Walt and John. The others rise, expecting a fight.)

John: By God, I'll make you. I'll make you pay every bill there is.

Walt: How'll you make me? By havin the law on me? You done that oncet and you ain't got much out'n it.

John: I'll find a way of makin you . . .

(Thompson, to avoid the fight which seems inevitable, takes John by the arm and leads him toward the front of the store.)

Walt: If you so much as touch me I'll have the law on you. You had your chancet and I'm as free as I ever was.

Thompson: Come on, John. I want to talk to you. Going home?

John: Yes. Has the woman gone up?

Thompson: Been gone for ten minutes. You'd better go on up yourself. I'll see if I can't fix this up for you and I'll be up later with Andy.

John: No. I ain't goin to leave without fixin that young whelp there . . .

Walt: You lay a finger on me . . .

Thompson: Come on, John. You don't want a fight here. It wouldn't do you any good. The lad's right. Only get you into trouble. Come on. There's something I want to talk to you about.

(Thompson leads John to the door with difficulty and goes outside with him.)

Nosse: (Admiringly) You talked right up to him that time, Walt. Didn't he, Tom? Yes, sir. Have another cigar?

Walt: I knowed he ain't got no hold on me and I ain't afraid of him, neither. Lawyer Thompson knows it, too. He's a friend of old John's and he'd helped him if there'd been a way to do it. Wouldn't he?

Two of the boys: He sure would.

Nosse: He can't do anything to you, that's certain.

Barnood: But if you had a bit of decency in you you'd be willin to live up to your acts.

(Thompson returns.)

Walt: I don't have to and I ain't goin to. Where's that cigar you was goin to give me, Tad?

(He goes over to the counter and gets another cigar while Thompson comes in and stands in front of the stove, his hands behind his back, his pose studied and severe.)

Thompson: If I were you, Roche, I'd keep rather quiet about what I would do and what I wouldn't do.

(There is a quality in his voice which makes Walt hold his lighted match until it burns his fingers. He does not light the cigar.)

Walt: Why not? He's had me arrested and it ain't done no good. He can't do a thing.

Thompson: That is just where you are very mistaken. He may have had you arrested but you've never been tried.

Walt: But old Sam Spenton . . .

Thompson: Is a justice of the peace and has just as much jurisdiction to try your case as Tad Nosse would have sitting on the top of that show case.

Walt: (Nervously) But these lads'll swear . . .

Thompson: (In the same monotonous, legal tone) If you produced a regiment, it wouldn't necessarily make any difference. It would only mean that they were equally guilty. (One of the three boys rises and makes his way as quietly *as possible toward the door. Thompson wheels on the other two.)* Have you chaps sworn to anything?

One of them: *(Eagerly)* No, no, Mr. Thompson. We ain't sworn to a thing.

Another: We didn't do it anyways. We just wanted to help Walt out'n a hole . . . We . . .

Another: No, Mr. Thompson, we . . .

Thompson: You're probably lying . . . but it doesn't matter. Now listen to me, Roche. If Serang ever takes this before a court of competent jurisdiction you could be sent down for twenty years.

Walt: *(Chokingly)* Twenty years?

(The air seems to have grown close to everyone.)

Thompson: Yes. Twenty years.

Walt: I . . . I . . . God! Twenty years. They couldn't do it.

Thompson: They could and after what you've said here today, they probably would.

Walt: What'll I do. Beat it.

Barnood: That wouldn't do you any good. They'd get you sooner or later.

Thompson: Serang asked my advice as a lawyer and I told him what I've told you but I don't like to see a lad of your age sent down for the best part of his life just because he's got a damn fool tongue in his head. You'd stand a very poor chance if this ever went to trial.

(One by one the three boys slink out, very frightened, despicable figures.)

Walt: What'll I do. Please, Mr. Thompson.

Thompson: You'd better see Serang as soon as you can. Perhaps he'll let you off if you'll marry her.

Walt: Where is he? Where did he go? I've got to catch him.

Thompson: He was going up home. You could catch him, if you ran.

(Walt rushes to the door, followed by Tom, and goes out. The three men remain silent for an instant; Nosse behind the counter; Barnood and Thompson near the stove.)

Barnood: Is that right, Mr. Thompson?

Thompson: *(Filling his pipe)* Well . . . it's a possibility.

Nosse: John ought to shot him, like I said.

Thompson: *(Infuriated)* By God, Nosse. I'd like to see you in that lad's shoes and hear how you'd talk then. Come on Andy.

(Thompson and Barnood go toward the door.)

Curtain

A29

Noon of the same December day as Act two.

The kitchen of the Serang home has altered entirely in its atmosphere. Where before was a feeling of extreme squalor, poverty, tragic futility, there is a feeling of regeneration. The place lacked self respect before. The curtains on the windows; the kept, black look of the stove; the red table cloth on the table, piled high with dirty dishes before, and the tin can covered with birch bark and the geranium it holds, all echo the evident attempt to make the place decent to live in. A new roller towel hangs by the door.

Jo is sweeping near the open door, which looks out on a desolation of grey stone. As he gives the broom a few vigorous strokes to scatter the dust outside, Sarilin's voice is heard calling from the room at the left. Jo listens and she calls again. There is an imperious quality in the call. Jo puts the broom down by the door, makes a gesture which starts with a hint of impatience and terminates with one of necessary compliance. He goes to the door and opens it.

Sarilin: Joey! Joey!

Jo: What is it, Sarilin?

(Her answer is unheard but he draws back from the open door and goes over to the wash bench and gets a dipper of water. He carries this into the room and comes out an instant later and goes to the table, pulls out a drawer, takes a glass from it, pours the water into the glass and goes back into the room. He comes out empty handed, goes to his broom, looks around. He straightens a curtain. The sound of voices comes from the room on the left.)

Jo: *(Calling)* You'd best be gettin out of here, Tessie, if you don't want maw and paw to catch you. They ought to be gettin back pretty soon now.

(He goes on with his work and Tessie appears at the door and turns, with her hand on the knob. She speaks into the room, to Sarilin.)

Tessie: You're a fool, I tell you. Why don't you do as I say. It'd make it away easier for you in the long run. *(Pause)* Oh, I don't blame you for makin the best of this while it lasts. I'd stay in bed all day too if I could get anybody to wait on me, the way you have.

Jo: Tessie, go on home.

Tessie: I guess I'd better. *(Speaking inside the room again)* You can do as you like, but I'm tellin you. You're a fool if you don't. *(A pause)* Oh. Tell 'em anythin. Tell 'em you fell. They'd never know. *(She turns from the door, half closing it, and comes into the room. Looks around and sneers)* Kinda changed, ain't it? I suppose paw says prayers every night?

Jo: *(Coming nearer to her)* What've you been talkin to Sarilin about, again? You been tryin to fill her up with some idea.

Tessie: There's some things it'd be better for little boys not to know. Give my love to paw. *(She starts to go out the door and then hesitates)* She ain't sick. She's just as able to do that sweepin as you are.

Jo: *(Flaring)* She ain't goin to have to do none. Maw says she's to rest. *(Tessie laughs)* And if you come around again tryin to fill her with your ideas I'll tell maw.

Tessie: Hunh! You're as crazy as maw is.

(She goes out this time. She can be seen standing in front of the open door. She moves to the right, then turns quickly to the left and passes the window, running. Jo sees her and goes to the door, looks after her and then to the right.)

Jo: Hello, Pete. Maw come back too?

Pete: *(Coming into the house)* She's out at the buggy with Mrs. Clantch. Was that Tessie? I seen someone runnin around the corner of the house, just now. It looked like her.

Jo: She just went. She's been talkin to Sarilin for the best part of an hour. *(Pete lays his bundles on the table.)* You ain't heard how Walt Roche came out down at Hendale?

Pete: They wasn't back when we left Bronton. *(Nodding his head toward the room)* Is she still in bed?

Jo: Ain't been up this mornin.

Pete: Seems to me sometimes maw is a fool to let her have her own way about everythin.

Jo: It's been away better for us anyways. Remember what it used to look like? When Tessie was home?

Pete: Yes . . . I wonder what changed maw, anyways?

Jo: I ain't sure but they was a city woman that went through to Pembroke in a car and she had a puncture outside our gate and she come in. It was just after maw learned about Sarilin. She talked to her.

Pete: It might've been somethun like that. It wasn't the minister. He was for sendin her to some girl's home somewheres. What did she say to maw?

Jo: The city woman? I ain't sure but after she went maw stayed out there by the gate for an hour, lookin down the road. 'N she went round in a kind of a daze and wouldn't speak to no one. You remember.

(Sarilin is heard calling. Pete goes to the door of her room.)

Pete: What is it, Sarilin? *(Pause)* All right, I'll tell her. *(To Jo)* She wants maw. *(He goes to the outer door and calls)* Maw! Maw! *(He comes in again)* She's comin.

(Lena comes in the door, carrying the parcels.)

Lena: What is it, Peter? Does Sarilin want me?

(Pete nods and she goes into Sarilin's room. Mrs. Clantch, very prim, her air of injury most pronounced, appears at the outer door.)

Mrs. Clantch: Good mornin, Joey.

Jo: Hello, Mrs. Clantch. Did you drive maw up?

Mrs. Clantch: We came up together along with Pete. How is your sister?

Jo: Oh, she's all right. She's restin.

Mrs. Clantch: *(Sitting down with a snort of disapproval)* Hunh! It's all foolishness lettin that girl loll round that way. I can't see what your mother's thinkin about.

(Lena returns.)

Lena: The poor child wants some tea. Joey, put the kettle on. Peter, open that package of tea we got down at Nosse's.

(Jo fixes the kettle and Pete rummages over the parcels and opens the one containing the tea.)

Mrs. Clantch: Hunh! If she was my girl she wouldn't be in bed at this hour. Havin tea. She's as fit to work as you are, Lena.

Lena: May be she is. But she ain't your girl . . . she's mine.

Mrs. Clantch: Then you're more the fool to put up with them kind of actions. Her in disgrace and you treatin her like she was a queen. I'd teach her a few lessons, if she was mine.

(Lena has gone to the stove and taken the kettle from Jo.)

Lena: *(Wrathfully)* Don't ever say that word in my house again. She's in no more disgrace than you or me. Disgrace? If it's anybody's disgrace it's her paw's for givin her no chancet.

Mrs. Clantch: *(Drawing back)* I ain't meanin no harm, Lena. Only it seems to me you're gettin the queerest ideas into your head and I don't see where you got them.

(Sarilin calls.)

Lena: In a minute, dearie.

Mrs. Clantch: I'd feel better if you hadn't talked to the minister the way you did.

Lena: The minister? Why, he come into this house and says Sarilin was steeped in sin . . . and damned. Why . . . he was lucky to get out of this house alive. Damned forever, because she didn't have him say some words over her first.

(Sarilin calls and Lena goes into her room.)

Mrs. Clantch: *(To Pete)* How did your maw come by such ideas?

Pete: Jo says they was a woman come by here in a car one day and talked to her. But I don't know for sure. Jo! You'd best put some more wood on that fire. This kettle ain't doin very well.

(Lena calls to Pete from the room and he goes in. Jo shoves another stick of wood in the stove.)

Mrs. Clantch: Is that so, Joey? Was there someone stopped here and give your maw these sinful ideas?

Jo: They was a woman goin to Pembroke in a car and they had a puncture under that maple tree down by the gate. She come in while he was fixin it. She and maw talked a long time and maw walked out to the car with her and kissed her hand when she went. Maw went around like she was in a dream for the best part of a day and then she started to clean the place up and wouldn't let Sarilin do a thing.

(Lena and Pete return from the other room.)

Lena: She wanted her bed moved so's she could see out. *(She goes to the table)* Look at the nice picture Andrew Barnood give me down at Bronton. Look, Joey! Ain't that nice? We'll put it up in Sarilin's room where she can see it. *(Jo and Pete look at the calendar. Lena puts it down on the table and Jo picks it up.)* You get the hammer and tack it up, Joey. *(Her eye lights on the tea. Proudly, to Mrs. Clantch.)* It's the best that Tad Nosse sells. Seventy-five cents a pound. It's for her.

Mrs. Clantch: I bought the same kind for fifty. *(Lena smiles and goes over to the tea pot.)*

Lena: I guess you've mistook it for some other kind.

Mrs. Clantch: No I ain't. *(Accusingly)* Lena. What is this Joey says about some woman stoppin here and talkin to you and convertin you to some heathen religion?

Lena: What're you talkin about?

Mrs. Clantch: Jo says some woman had a puncturn outside the gate and come in and talked to you. He says you kissed her hand when she went away.

(Lena's face lights up with a really beautiful smile. She moves absently around and seems to be recalling some happy memory. Mrs. Clantch watches her narrowly and suspiciously. Pete has been busying himself putting things away from the table. He goes out.)

Lena: Yes. I didn't think anybody knowed about her. Her and her husband stopped outside while he fixed a puncture and she come in and talked to me. (She turns to her work.)

Mrs. Clantch: (Very suspiciously) Who was she?

Lena: She give me her name, printed on a little card but I ain't been able to find it since.

Mrs. Clantch: It sounds awful queer to me. What did she talk about?

Lena: I can't see that there's anythin queer about a woman stoppin in front of your door and comin inside out'n the sun. What's queer about it?

(Jo comes back from Sarilin's room.)

Lena: Jo, get a cup and saucer.

Mrs. Clantch: It all sounds queer to me. And the way you look.

Lena: Put them on the table. No, there's nothin queer about it.

Mrs. Clantch: (Reeking with suspicion) Well. Did she convert you? Did you get religion or what happened to you? Although it must have been some heathen creed from the way you acted when the minister was here.

Lena: (looking around the spotless room) I guess I was converted to somethun . . . new! And it must've been a heathen creed like you say. It ain't like the minister's.

Mrs. Clantch: (Trembling with curiosity) What did she talk about?

Lena: About lots of things. About Sarilin. It was just after she told me.

Mrs. Clantch: Didn't she think it was a dis . . .

Lena: (Quickly) I warned you, oncet! (Coming to the table and leaning on it) No, she didn't. She says that it seemed hardly fair to bring a baby into the world to live in a place like this was . . . then. It's clean now, anyways. And she said it was natural . . . she told me people is ruled by laws . . . just like a tree is . . . and she says no one was to blame.

Mrs. Clantch: Did she think an illegitimate was as good as a young one born in holy wedlock, to man and wife.

Lena: I don't know. I can hear her now, sittin right in that chair where you are. Her voice kinda rang like a bell. She says to call a baby illegitimate . . . was an awful thing. (Sarilin calls again) Yes, dearie! (She goes to the door of the room) The kettle is just comin to a boil now. You'll have it in a minute.

(Lena proceeds to make the tea and Mrs. Clantch rises, undecided whether she should leave on the instant or whether duty doesn't demand that she try to worm more information out of Lena. Jo has gone into Sarilin's room.)

Mrs. Clantch: Well . . . it's certainly strange ideas you got into your head now. What does John think about all this.

Lena: He ain't home very much. I got him to take a job teamin so's that we could do what she said.

Mrs. Clantch: (Shocked) Did she say more than that?

Lena: Yes. She says now that the baby was comin the only thing to do was to give it the best chancet as we could. I never told John. She says not to ever let Sarilin feel ashamed . . .

Mrs. Clantch: (Utterly shocked) Well. I ain't heard such a story in my life. And that's why you've been cleanin and workin and treatin that young strumpet in there . . .

Lena: *(White with rage)* I think . . . I think . . . you'd best go now.

(Mrs. Clantch does not realize the full, suppressed fury of Lena and she moves as if to continue.)

Lena: Go on! Go on! Get our of here before I . . . *(She turns as if searching for some weapon)* You're one with the minister . . .

(She moves quickly this time. Lena is a very menacing figure but Mrs. Clantch attempts to force as much virtuous dignity as she can into her exit. Lena regains control of herself as she sees the other woman leaving. Pete comes in the door and stands behind Mrs. Clantch.)

Mrs. Clantch: Hunh! Not let Sarilin feel ashamed . . .

(Lena either does not hear her or ignores her. Mrs. Clantch goes out.)

Lena: I guess the tea's steeped, Peter.

Pete: Yes, maw, I'll take it in to her.

(Through the window to the right Mrs. Clantch is seen giving the cut direct to John, who is coming toward the house. It is so obvious that John stops in astonishment and looks after her.)

Lena: You'd best get some more wood, Peter. Joey can take this in. Joey!

Pete: *(Turning toward the door)* I'll get some.

(He opens the door and goes out. John turns toward the house and the two meet outside. Jo opens the other door.)

Jo: What is it, Maw?

Lena: Here's Sarilin's cup of tea. You can take it in to her.

(He comes to the table and is given the tea and goes back into the room. John comes in the door, stops an instant as if he were entering a strange house and then hangs his hat on a nail. Lena goes to the other door and closes it tightly.)

John: Well, he got off.

Lena: You mean Walt?

John: Who else'd I mean?

Lena: But how was that, John? Did he offer to do somethun?

John: Won't do nothin. He had three lads down there with him that was willin to swear that they had as much to do with it as he had. *(Lena looks at him in stupefaction. He looks around the room)* Hunh! Ain't been home for so long, it don't look natural. I suppose you know this is runnin away with a lot of money?

Lena: John? Did Mr. Spenton believe that? Do you believe that? John?

John: Spenton let him go. Told him and me to settle it between ourselves. I saw Lawyer Thompson down at Bronton and he's comin up to have a talk with me.

Lena: What did he say?

John: I seen him only a minute. He didn't say much except that he'd see what he could do. He's comin up in his car later.

Lena: Oh, John, it's a lie about Sarilin. You know it's a lie.

John: May be it is but he got off by tellin it. If it is a lie. *(Looking at the table)* What's them?

Lena: Just a few things I got down at Bronton for Sarilin. *(Coming close to him)* I know it's a lie, John. I know it is.

John: *(Quite indifferent)* What if it is? It worked

Lena: But you'll do somethun?

John: What can I do more'n I have? Perhaps Lawyer Thompson'll do somethun.

(Lena realizes the futility of trying to make John feel as she does and turns away, limp, till her eye catches the door.)

Lena: If he can only prove it's a lie.

John: *(Looking at her with a new gleam of understanding)* You seem to be believin in somethun awful hard, Lena;

Lena: *(Starting to clear the table)* Perhaps I am.

John: I can't figger what's got into you. Whatever it is, you got me half believin in it too. You must or I wouldn't be damn fool enough to let you carry on this way, spendin all the money you are. You've put more into this room and them sheets for her bed than the whole place is worth. Where is she?

Lena: She's restin this mornin. Joey just took some tea into her.

John: Restin, eh? Till noon. And don't the rest of us get anythin to eat? *(He smiles his twisted smile)* Joey's just taken some tea in to her. *(He laughs shortly)* You'd almost think you was proud of her.

Lena: If you'll move I'll set the table.

John: What's this I hear about the minister comin here?

Lena: He was here and talked to me. He went away.

John: I believe you are proud. Why, I don't see.

Lena: Whatever I am I ain't ashamed, anyways. And Sarilin ain't goin to be ashamed neither. She's in bed in there. She's just as able to be up as you or me. But she's been cuffed and beaten and set upon her whole life by you . . . yes and by me, too. She's drudged, that's what she's done, John. Drudged. Her whole life. And now . . . she's goin to be a mother . . . I ain't goin to have her hate her baby . . . like I've hated mine. And I ain't goin to have her ashamed John. Do you hear me? She's goin to want her baby and be proud . . .

John: What difference'll make if she wants it or don't want it? She'll have it anyways.

Lena: Oh, you wouldn't understand but I do. I know now. That's why I've tried to make this place pretty and clean. So's it would be nice for her. *(Fiercely)* She will want her baby, John.

She will.

(The tenseness of Lena leaves John half believing in her words. They are standing looking at each other, when Pete bursts in the door.)

Pete: *(Excitedly)* Lawyer Thompson and Andy Barnood and young Walt Roche just come up in a car. They's out at the gate, there. They's comin in, I think.

Lena: Roche?

Pete: He was there with Lawyer Thompson and . . .

(Jo re-enters.)

John: *(Going to the door)* He's right, Lena. Lawyer Thompson's fixed somethun up.

(Lena moves quickly to the door to Sarilin's room and stands there as if she wished to protect the girl within. Thompson and Barnood are seen rapidly coming up the path. They enter and Thompson walks directly to John.)

Thompson: Andy and I have brought young Roche up in the car. He's pretty scared and he'll do just about what you want him to do, I think. I'd advise you to be as easy with him as you can.

John: Scared? How did you scare him?

Thompson: That hearing before old Sam Spenton might just as well have been before one of those grey stones out yonder for all it mean't. He's only a J.P. and where he got it into his head that he could try such a case, I don't know.

John: You mean that young Roche ain't really been tried?

Barnood: No. He ain't been tried, John. Lawyer Thompson says you can send him down, if you want to.

John: *(Excitedly)* By God! If that's right, I'll . . .

Barnood: I wouldn't be too rough on him, John. Let him marry her. Don't try and send him to prison.

Thompson: It would mean the best part of his life, John. He's just a youngster. He'll probably be willing to marry her now and that's all you want.

John: I suppose it is. If he does it'll be all right.

Barnood: We'll bring him in, eh? Mr. Thompson?

Thompson: Yes, bring him in, Andy. *(Barnood goes out and Thompson observes Lena for the first time)* How are you, Mrs. Serang. I didn't know it was you down at the store this morning. You've changed.

Lena: Yes, Mr. Thompson . . . some say I have.

(Thompson looks around the room, noting its changes, and sees the two boys.)

Thompson: These boys had better be sent out.

John: Get out, you two.

(There is no hesitancy about their going.)

Thompson: Perhaps it would be better if you left, too, Mrs. Serang.

Lena: I'll stay right here, thanks.

(It would seem that John was about to order her out but he changes his mind when he looks at her, leaning against the door. Andy comes up the path with Roche, a very frightened boy.)

Barnood: Get in there and take your medicine.

(The boy comes through the open door. Thompson has withdrawn to one side and, like John, is standing as if he were a black executioner of the inquisition. Against the other door is Lena, as if she would protect the girl within from the very words that will be spoken. The boy looks around nervously, his hands twitching. No one says a word.)

Walt: *(With evident effort)* I come up to see you about . . . Lawyer Thompson told me . . .

John: Go on. I'm listenin.

Walt: Well . . . down at Hendale . . . Sam Spenton said we'd do best to settle this between ourselves 'n I . . .

John: You come up to settle it, eh? You seem a lot more anxious to settle it now than you was half an hour ago at Nosse's.

Walt: *(Swallowing hard)* I'll pay you the two hundred dollars you said you wanted.

John: *(With a short laugh)* Where'd you ever get two hundred dollars?

Walt: Paw can raise it for me. To-day . . . this afternoon, if you want it.

John: All right. *(A long pause)* But that ain't enough.

Walt: *(Getting more frightened)* I'll pay all the doctor's bills, too . . . and give you so much a week.

John: That won't do, neither.

(Thompson and Barnood are wondering if they have been well advised in bringing the boy.)

Thompson: *(With a nervous cough and in a low low voice)* Don't be too hard on him, John.

(John's attitude lacks any suggestion of compromise.)

Walt: *(With a sob)* I'll marry her . . . if I have to . . .

Barnood: Now you're talkin sense. That'll give the young one a name.

John: Hunh! You're willin enough to marry her now, eh? *(A pause)* I don't know . . .

Walt: My God, John . . . Mr. Serang, don't send me down. Don't send me down. It might mean twenty years of my life. *(He breaks down completely and grovels on his knees at the other man's feet)* Don't send me down. I'll marry her this afternoon.

Thompson: That's all you can ask, John.

John: Hunh! Get up out of there, you poor snivelling rat. You'll marry her this afternoon . . .

(Into the centre of the room stalks Lena, the personification of cold insensate rage.)

Lena: He'll do no such thing!

Thompson: Don't be foolish, Mrs. Serang.

John: You keep out of this. This ain't no affair of yours.

Lena: No affair of mine? You say that? You, that called me a sow in this very room because I'd born you twelve children . . . and you talked then as if they wasn't as much yours as they was mine. No affair of mine, you say? No affair of mine? It's more my affair than anybody else's and I say she ain't going to be forced into no marriage with a thing like that *(Pointing to Walt)* just to serve your grudge, John, or to fit some lawyer's idea of what is right.

Thompson: You're acting very foolishly.

Lena: She'll not be married! She'll stay here in this house and have as much care and kindness as I can give her and she'll not be ashamed.

Barnood: But the child will have no name!

Lena: Name! Name! It'll have my name, Serang! It's just as good a name as Roche . . . or Barnood or Thompson, even! You'd tie my girl to that *(Pointing to Walt)* for her whole life, for its name?

John: You've gone crazy. You and your ideas about Sarilin. You can't stay in my house if you go on this fool way.

Lena: Then I'll leave your house and your fifty acres of grey stone. I'll take her and I'll go out front. And whatever I do, that baby is goin to be born into the world with the best chancet I can give it.

Walt: What'll I do?

Lena: You? Oh, get out. Go! You wasn't no more to blame than she was. Young fools, that's all. It wouldn't've been so bad if you hadn't got your lying friends to say that they . . . they . . . they'd been with her too. Go.

John: Here, wait! The money.

Lena: We'll not take his money, no more than his name.

(Walt moves toward the door but Barnood steps in front of it. They all watch Lena, who seems let down and then speaks . . . as if repeating her faith.)

Lena: She told me a baby that wasn't wanted by its mother ought never to be born. Sarilin'll want her baby . . .

(A piercing scream is heard from Sarilin's room. All turn and look and Lena, terror in her every gesture, rushes to the door. She is gone an instant and then calls.)

Lena: John! John!

(John goes into the room quickly and comes out an instant later.)

Thompson: *(Anxiously)* What's the matter? Is she hurt?

John: Will you take your car and go and get the doctor down at Hendale?

Thompson: Yes, of course. What's wrong?

John: She fell.

Curtain

A39

Four months later.

The Serang living room has sunk back into its old dilapidation. The table is piled with the dirty dishes of many meals and under them is the red table cloth, soiled and bedraggled. The remaining muslin curtains on the windows are stringy and torn. Sarilin bends over the dishpan on the stove and the two boys are seated at the table, finishing their supper. Lena, dishevelled and tired, her valiant air completely gone, is moving about the room. The oil lamp is burning on the table and the windows are becoming a deep purple.

John is lounging listlessly against the jamb of the open door, talking to Nosse, who is inside the room.

Nosse: *(Putting on his hat with an air of finality)* Well, John, this ain't the first time or the second time even I've come and seen about this bill but it's got to be the last. I hate to close down on a feller but I got to think of myself oncet in a while.

John: Lookut her, Tad. I'd give it to you if I had it but I ain't got it. I ain't found a thing to do all winter.

Nosse: Well, I can't wait much longer. John, I'm tellin you. And this farm ain't worth nothin. Wouldn't cover this here. *(Unfolding the bill he has had in his hands)*

John: *(Looking out the door)* No, it ain't worth much.

Nosse: *(Abruptly)* I can't wait here all night. Will you pay somethun towards it?

John: *(Wearily)* I tell you I ain't got a thing.

Nosse: *(Buttoning his coat)* Well, I got to shut down on you then.

John: *(Moving to let him pass)* I suppose you have.

Nosse: You know me, John. You know it ain't to my likin . . .

John: *(With a sardonic laugh)* I know, Tad. Good night.

(Nosse goes out and John continues to lean against the door.)

Lena: *(Anxiously)* He ain't goin to shut down on us at the store? He wouldn't do that?

John: Why wouldn't he? He's got to live, I suppose, like anybody else. He can't help hisself.

Lena: He wouldn't take the farm, would he?

John: *(Derisively)* It ain't worth half the bill. He's got some sense.

Lena: What'll we do, John? Where'll we buy anythin?

John: No place I know of. I suppose we'll starve like we done before.

Lena: If you'd kept on teamin . . .

John: *(Angrily)* Shut up about me teamin . . . If you hadn't gone on like a crazy person we wouldn't've been shut off at the store.

Sarilin: *(Looking into the kettle)* Pete, put some more water in this here kettle.

Pete: Put it in yourself. You're nearer to it'n I am.

Sarilin: Aw, Pete . . . Jo, you put some in.

Pete: Let her do it herself. She think we're goin to wait on her all our lives?

Lena: *(Snappishly)* Sarilin, if you want that kettle filled, do it yourself.

(Thompson and Barnood appear at the outer door.)

Thompson: Hello, John. Taking a bit of air. Kind of chilly.

John: Evenin, Lawyer Thompson. Harye, Andy? Comin in?

(The three men come into the house and close the door.)

Thompson: Good evening, Mrs. Serang.

Lena: 'Ll you have a chair?

Thompson: Well, thanks. *(He sits down)* We can't stay but a minute though.

John: It ain't late.

Barnood: We got to be up pretty early if we're countin on makin Duck Lake to-morrow.

John: Prospectin?

Thompson: Andy says he's found a likely showing.

John: Andy's been findin them showin's for fifty years. *(Sneeringly)* Andy, I suppose you're feelin a lot better since the new government's in power. Things is so much nicer. The weather's been so good . . .

Andy: Give them time, John. Give them time.

John: *(With bitter sarcasm)* I suppose the hay'll be standin shoulder high in the marshes this summer, eh, Andy? 'N they'll be buildin railroads all through the back country. Up to this here minen of yourn back of Duck Lake.

Barnood: *(With a trace of belligerence)* They can't be no worse'n the last.

Thompson: And there isn't much chance of them being any better, I'm afraid.

John: Andy thinks the new government could vote a crop of wheat onto this fifty acres of grey stone I got here.

Barnood: I don't think nothin of the sort. What I does say is, we'll have better times all round.

John: Better times for who? Tad Nosse, perhaps. No, Andy, you'll still go miles to cut marsh hay to winter your cattle and you'll still hope they's enough snow to haul it out on. And you'll still say what we need's a change in the government.

(Jo and Pete get up from the table and shuffle to the back of the room.)

Sarilin: You might do somethun besides sittin there doin nothin.

Pete: You'd think we was your slaves . . .

Lena: That'll do, Jo. You boys keep quiet.

(Lena goes into the other room.)

John: How long're you back for, Mr. Thompson?

Thompson: Just a few days, John. Long enough to see this claim Andy tells me about. I find it hard to keep out the back country this time of the year, too.

Barnood: Seems to me you find it pretty hard most any time of the year to keep out'n the back country.

John: I often wondered what you seen in the back country. It ain't nothin but a popple wilderness of granite, sickly farms'n lakes . . . A feller can't scrape a livin off'n it.

Thompson: It's a great country, John. With any sort of care it will be a pinery once more.

John: *(Disgustedly)* A lot of good a pinery'll do us a hundred years from now. People like you that don't have to make their livin back here think it's fine country, Mr. Thompson. *(Dejectedly)* Try and scrape a livin off'n this farm of mine that you can't drive a plow straight for ten feet on and you'd change your mind.

Barnood: Look at all the summer people that comes here, John. They like it.

John: They only spend money. They don't have to make none, here. 'N it'll be a long time before you'll ever see a government that'll sink a cent of money back here, Andy. They's townships that ain't got twenty voters if they got that many.

Thompson: If I hated it as much as you do, I'd leave it.

John: I suppose you'd walk to Alberta and pick choke cherries to feed yourself. If one of these damn governments Andy is always harpin on'd help a feller get off'n God forsaken farms like these here and get on land where a feller's work'd show for somethun there might be some sense to it. But there ain't . . . They bring 'em from Russia and they don't care what happens right here.

I'll bet them head lads down there to Toronto ain't never heard of Bronton or Hendale.

Barnood: You're expectin too much . . .

John: *(With his twisted smile)* I ain't expectin nothin, Andy. I ain't crazy.

Thompson: There's no law to compel you to work the farm, you know. There are lots of jobs around.

John: And they's twicet the men to fill'em, what they is. The mines ain't workin, no shantys runnin, no haulin . . . nothin . . . *(He gets up and goes to the door, opens it and looks out)* Fifty acres of grey stone. You can't get off'n it and you can't live on it.

(Sarilin has been going on with the dishes in a haphazard way. She opens the door to the other room.)

Sarilin: *(Calling)* Ain't there no more soap, Maw?

(Lena appears, helpless and a little embarassed.)

Lena: No, there ain't. Make what you've got there do.

(Thompson and Barnood watch this interchange of remarks about the soap. John pays no attention. Jo has slipped outside. Lena fusses at the dishpan for a moment and returns to the side room.)

Barnood: Well, John, we'd best be goin. What do you think, Mr. Thompson.

(Barnood and Thompson rise.)

Thompson: Yes, I think we had. *(He stretches and looks around)* The place looks different than when I was last here, John.

John: *(With his twisted smile)* I never could figger out what got into the old woman there for awhile. *(Smiles again)* It ain't lasted, anyways.

Thompson: What's happened to young Walt Roche?

John: Nothin that I know of. He's around. Trap-

pin, I suppose.

Thompson: You didn't keep on teaming very long, John.

John: Got histed out'n my job. Some fellow from Hendale come along and offered to do the teamin for fifty cents a day less. I quit.

Thompson: *(He nods his head toward Sarilin)* How is the young one, all right again?

John: *(Looking at Sarilin, contemptuously)* You don't need to waste no worry on her.

Thompson: She was pretty ill when I left here last winter.

John: Aw! Tessie put her up to it. *(Sneers)* I don't know but what she showed pretty good sense, too. I'll walk out to the gate with you.

(The three men go out, nodding to Pete and ignoring Sarilin.)

Sarilin: *(To Pete)* You might help with these dishes. I'd get them done quicker.

Pete: What do you want 'em done for. You ain't goin no place.

Sarilin: I'm goin over to see Tessie.

Pete: Hunh! Think I believe that? You're gettin pretty fond of Tessie. Goin out to see her every night.

Sarilin: Well, it ain't none of your business anyways. Here! Throw this dishwater out.

Pete: Throw it out yourself. That's your work. I done enough for you and so did maw and Jo last winter. You needn't think you can get any help out'n me again.

(Sarilin goes outside to empty the dishpan and Lena comes into the room. She kicks before her the calendar and bends and picks it up.)

Lena: Put that in the stove, Pete. It's been kickin around for a week or more. *(Pete takes it, looks at it and then puts it in the stove)* Where is your paw?

Pete: He went out with Mr. Thompson.

Lena: Where's Jo?

Pete: Outside.

Lena: Tell him to get in here and get to bed. *(To Sarilin)* You'd best be gettin in there too.

(Pete goes out and calls Jo. They both come in.)

Sarilin: I don't want to go to bed yet. I'm goin out. I'm goin over to see Tessie for a while.

Jo: I don't want to come in, Maw. I was talkin to Jim Relmer. It ain't hardly dark yet.

Lena: *(To Sarilin)* Ain't you got no sense at all? Can't you remember nothin?

Sarilin: I don't care. I'm goin out.

Lena: We'll see what your paw says. Go on up to bed you two.

Pete: She ought to be sent too.

(John returns.)

John: I wonder what young Relmer sees in this part of the woods. I seen him around three or four times now.

Lena: *(Naggingly)* It's a wonder to me what anybody sees in this part of the woods. If you'd kept on workin for a year we could've left . . . instead of stayin on here. *(To Sarilin)* You go in there to bed.

John: *(Angrily)* I wish you'd shut up once and for all about leavin here. We can't, that's all they is to it. We're here and here we'll stick till we die. Even then they'll find a hole someplace in the grey stones and . . .

Lena: *(Interrupting)* There ain't any soap in the house, even.

John: It's a damn wonder they's any house left after the money you run me into last year with that young one. *(To Sarilin)* Go in there and get to bed. Get!

Sarilin: It ain't fair. I'm old enough to have some fun.

John: You ain't old enough to be left three feet out'n a person's sight. I'd as soon trust a four months old pup. *(She doesn't move and John comes to her)* Will you never learn nothin? *(He takes her roughly by the arm, opens the door, and almost throws her into the room)* See you go to bed, too!

Lena: *(Standing by the table in the centre of the room)* It's a wonder I ever stood it.

John: Stood what?

Lena: Livin here with you all these years. Twelve young ones . . . five of them dead . . . two gone fightin for their country . . . three of them left home . . . *(She sighs in a hopeless way. Then, seeing John leaning across the table, his face black and angry)* Yes, and half starved, too, the best part of the time.

John: *(Slowly and bitterly)* And what about me? The best twenty years of a man's life gone into fifty acres of grey stone. Twenty year! And what have we got to show for it? Nothin. When we might've gone, you wouldn't leave your people. You wanted friends. Now they's hardly a soul in the country side'll come inside your door because of the fool way you went on with Sarilin. **You** kept us here. Scratchin away like the scrawny chickens you got, tryin to feed twelve mouths on this fifty acres of grey stone. *(He strides to the door and flings it open)* Fifty acres of grey stone. And you rail at me? Me, that's put in my whole life on your father's damn farm. What about me?

Lena: *(With a tired, broken sigh)* Oh, well. I guess we're pretty much in the same boat. *(She goes to the window, looks out for a moment and turns toward him)* We must've been kinda fond of each other to stick together all these years, John?

John: *(Brutal and uncompromising)* Fond? Fond be damned. We stuck together because we couldn't get away from each other. That's why we stuck. We're chained here. That's what we are. Just like them stones outside the door, there. Fond? Bah! *(He picks up the lamp)*

Well, are you goin to stay up all night?

Lena: No, I'll come now.

(She closes the rear door, goes to the door of Sarilin's room, opens it, listens and closes it. She follows John upstairs and as soon as the last ray of light has gone there is a low whistle. The door at the left opens and Sarilin tip-toes into the room. Against the window appears the silhouette of a man's head. There is a tap on the window and Sarilin crosses to the outer door. She opens it with an admonitory, "sh"! A man steps in and takes her arm roughly.)

The man: *(In an intense whisper)* What kept you?

Sarilin: Sh! Maw and paw sent me to bed.

The man: I been waitin an hour. Come on!

Sarilin: All right.

(He takes her arms roughly and just before they go swings her to him and kisses her viciously, her head bent far back.)

Curtain

The Unreasonable Act of Julian Waterman

Ron Taylor

Ron Taylor was born in Toronto, Ontario, and began his dramatic life as an actor rather than a writer. He received his early training from Sterndale Bennett at the Royal Conservatory, and later studied with Wynn Handman in New York. As an actor, he has performed in summer stock at Port Carling; on CBC television; and in films.

His first plays, "The Door" and "The Songwriter" were produced at Toronto's Theatre in The Dell in 1962. Since then he has written innumerable plays for both radio and television, including the series "To See Ourselves", "Sunday at Nine", "Program X" and "Teleplay". His successful half hour television play "Ride to the Hill", has been published in an anthology.

Mr. Taylor's contribution to this volume is a witty and sophisticated comedy which has enjoyed considerable success in the theatre, to the point of outstripping a Neil Simon comedy at the same theatre, in terms of both ticket sales and length of run. "The Unreasonable Act of Julian Waterman" is, however, an extremely difficult play to do. In order for it to succeed, it requires three important elements: split-second timing, acting of the highest professional calibre, and a director with a firm hand. Ron Taylor himself does not hesitate to quote the late Sir Noel Coward on the subject. Speaking of his play "Hay Fever", Coward wrote:

"It has certainly proved to be a great joy to amateurs, owing I suppose to the smallness of its cast and the fact that it has only one set, which must lead them to imagine that it is easy to act . . . no word of mine shall be spoken, no warning finger of experience raised to discourage them, beyond the timorous suggestion that from the professional standpoint, it is far and away one of the most difficult plays to perform that I have ever encountered . . . "

We suggest that the same may be said of "The Unreasonable Act of Julian Waterman". Amateurs beware!

Cast of characters

Barb and Julian — a fashionable couple in their
early thirties
Hank — their world-travelled writer friend
Officer — a young policeman

Act one

Setting: Julian and Barb's apartment.

The two-bedroom apartment is expensive, for Julian Waterman is a good provider. There is fine furniture. There are oil paintings, signed lithos, vases, sculpture, books, records, everything a well-to-do urbanite could wish for.

It is mid-afternoon.

The front door flies open and Barb rushes in. Julian follows at his own pace.

Barb: He's not here.

(Julian closes the door.)

Julian: I didn't think he would be.

Barb: The superintendent could have let him in.

Julian: If we just sit down and be calm, I'm sure he'll turn up.

Barb: How the hell could a thing like this happen? It's so embarrassing. He'll think we didn't bother to meet him.

Julian: When he gets here we'll simply explain that we went to the airport and somehow missed him.

Barb: No wonder. We didn't even get into the parking lot.

Julian: It's true.

Barb: One more car and we would have made it. Why did you have to let those people cut in like that?

Julian: I was just being courteous.

Barb: You were being considerate, Julian. That's your whole problem. You're too damn considerate. People walk all over you.

Julian: They did not walk all over me.

Barb: They got into the parking lot and we didn't. It's the same thing.

Julian: I didn't know the parking lot was going to be full.

Barb: It wasn't going to be full. It was going to have room for one more car, us, if you hadn't let those people cut in like that.

Julian: We should have allowed more time.

Barb: I couldn't get an earlier hair appointment. I thought it was important to look my best for him.

Julian: They build these planes so . . .

(Barb suddenly disappears into the bedroom.)

Julian: *(Louder)* I say, they build these planes so big you could have a thousand people going out to meet one flight. No wonder the parking lots can't keep up.

(Barb reappears with a dress box. She opens it and holds up an outrageously sexy negligee.)

Barb: Tell me the truth. What do you think?

Julian: It's very nice.

Barb: Do you think he'll like it?

Julian: I don't see why he shouldn't.

Barb: It cost an arm and a leg.

Julian: I can imagine.

Barb: Julian, I don't care what it cost, as long as it makes him happy. Do you realise that inviting him here is the most exciting thing that's ever happened to us. Whoever said that two is company and three's a crowd didn't know what the hell he was talking about. The first thing we should do is make a schedule. What do you think? Alternate nights, or alternate weeks?

Julian: I think that's something we're going to have to sit down and discuss together.

Barb: You're right. From now on, whatever we decide, it has to be decided by the three of us.

Julian: It seems only fair.

Barb: Julian, this'll be very good for you, too. It's going to allow you more free time. You won't have to worry about entertaining me every night. You can find new hobbies. You can even devote more time to your business without feeling guilty about it.

Julian: Yes, I suppose I can.

Barb: The trouble with us, Julian, is that we're too damn comfortable. We're too well off. We're too secure. Nothing ever happens to us. Where's the adventure, the romance, new things and fresh experiences that should be happening every minute of the day? I'm not blaming you, Julian. A thing like this is as much my responsibility as it is yours. We owe it to ourselves to make life as interesting as possible.

Julian: You could always take another extension course.

Barb: Julian, I'm sick to death of taking extension courses. If I see one more Yoga twisted up like a pretzel, I think I'll bring up. All that rhythmic dancing with those damn balls. And interior decorating! How many times can we repaint the apartment?

Julian: I enjoyed your gourmet cooking.

Barb: Gourmet cooking was fine, but who wants to spend the rest of their life with a roast duckling in orange sauce. Where's the exchange, Julian? Where's the contact with another human being? The thrill of human intercourse?

Julian: How about pottery making?

Barb: Julian, I'm not looking for self-expression. I'm looking for excitement, and a handful of wet clay just isn't going to do it for me. We're getting on. This may be our last chance. Before you know it we'll be out shopping for his and her rocking chairs. The worst thing we can do is to go through life wondering what might have happened if we just had the courage to try something a little out of the ordinary.

Julian: That's true. I wonder what the neighbours are going to think?

Barb: Who worries about neighbours in a high-rise apartment? I don't even know any neighbours.

Julian: Come to think of it. Neither do I.

Barb: The point is that you have to use your imagination, Julian. You have to be creative. If it weren't for people like us, there'd never be any progress. This could turn out to be a very important social experiment.

Julian: Maybe I should keep notes.

Barb: I don't think that will be necessary.

Julian: It was just a thought.

Barb: Forget it. Julian, when he gets here it'll be like throwing open the windows and airing out our whole lives. The man has travelled all over the world going from one adventure to another. If anyone knows how to live it's him.

Julian: He's certainly enjoyed a different life-style.

Barb: I'll say he has.

Julian: After all that free-wheeling adventure, I wonder how he's going to adjust.

Barb: How do you mean?

Julian: He might find it difficult to settle down.

Barb: My God, I never thought of that. You're right. One week with us and he'll be like a caged lion.

Julian: It's possible.

Barb: Julian, I'm not taking any chances. I'll order another nightgown.

(She stuffs the negligee into the dress box and carries it back into the bedroom.)

Julian: On the other hand, he might be just as content to put his feet up and relax. I wonder what he's planning to do. I suppose I could always take him into the firm.

Barb: (Off) Julian, he's the last person in the

world to go into an accounting firm. I don't think you have to worry about him anyway. I'm sure he'll find something. Something really exciting. *(She comes back into the living-room.)* I don't understand what's taking him so long.

Julian: I don't understand why he didn't sit tight and wait for us.

Barb: Can you imagine him sitting and waiting? As soon as he saw we weren't there he'd say, the hell with us, and grab the first cab into town. I wonder why he isn't here already?

Julian: Maybe he stopped off for a drink.

Barb: Oh my God yes. Of course he did. He probably stopped in at . . .

(Her eyes cloud over with memories.)

Julian: At Vardy's.

Barb: Yes, at Vardy's. Julian, I just want you to know that what you're doing is one of the kindest, most wonderful things that any husband has ever done. You're a very brave, generous and considerate man.

(She kisses him gently.)

Julian: I think we should all go out to dinner tonight.

Barb: I was going to make a roast. I thought a nice home-cooked meal. He's spent his whole life eating in restaurants.

Julian: That's true. He has. My God, what a way to live.

Barb: Mind you, it's always nice to eat out.

Julian: I thought it would give us a chance to talk.

Barb: That's right. How can we talk if I'm cooking and washing dishes?

Julian: That's what I thought. Besides, he has the rest of his life to eat home-cooked meals.

Barb: He has, hasn't he. And what a lovely way to put it. My Julian always knows the right thing to say.

(She kisses him once more.)

Julian: It might not be a bad idea to call Vardy's and see if he's there.

Barb: You're right. That's a wonderful idea. *(She rushes to the phone.)*

Julian: He's liable to get started and forget all about us.

(Barb picks up the phone; then puts it down.)

Barb: Julian, maybe you'd better call. I wouldn't want him to think I was pushing.

Julian: Why should he think that? He seemed quite interested in his letter.

Barb: Interested! He'd better be a hell of a lot more than that.

Julian: I used the wrong word. I should have said 'anxious.'

Barb: Anxious! Julian, do you really think he's anxious?

Julian: Of course I do. He was always very fond of you.

Barb: Fond of me! He was **crazy** about me! The man was falling at my feet.

Julian: Yes, he certainly was.

Barb: When I think of the way he used to worship me. If he's only half as interested there's nothing to worry about.

Julian: Exactly.

Barb: Julian, I'm worried. What if he's having second thoughts? People change. You can't expect a person to feel the same way forever.

Julian: That's something we won't know until he gets here. Besides, it all depends how deep those feelings really go.

Barb: They go deep, Julian. They go very deep.

Julian: Then there's nothing to worry about.

(He picks up the phone.)

Julian: I'd better call before he gets too far along.

Barb: That's a good idea.

(Julian dials and gets an answer almost immediately.)

Julian: Hello, Mr. Vardy? It's Julian Waterman calling. I wonder if you'd mind paging a Mr. Hank Grant for me. Oh you don't. You're sure. I see. Thank you, Mr. Vardy. Yes, if he comes in. Thank you. Goodbye.

(Barb looks worried.)

Julian: He's not there. Mr. Vardy remembers him very well. I suppose he could have stopped in somewhere else.

Barb: Julian, do you think he's changed his mind?

Julian: I think we'd be jumping to conclusions if we didn't wait this out a little longer.

Barb: I'm not blaming him if he has. After all, it's been years. I haven't gotten any younger.

Julian: None of us have.

Barb: The son-of-a-bitch could at least have had the decency to call.

Julian: Maybe he hasn't had a chance.

Barb: Oh my God. Maybe he's had an accident.

Julian: That's possible.

Barb: Julian, call the police. Call the hospitals. If anything's happened to him I'll kill myself.

(Julian goes to the phone.)

Julian: There's no point in getting upset.

Barb: I can't help it. This whole damn thing is my fault. I've been too damn selfish and you know it. You've got to stop giving in to me, Julian. You've got to stop pampering me. Nobody has a right to get their own way all the time.

Julian: I don't think you're being fair to yourself.

Barb: There you go being considerate again.

(Julian hesitates at the telephone.)

Julian: Do you mind if I call the hospitals first?

Barb: Wouldn't it be faster to call the police? They'd know if there was an accident.

Julian: Yes, I suppose they would.

(He hesitates . . . then begins to dial.)

Julian: I think I'll call the hospitals first.

Barb: Julian, we just agreed that it would be faster to call the police.

Julian: Yes I know. Just the same, I'd like to try the hospitals first.

Barb: Julian, call the police.

Julian: It may not even be necessary. We'll see what the hospitals have to say.

Barb: Will you call the goddam police for crissake!

Julian: No.

Barb: What do you mean, no?

Julian: I mean that you can't expect to have your own way all the time.

Barb: Julian, this is an emergency. It is not the time to assert yourself. I appreciate what you're trying to do for me, but I'd much rather you called the police.

Julian: I can't.

Barb: Why not?

Julian: It upsets me.

Barb: In what way?

Julian: It just upsets me. Policemen make me nervous. They always have. I'm afraid of them.

Barb: Why?

Julian: I don't know why. All I know is that I am very uncomfortable in the presence of a policeman. I always feel as though I've done something.

Barb: Done what?

Julian: Anything. I feel guilty.

Barb: Then you must have done something.

Julian: Whose side are you on?

Barb: I don't mean now. I mean in your childhood.

Julian: I wonder if that's possible. *(Interested)* As a matter of fact, now that I think of it . . .

Barb: Julian, not now. Give me the telephone.

(She takes it from him.)

Julian: I'm sorry if I let you down.

Barb: It's not your fault. You couldn't help it. My poor sweet Julian who wouldn't hurt a fly.

Julian: When any twenty-year-old kid of a policeman can make me feel like a bad little boy, there must be something wrong.

Barb: I don't think it's serious. *(Into the phone)* Yes. I'd like to inquire about an accident. I said, 'inquire' not report. My name?

(Julian begins signalling not to tell.)

Barb: Why do you have to know my name? Alright, my name is Mrs. Julian Waterman.

(Julian slaps his forehead in exasperation.)

Barb: My address? Oh for God sake. I told you, I just want to ask about . . .

(Julian signals frantically.)

Alright, my address is 560 Avenue Road, apartment 802.

(How could she do this to him?)

Yes, I want to find out if there's been an accident. No, my husband is right here. This man is a friend of ours.

(There is a knock at the door.)

Barb: Julian, get the door. *(Into the phone)* His name is . . . Oh my God it must be him. I'm sorry. Goodbye.

(She hangs up the phone.)

(Julian opens the door to reveal Hank Grant with a huge suitcase, a rifle, a portable typewriter, a tennis racquet and a set of golf clubs.)

Hank: Julian.

Julian: Well, well, well.

Hank: I didn't bother to buzz. I just came on through with one of your neighbours.

Julian: Come in. Come in. We were just . . .

(Hank is looking past Julian to Barb. She in turn is looking at him. Their eyes are rivetted to one another. Their bodies tense like two springs ready to uncoil.)

Hank: Barb.

Barb: Hank.

Julian: I'll get your things.

(Julian steps into the hall. He lifts the bag with some difficulty and drags it into the apartment.

Just then a spring uncoils. Barb rushes across the room. Hank comes to meet her. Julian is almost caught between the two of them as they embrace and kiss passionately.)

Barb: It's been so long.

Hank: Yes, yes, I know.

Barb: I waited and waited.

Hank: Thought I'd go mad.

Barb: Out of my mind.

Hank: Couldn't stand it.

Barb: Going to explode.

(They continue kissing as Julian brings in the other things.)

Julian: We were just about to call the hospital. We thought you had an accident.

(Hank stops kissing.)

Hank: Accident?

Julian: Yes, we couldn't understand what was taking you so long.

Barb: That's right. Where the hell were you?

Hank: As a matter of fact, I was wondering why you didn't come out to the airport.

Barb: We did, but Julian couldn't find a place to park.

Julian: We should have left a little sooner.

Barb: By the time we got to the terminal you were gone.

Hank: I thought you weren't coming, so I hailed a cab.

Barb: That's what I told Julian.

Hank: *(To Julian)* She knows me.

Barb: *(Suspiciously)* Then why didn't you get here ahead of us?

Hank: We had a flat tire.

Julian: I knew there was an explanation.

Hank: The jack broke and we couldn't change it. Have you ever tried to get somebody to stop and help you on one of those expressways? We could have sat there all day.

Barb: It's too bad we didn't take the expressway. Julian would have stopped.

Hank: You probably wouldn't have known it was me.

Barb: It doesn't matter. Julian would have stopped.

Hank: *(Impressed)* Is that right?

Julian: Can I get you a drink, Hank?

Hank: Yes thank you, Julian. Scotch please. On the rocks.

Julian: On the rocks. *(To Barb)* Dear?

Barb: I'm so excited I don't know what to have.

Hank: Why don't you have the usual?

Barb: There's no Vermouth. We hardly drink at all anymore.

Julian: I wouldn't say that. I like a brandy in the evening when I read.

Barb: He likes to read in the evening.

Hank: Oh really.

(Hank and Barb exchange knowing looks. Hank begins to chuckle. Barb giggles. They come together for an intense, hungry kiss.)

Julian: Why don't we have a sherry?

(Julian pours the drinks as Hank and Barb continue to smooch on the couch. When the drinks are ready, Julian clears his throat loudly and presents the scotch to Hank, the sherry to Barb.)

Hank: Thank you, Julian.

Barb: Thank you, Julian.

(Julian picks up his own sherry.)

Julian: I believe this calls for a toast. *(He raises his glass.)* To peace and harmony.

Hank: To good times.

Barb: To our happiness.

(They all drink.)

Hank: Julian, I just want you to know how grateful I am.

Barb: So do I, Julian.

Hank: There comes a time when a man has to settle down, when he's weary of travelling all over the world, living in hotel rooms.

Barb: Eating in restaurants.

Hank: I've needed a home for quite some time, Julian. Some place where I could put my feet up and feel comfortable.

(He is about to swing his legs up on the coffee table when Barb stops him.)

Barb: It's an antique.

Hank: Sorry. *(To Julian)* And to be perfectly frank, I'm getting pretty damn tired of chasing around after it. Sometimes I listen to myself trying to make out with some girl and it almost makes me sick, saying the same things over and over, meeting a new woman and telling her all about me. I get bored just listening to myself. What I'd like is to be able to come home in the evening, put my arm around the woman I love, and know that it's there when I want it.

Barb: Oh, God, he puts it so beautifully.

(She begins biting his neck.)

Hank: I have to admit that when I first got your letter I was, frankly, quite shocked. Then I got thinking about it, and, what the hell. We're living in new times. People don't think of these things the way they used to. You live the way you want to live. Life is too short, Julian. The whole damn world could blow up any minute. Besides, none of us is getting any younger. *(To Barb)* I'm sorry Barb. I didn't mean that you

don't look as delicious as you ever did. In fact, more so. You seem somehow so ripe, Barbara.

Barb: Ripe?

Hank: Yes, ripe. I've never seen you look like this before. It's wonderful. You're more beautiful than ever.

Barb: And you're more handsome than ever. There's something even more solid, more masculine about you. Those touches of grey in your hair, they're something a woman finds hard to resist.

Hank: It's nice of you to say so. Of course it is thinning out a bit on top, but I suppose it's still alright for a man of my age.

Barb: You're magnificent. You couldn't be better.

Hank: And Julian. Well . . .

Barb: Julian is Julian.

Hank: He certainly is. You haven't changed, Julian. You look the same as you always did.

Julian: Thank you. I think.

Hank: I meant that as a compliment.

Julian: I'm sorry. Of course.

Hank: When I think of the opportunity I missed ten years ago, and now to have a second chance. I can't tell you how grateful I am, Julian. It's very manly of you. I just don't know what I was thinking about in those days.

Barb: You were younger. We all were.

Hank: All I knew was, I had to travel light. No burdens. Nothing to slow me down on that one road ahead. And then one day I suddenly realised that I was still going down that same old road, only I really had nothing to show for it.

Barb: I don't see how you can say that. You've been all over the world. Your stories have been in all the papers. You've had enough adventure for a dozen men.

Hank: I suppose it sounds that way to you people back here, but after you've lived with it as long as I have it's just another job. I'm a correspondent and I travel around looking for news and most of the news is about war; so I see a lot of war and after a while I get so confused I can't tell one war from the other. I get the sides mixed up too. I keep forgetting who the good guys are. Maybe I'm suffering from fatigue. What the hell, soldiers get it. Why shouldn't it happen to a correspondent? Someday I'm going to total up all the casualty lists I've reported in my career. I think the figures would be astounding. Maybe you could do that for me, Julian. You're an expert in that field.

Julian: I'd be glad to, if you think it would help.

Hank: I think it would be of interest to people to know just how many casualties I've reported in the course of my work.

Barb: (Seductively) I'd like to bet that you've reported more casualties than any other man in the business.

Hank: I certainly think I've done my share.

Barb: Of course you have. Now let somebody else do the dirty work for a change.

Hank: That's exactly the way I feel about it. I just want to wash my hands of the whole thing. You see, what I'd like to do is get a nice quiet job on one of the dailies. I don't care if they have me covering garden parties. All I'm looking for is a little peace and quiet. I'll go down and see Pete Harris on Monday. He's managing editor here. We used to be very good friends. I'm sure he can do something for me.

Julian: Maybe he can get you into the sports department.

Hank: As a matter of fact, that's just what I had in mind. I have a pretty good background there. Played a lot of football, you know.

Barb: (Very sexy) Oh my God, I'll say you did.

Hank: I almost turned pro there at one time.

Julian: I didn't know that.

Hank: Oh yes. I had a couple of very good offers.

Julian: I suppose a thing like that could bother you for the rest of your life.

Hank: How do you mean?

Julian: Wondering how things might have turned out if you'd taken one of those offers.

Hank: Well no, not really.

Barb: How could he take a football offer when he wanted to be a correspondent?

Hank: That's right, Julian. You see, I had this . . . this thing.

Barb: He wanted to be a correspondent.

Hank: That's not quite correct, Barb.

Barb: I thought that's what you wanted.

Hank: I did, but there's more to it than that. Do you understand what I mean, Julian?

Julian: Not quite.

Hank: I wanted the experience, the adventure . . . the background.

Barb: The background for what, for crissake?

Hank: Julian knows what I mean. Don't you, Julian?

Julian: I really can't say that I do.

Hank: Who do we know that wrote for a newspaper, involved himself in a war, and went through one adventure after another?

Barb: You! You're the only one we know who's ever done anything even remotely exciting.

Hank: I don't mean someone we know personally. I mean someone we know of. Someone very famous. Someone we all love. Julian knows who I'm talking about.

Julian: I can't honestly say that I do.

Hank: Take a guess.

Julian: I really don't think I'm qualified.

Hank: Hemingway. Ernest Hemingway.

Barb: What about him?

Hank: That's what I wanted to be.

Barb: You wanted to be Ernest Hemingway?

Hank: I didn't want to **be** Ernest Hemingway. I wanted to be **like** the man. Don't you understand? These past fifteen years have been a storing of experience, a gathering of material, a period of preparation.

Barb: Preparation for what?

Hank: Tell her, Julian.

Barb: Will you leave Julian out of this.

Hank: I feel that Julian understands.

Barb: How can he understand if he doesn't know what the hell you're talking about? A preparation for what? For what has this been a period of preparation for?

Hank: *(He would rather have told Julian)* My novel.

Barb: *(In awe)* My God, Julian. He's written a novel.

Julian: Congratulations, Hank.

Barb: A whole bloody novel. He'll win a Pulitzer prize. I know he will.

Julian: Who's the publisher?

Barb: He even looks like Hemingway. Julian, doesn't he look like Hemingway?

Julian: I hope we'll have an opportunity of reading it before . . .

Barb: Why don't we read it now?

Julian: Maybe he'd rather wait until we've all

had a chance to . . .

Barb: I'm too excited. I know exactly what we'll do. We'll forget about going out. We'll order Chinese food. We'll just stay in and sit here while Hank reads his novel to us. We'll stay up all night. Julian, it's the most exciting thing that's ever happened to us. How many people have had an author read his novel to them right in their own livingroom?

Julian: He may not have a copy with him.

Barb: Of course he has a copy. Why would he come here without a copy of his novel? Julian, get the bags.

Hank: I don't have a copy.

Julian: I didn't feel like Chinese food anyway.

Barb: Why not?

Julian: We had it last night.

Barb: Julian, I'm asking him why he didn't bring a copy of his novel.

Julian: I'm sorry.

Hank: Well, the fact is, I haven't written it yet.

Barb: You mean it isn't finished.

Julian: These things take time.

Hank: It isn't started.

Barb: What the hell have you been doing all these years?

Hank: I told you. I've been storing up experiences. Drinking great gulps from the cup of life, as it were.

Julian: And now he feels that he's ready.

Hank: Exactly.

Barb: I'm sorry. I can't help feeling cheated.

Hank: There's nothing to feel cheated about. As soon as I get settled, I'm going to begin. I don't expect my work at the newspaper to take up too much time. I figure about six months.

Barb: (Impressed) For a whole novel?

Hank: Why not? I'm a professional. It's not as though I've never put one sentence in front of another before. I tell you what. Is there a calendar around here?

Julian: On the desk.

(Hank goes to the desk.)

Hank: O.K. I'm going to mark this calendar six months from today, and you just see if I haven't given birth by then. (He is about to mark it.) Somebody's already marked it.

Julian: Let me see that.

(Julian looks at the calendar.)

Julian: Well, for goodness sake. That was an apt phrase.

Hank: What was?

Julian: Your giving birth to a novel.

Hank: It's really not that original, Julian.

Barb: I forgot all about it.

Hank: Forgot about what? (To Julian) What did she forget?

Julian: The circle on the calendar. It's the same date as the baby.

Hank: What baby?

Barb: I forgot all about it.

Hank: She's going to have a baby?

(Julian points to the spot on the calendar.)

Julian: Right about there.

Hank: (Truly staggered) I think someone should have told me.

Barb: I forgot.

Hank: How can you forget a thing like that?

Barb: I forget all the time. Don't I, Julian?

Julian: I had to mark the calendar so she'd remember.

Hank: I've never heard of anyone who couldn't remember. No wonder she looked so ripe. Of course this changes everything.

Barb: Oh no. No it doesn't. Does it, Julian.

Julian: I really don't see why it should.

Hank: She's going to have a baby. Your baby. (To Barb) Isn't it?

Barb: Of course. What a cruel thing to say.

Hank: I'm sorry. (To Julian) She's going to have your baby, and you don't think it makes any difference?

Julian: Not really. No.

Barb: Julian feels that the baby can only benefit by having two fathers with such diverse interests.

Hank: I really don't think I should have come.

Barb: Of course you should. Don't you see. It's not a matter of the baby being mine and Julian's. It's going to belong to all of us. The baby is simply ours.

Hank: It's still his.

Barb: Not quite.

Hank: You just got through telling me it was his.

Barb: It is, and it isn't.

Hank: I don't understand that. Either it is or it isn't.

Barb: It is, but it isn't.

B12

Hank: Now that's impossible.

Barb: The fact is, that at the time, I happened to be thinking of you.

Hank: At what time?

Barb: The time of conception.

Hank: You were thinking of me?

Barb: Exactly.

Hank: In bed?

Barb: Where else?

Hank: Julian, this is very embarassing.

Barb: Julian knows all about it.

Hank: You told Julian a thing like that?

Barb: Either you're honest with one another or you're not.

Hank: Of course. (A flash of inspiration) How do you know that this baby . . . ?

Barb: (Beating him to the punch) Julian keeps a diary.

Hank: I see.

Barb: The point is that I feel the baby is as much yours as it is Julian's.

Hank: I was three thousand miles away.

Barb: Not to me you weren't.

Hank: I really wasn't expecting anything like this.

Julian: Let me get you another drink.

Hank: Thank you, Julian. (To Barb) All these years of preparation, and now, just when everything seemed to be falling into place, when I thought I'd finally found the right atmosphere for my novel, the last thing in the world I wanted was to be burdened with parenthood. A man has to come into these things gradually. I haven't even

been married. How can you expect me to accept parenthood?

Barb: That's the beauty of the whole thing. Julian is here to accept it for you.

Hank: Frankly, I don't think this is being very fair to Julian.

Barb: (Strongly) Julian is perfectly happy with the arrangement.

Hank: (Thinking it out) Frankly, I can't help feeling that we're taking advantage of him.

Barb: (Very strongly) He is not being taken advantage of.

Hank: (Still working on it) If he's happy with the arrangement, and he doesn't think he's being taken advantage of, then . . .

Barb: Then what?

Hank: (Reaching his conclusion) Then Julian is a sap.

(Barb slaps him a terrific wallop across the face.)

Barb: My Julian is not a sap. He is a very considerate person.

(Julian arrives with Hank's drink. Barb takes it instead.)

Julian: I really don't think there's any need for this hostility.

(Hank touches his face gingerly and explores the inside of his mouth with his fingers.)

Hank: (To Barb) I think you've broken my dentures.

Barb: I didn't know you had dentures.

Hank: It's only a partial. I think you've broken it.

Julian: What ever has to be done, you can send me the bill.

Hank: (Losing all patience) Now look here,

Julian. I wish you'd stop being so damned considerate. First you're willing to share your wife; then you're willing to share your child, and now you want to pay my dental bills. If you were half a man, you'd punch me right on the nose.

(Julian promptly punches Hank right on the nose. It bleeds profusely.)

Hank: *(In agony)* Oh my nose.

Barb: Julian, if you've broken his nose I'll never speak to you again.

(Julian stares at his own fist in amazement.)

Julian: I'm sorry. I don't know what in the world came over me. I'll get a towel.

(There is a knock on the door as Julian goes into the bathroom.)

Barb: Julian, it's the paperboy.

(Julian comes out with a towel, hands it to Barb and goes to the door. Barb leads Hank into the bathroom.)

Barb: If he's broken your nose, I'll never speak to him again.

(Julian opens the door. A Police Officer, looking more like a young military cadet, faces him.)

Officer: We had a call here from a Mrs. Julian Waterman.

(Julian is like someone suffering a violent reaction to an allergy.)

Julian: Yes.

Officer: Are you Mr. Waterman?

Julian: Who? Me?

Officer: Yes sir, you.

(Julian shakes his head in denial.)

Officer: Is Mrs. Waterman at home?

Julian: No. There's nobody home. Thank you for calling.

(He is about to close the door when Barb and Hank come out of the bathroom. Hank holds a towel to his nose.
The Officer steps into the apartment.)

Officer: Mrs. Waterman?

Barb: Yes.

(Julian winces.)

Officer: You called about an accident?

Hank: It was no accident. *(Pointing to Julian)* He hit me right on the nose.

Officer: *(Interested)* Oh really.

(He takes out his notebook like an eager young salesman about to write his first order.)

(To Hank) Would you like to lay a charge of assault?

Hank: Yes.

Barb: *(Astonished)* Yes?

Hank: He punched me on the nose, didn't he?

Barb: You can always punch him back.

Hank: Why should I get charged with assault.

Barb: Julian would not charge you with assault.

Officer: *(To Barb)* Excuse me. Did you say, 'Julian?'

Barb: Yes.

(Julian is in agony. The officer is delighted at having caught somebody.)

Officer: *(To Julian)* I thought you were lying. *(To Hank)* I'll have to have your name, sir.

Hank: Hank Grant. *(Aside to Barb)* How did he get here so fast?

Officer: And your address, sir.

Hank: My address?

Officer: Yes sir.

Hank: I don't have an address. That is, I was supposed to live here, but right now I'm not so sure that I'm going to stay.

Barb: You'd damn well better be sure if you're going to charge Julian with assault.

Hank: He shouldn't have punched me like that.

Barb: You asked for it.

Hank: Only because I didn't think he was capable of violence.

Barb: *(Meaningfully)* You underestimate my Julian.

Hank: What is that supposed to mean?

Barb: *(Laying it on)* What do you think it means?

Hank: Surely you're not suggesting . . .

Barb: I certainly am.

Hank: *(Incredulous)* He beats you?

(Barb turns to Julian proudly.)

Barb: Brutally!

(Julian is numb. His lips move, but no sound comes out.)

Hank: *(Horrified)* My God.

Officer: *(Eagerly)* Would you like to lay a charge of assault, m'am?

Barb: Mind your own business.

Hank: Now look here, Julian. I won't have this. Do you hear. She may be your wife, but she happens to be the woman I love.

(Julian is verging on the state of catalepsy.)

Barb: *(To Hank)* I don't see what you can do about it.

Hank: I can stay here and protect you from this Jekyll and Hyde. That's what I can do about it.

Barb: If you think you're man enough.

Hank: I'm man enough to handle him. Don't you worry about that. Besides, there's the baby to think about.

Officer: What baby?

Hank: *(Proudly)* Our baby.

Officer: *(Aghast)* He beats the baby, too?!!

(All turn as Julian falls in a dead faint.)

Curtain on Act one

Act two *Evening. Two days later.*

The drapes are drawn. The lighting is low. The music from the record player is romantic.

An elegant dinner table is set for two. Barb, in an outlandishly sexy costume, is just lighting the candles. She fusses with the place settings; then makes a tour of the livingroom, turning down a lamp here, turning up another there, trying to make the setting as seductive as possible.

Finally she goes off into the kitchen.

The front door opens and Hank enters with a newspaper under his arm. He walks into the livingroom without noticing the dinner arrangements and sinks into the sofa shaking his head.

Barb comes out of the kitchen, sees Hank, and strikes a pose.

Barb: *(Very sexy)* Hi there.

(Hank turns to see her and is overwhelmed by the costume. He stands.)

Hank: Barb. You look ravishing.

Barb: Thank you.

(Barb disappears into Hank's bedroom and returns with his slippers.)

Hank: What's going on here?

Barb: Never mind. Sit down.

(Hank hesitates.)

Barb: Sit.

(She pushes him back onto the sofa; then proceeds to take off his shoes and put on his slippers.)

Hank: *(Embarrassed)* Say, you don't have to do that.

Barb: I want to. There. Comfy?

Hank: *(Pleased in spite of himself)* Very.

Barb: I'll fix you a drink.

(She goes to the bar.)

Hank: Where's Julian?

Barb: He's working late tonight.

Hank: Oh.

Barb: I've made a special dinner, just for the two of us. It's the first chance we've had to be alone.

Hank: To tell you the truth, Barb, I'm really not that hungry. Why don't we just wait for Julian?

Barb: Julian's eating downtown. *(She holds up a glass.)* Guess what I'm drinking.

Hank: *(Worried)* The usual?

Barb: The usual.

(She presents him with his Scotch and holds her own Martini.)

Barb: Cheers.

Hank: Cheers.

(She sinks into the sofa beside him, and like the perfect wife . . .)

Barb: Now. Tell me all about the newspaper. I want to hear everything.

Hank: Well . . . I got the job.

Barb: I knew it. I knew they couldn't resist you. Good old Pete what's-his-name.

Hank: Pete Harris.

Barb: Good old Pete Harris. Oh God, we're going to have such marvelous times. I love football games. All that running and kicking. And hockey. The way they come flying down the ice, slamming into one another like that. I don't think there's anything as exciting as . . . *(Suddenly)* the **fights!** We'll be able to go to all the fights.

Hank: I don't think they have too many of those anymore.

Barb: Whatever it is. I want to share every exciting moment with you.

Hank: The fact is, Barb, I don't think you'll find it all that exciting.

Barb: Of course I will. I love sports. I've always loved sports.

Hank: Yes, I know. The point is, I won't be writing for the sports department.

Barb: Why not?

Hank: They don't have any openings. We can still go to the football games.

Barb: What department are you writing for?

Hank: It's really not that important, Barb. It's only a means to an end. The main thing in my life is this novel. I'm willing to do anything as long as I . . .

Barb: I think I have a right to know what department you're writing for.

Hank: Alright. This may sound a little strange, but when you think about it, it's not all that bad.

Barb: It sounds horrible. What is it?

Hank: Well, as I say, they didn't have any room in the sports department.

Barb: You said that.

Hank: I probably could have gone into general reporting or even politics, but that's the very thing I'm trying to get away from.

Barb: So?

Hank: So, that really leaves only one area.

Barb: What's that?

Hank: Social.

Barb: Social?

Hank: I'm going to be writing a society column.

(Barb rises.)

Barb: I think I'll have another drink.

Hank: It's really not as bad as it sounds, Barb. Actually it makes pretty good sense. It'll get me away from all that tension. I'll probably find it very relaxing.

Barb: How about dull.

Hank: It's only a stop-gap job. As soon as my novel is published I can forget about it. In six months we'll be laughing about this.

Barb: Ha, ha.

Hank: (Holding his head in his hands) To tell you the truth, I don't even know how it happened. One minute I made that crack about garden parties, and . . .

Barb: What crack?

Hank: The one I made to you and Julian. I said I didn't care if they had me covering garden parties.

Barb: You said that to Pete Harris?

Hank: Only as a figure of speech. How did I know the man was going to take me seriously. I can't understand it. We were always such good friends. I can remember in college we used to call him Spindle Legs. Poor old Peter couldn't catch a football if you painted it with glue. Did I ever tell you about the time he couldn't find his glasses? It was right before exams. The poor guy was going crazy. To this day he still believes I'm the one who hid his glasses.

Barb: Did you?

Hank: Now would I do a thing like that to poor old Pete? I tell you we had some good times. You'd think he'd have gone out of his way to get me into that sports department.

Barb: You'd certainly think so, after all the good

times you two shared.

Hank: Exactly. *(He gets up and fixes another Scotch)* Can you imagine the nerve of these people. I tell you, Barb, if I wasn't so anxious to start on this novel I'd have told old . . .

Barb: Spindle Legs.

Hank: Spindle Legs exactly where he could stick that social column.

Barb: I think you should have told him anyway.

Hank: I need that job, Barb. I can't expect to come in here and free-load off you and Julian.

Barb: I wouldn't exactly call it free-loading.

Hank: I would. I've always paid my own way. I don't see any reason to change now.

Barb: Nobody's asking you to change. I just don't see why you have to humiliate yourself this way.

Hank: Every artist has to make sacrifices, Barb.

(Barb pauses thoughtfully.)

Barb: Isn't that funny. I've never thought of you as an artist. I've always thought of you as . . . as . . .

Hank: Somebody charging down a football field?

Barb: As a matter of fact, yes.

Hank: That was a long time ago, Barb.

Barb: I haven't forgotten.

Hank: You were the most beautiful kid I've ever seen.

Barb: You were like a bull moose. You could run through the whole damn team.

Hank: I used to look for you in the stands. No matter how many people were yelling, I always felt I could hear you.

Barb: That's funny. I never yelled.

Hank: I thought you were cheering for me.

Barb: I was too embarrassed. I had braces on my teeth.

Hank: They didn't detract one bit.

Barb: I couldn't understand what you saw in me.

Hank: You were a vision of loveliness.

Barb: You were so much older.

Hank: It was my last year of high school.

Barb: And my first.

Hank: I'd spent so much time at sports that I'd fallen behind, but I've never regretted it.

Barb: The first time you asked me to dance I thought I was being abducted.

Hank: The fellows used to kid me about robbing the cradle, but I didn't care as long as I could hold you.

Barb: It was like fox-trotting with King Kong.

Hank: I can still remember my hand on your back. The touch of you under your sweater.

Barb: *(Interested)* You touched me under my sweater?

Hank: Of course not. I mean with my hand over your sweater I could feel you underneath it.

Barb: Front or back?

Hank: The back, Barb. For God sake we were dancing. What kind of a guy do you think I was?

Barb: How the hell would I know. I was only thirteen years old.

Hank: Well I certainly wasn't about to take advantage of you.

Barb: What's a little touch under the sweater?

Hank: If anybody had done a thing like that to you I think I would have killed them.

Barb: Nobody came near me all year. They were afraid of you.

Hank: I felt very protective towards you.

Barb: To tell you the truth, I was happy as hell when you graduated.

Hank: I wish I could have stayed on to look after you.

Barb: You would have been older than some of the teachers.

Hank: All those years when I didn't see you.

Barb: You had your own life to live.

Hank: And then suddenly there you were, a grown woman engaged to be married. It was such a shock to realise that I still felt the same way about you.

Barb: You were already involved with your career.

Hank: And then those wonderful, happy months when the three of us . . .

Barb: Four of us. You brought a different one every time.

Hank: Those women meant nothing to me.

Barb: I don't know where you found them all.

Hank: It was only out of respect for Julian.

Barb: You didn't have to bother. Julian wasn't fooled for a moment.

Hank: I was desperate to be near you.

Barb: You were going to Europe.

Hank: If only you had of come with me.

Barb: If only you had of asked.

Hank: Of course Julian would never have let you go.

Barb: Yes he would.

Hank: How do you know?

Barb: We talked about it.

Hank: What did he say?

Barb: He said I might regret it later if I didn't go.

Hank: What kind of a way is that to hold on to a girl?

Barb: Julian is very understanding.

Hank: Didn't he realise you could have run off?

Barb: Why would I run off when he told me to go? If he told me **not** to go, I might have run off.

Hank: What kind of reasoning is that?

Barb: It must work. He got me and you didn't.

Hank: But all I had to do was ask.

Barb: I guess he knew you wouldn't ask.

(Hank moves closer to her.)

Hank: Barb, I was so close. You don't know how much I wanted you with me.

Barb: You had your career.

Hank: All those years when we could have been together. It must have been hell for you.

Barb: Why?

Hank: Living with a man you don't love.

Barb: Who said I don't love Julian?

Hank: I just naturally assumed . . .

Barb: Why should you assume a thing like that?

Hank: Because you asked me to come and live here.

Barb: What has that got to do with loving Julian?

Hank: Barb, for heaven sake! Happily married people simply do not ask another party to come and live with them.

Barb: *(Truly amazed)* I thought we were happily married.

Hank: How could you be happily married and enter into an arrangement like this?

Barb: My God, do you honestly think that Julian isn't happy?

Hank: I wasn't thinking of Julian.

Barb: Of course not. Nobody ever thinks of Julian.

Hank: Barb, I'm trying to talk about us.

Barb: I think it's important to talk about Julian. I think it's time we stopped taking him for granted.

Hank: Nobody's taking him for granted.

Barb: That's the trouble with being married for ten years. Your senses become so dulled you can't even tell when someone is unhappy anymore. Poor Julian must be miserable.

Hank: If he is, he hides it very well.

Barb: Julian's a proud man. He wouldn't want anybody to know. Besides, he's so considerate he wouldn't want to upset anybody.

Hank: You make him sound like a saint.

Barb: That's exactly what he is. My Julian is a saint. Day after day, pretending to be happy, slugging his guts out at the office so I can have charge accounts all over town. Tonight's a perfect example. He couldn't even come home for dinner, he's working so hard. *(A thoughtful pause. A look at Hank.)* Isn't he?

Hank: What do you mean?

Barb: When a man is unhappy and he starts working late at the office, doesn't that usually mean something?

Hank: Oh no Barb, I'm sure Julian wouldn't do anything like that.

Barb: Like what?

Hank: What you're suggesting.

Barb: You're right. He wouldn't do a thing like that. I know my Julian.

(She is about to sit down and relax, when suddenly she makes a dash for the telephone.)

Hank: What are you doing?

Barb: If he's not at the office I'll kill him.

(She dials.)

Hank: Barb, this may not be such a good idea.

Barb: They always leave him a line when he works late.

(She lets the phone ring and ring. When it finally becomes clear that there is not going to be an answer she slowly lowers the receiver.)

Barb: *(Stunned)* Son-of-a-bitch.

Hank: Now Barb, don't jump to conclusions. He probably just went out for a sandwich.

Barb: If he's so unhappy, why didn't he say something.

Hank: Don't you think we should wait and hear his side of the story?

Barb: What is there to hear? He's out with another woman. Some saint!

Hank: We really don't know that. So far we only know that he doesn't answer the telephone.

Barb: You think he's got her right there in the office?

Hank: *(Exasperated)* I didn't say that.

Barb: (A howl of anguish) Oh my God!

Hank: What is it?

Barb: I picked out the couch myself. I gave it to him as an anniversary present.

Hank: In that case I'm sure Julian would never . . .

Barb: On my couch! How could he do such a thing?!

Hank: Barb, please.

Barb: Who is it? That's all I want to know. It can't be his secretary. (Second thoughts) Can it?

Hank: How would I know? I never met the woman.

Barb: It's a very common thing, you know, for a man to have an affair with his secretary. That's the first place they turn.

Hank: Barb, that whole idea is a myth. Believe me, it's highly exaggerated.

Barb: You're right. It couldn't be his secretary. After all, the woman is sixty-three years old. (Thoughtfully) I wonder who it is?

Hank: It may not be anybody. There's no sense flying off the handle, Barb. Why don't we just sit down here and wait for Julian to come home.

Barb: What if he doesn't come home?

Hank: He has to come home sometime. His clothes are still here.

(Barb allows herself to be seated on the sofa.)

Barb: You're right. As soon as he walks through the door we'll confront him with it.

Hank: The main thing right now is to stay absolutely calm.

Barb: That's a good idea. Let him make the first move.

Hank: Just don't do anything rash. That would be the worst thing you could possibly do.

Barb: I'll play it very cool.

Hank: We're all adults. We should be able to talk this out like sensible people. These things happen every day.

Barb: You're right. It happens all the time.

(For a few moments they sit quietly together like two people in a dentist's office. Suddenly:)

Barb: Not to me it doesn't.

(She jumps up and charges over to the hall closet.)

Hank: Barb, what are you doing?

(Barb puts on her coat and pulls open the door.)

Barb: I'm going down there and catch them in the act.

Hank: (With authority) Now wait a minute.

(Barb stops. She waits for Hank to say something profound. Hank can't think of anything. Finally:)

Hank: I'll go with you.

(They leave.)

The stage is empty for two beats, when Hank rushes back in. He goes to his room, retrieves his shoes, sits in a chair and hurriedly changes from his slippers. He tosses the slippers into his room and rushes out again.

The stage is empty once more.

After a couple of minutes, a key is turned in the lock. The door opens and Julian enters.

He places his briefcase on the hall table and steps into the apartment. He immediately notices the table is set for two, the candles, the unfinished drinks, the subdued lighting.

He looks in the kitchen. Nobody there. The door to the bathroom is open. The door to

Hank's room is open. The door to Julian and Barb's bedroom is closed.

Julian nods. It is a knowing nod, a resigned nod, a nod not without a touch of surprise.

He thinks of sitting down; then decides that it might be better if he announced his presence. He coughs a couple of times. No response. He goes to the bedroom door, is about to knock and changes his mind.

He quietly crosses to the hall table, picks up his briefcase and goes out, closing the door carefully behind him.

The lights fade.

Scene two

The set is exactly as we left it except that the candles are burned down to denote a passage of a couple of hours.

After a moment, the door opens and Barb enters, followed by Hank. They both look weary and dejected.

Barb goes straight to the bar. She pours a Scotch and hands it to Hank. She pours another for herself and drinks it quickly.

Hank: Maybe he went to a movie.

Barb: Sure. The back row of the balcony.

Hank: Barb, what can I say.

Barb: There's nothing to say. You think a thing like this could never happen, and suddenly it happens.

Hank: I want you to know that I intend to stand behind you one hundred per cent.

Barb: Thanks.

Hank: I just don't understand how the man can be so insensitive. To do a thing like this, at a time like this. Barb, I swear to you. I'll treat that baby as though he were my very own son. We'll call him Hank Junior.

Barb: I don't think it will fit.

Hank: Why not?

Barb: I'm hoping for a girl.

Hank: In that case I leave it up to you.

Barb: You must be starving.

Hank: Couldn't eat a thing. It might not be a bad idea for you to have something, especially when there's somebody else depending on you.

Barb: I'll take a look at the oven.

(She goes into the kitchen.)
(Hank pours another drink.)

Hank: *(Calling)* How is it?

(Barb reappears.)

Barb: It's not a meal. It's a cinder. I've got a casserole in the freezer. I'll put that on instead.

(She returns to the kitchen.

Hank settles down in a chair and is just beginning to relax with his drink, when . . .
Barb comes out of the kitchen, resets the record player, turns it up very loud and begins to move to the music.)

Hank: Isn't that a little loud?

Barb: I like it loud. Let's dance.

Hank: How can you dance at a time like this?

Barb: I feel like dancing.

(Hank rises.)

Hank: Are you sure it's alright? I wouldn't want anything to happen.

Barb: If I have any pains, I'll let you know.

(Hank takes her very carefully (like someone holding a rare egg-shell) and they begin to dance.)

Hank: Am I holding you too close?

Barb: Any closer and we'd be dancing together.

Hank: Do you mind if I turn this down a bit?

Barb: If it bothers you, turn it down.

(He does. The music is now soft and very romantic. Hank holds her once more, this time a little closer.)

Hank: Let me know if I'm hurting you.

Barb: I'll let you know.

(As they dance, Hank holds her closer and closer, until they are finally snuggled together in the old high school style of the forties.)

Hank: Gee Barb, this is wonderful. It's been a long time since we danced like this.

Barb: *(Very snugly)* Mmmm. Hmmmm.

Hank: I could go on like this all night.

Barb: Mmmmm.

Hank: It's hard to believe it's been more than twenty years.

Barb: Mmm.

Hank: Do you remember how smooth that floor used to be. They'd sprinkle powder all over it to make it smooth. I played a lot of basketball on that floor.

Barb: *(Dreamily)* It must have been slippery.

Hank: They only used the powder when we had a dance, Barb. Gosh, there's something about a high school gymnasium. Do you know, I've been all over the world, and I've never enjoyed dancing as much as I did then. Whoever set those lights did a beautiful job. It was always so romantic. Remember, Barb?

Barb: Mmmm. Hmmm.

Hank: I wonder if they'd let us go back there and dance sometime.

Barb: I think we'd be a little out of place.

Hank: I don't know about that. Kids are pretty tolerant these days. I'll bet they wouldn't mind a bit. I wonder if they're having a dance this weekend?

Barb: I wonder if Julian's coming home tonight.

Hank: Barb, why don't you relax and forget about Julian for a while.

Barb: You're right. I've got to stop thinking about him. He's out there, and there's nothing I can do about it. I might just as well relax and have a good time.

Hank: Exactly.

(They snuggle up once more and go on dancing, until . . .)

Barb: Maybe they're going to elope.

Hank: Barb, for heaven sake!

Barb: You're right. You're right. I've got to forget. *(She breaks away.)* I'll go in and put on a skirt and sweater right now.

Hank: Why do you have to do that?

Barb: It'll be like old times. When you had your hand on my sweater.

Hank: That's really not necessary, Barb.

Barb: Of course it is. Obviously it meant a great deal to you. If you've got a fetish about sweaters, I'll wear a sweater.

(She disappears into the bedroom.)

Hank: I haven't got a fetish about sweaters. All I said was . . .

Barb: *(Off)* Do you like a furry sweater or a smooth one?

Hank: It doesn't matter. Look Barb, you're misinterpreting the whole thing.

Barb: *(Off)* I've got a nice angora.
(She comes out of the bedroom with the sweater.)

Barb: How's that?

Hank: Barb, the sweater has nothing to do with it.

Barb: You don't like angora. I'll get something else.
(She goes back into the bedroom.)

Hank: Barb, you don't seem to understand. It wasn't so much the sweater as it was you.

Barb: *(Off)* I know. I feel better under a sweater. Do me a favour and look at the oven.

(Reluctantly, Hank goes into the kitchen.)

Barb: *(Off)* I know I've got one in here somewhere. *(Now in a half-slip and brassiere, she comes to the door of the bedroom and shouts across at the kitchen.)* Don't worry. I'll find something.

(She goes back into the bedroom.)

The front door opens and Julian enters. He places his briefcase on the hall table and is about to come into the livingroom when:

Hank comes out of the kitchen.)

Hank: Julian!

Barb: *(Off)* I found it!

(Barb comes out of the bedroom holding a sweater. She is still in the brassiere and half-slip. She sees Julian.)

Barb: Julian!

(Julian takes note of the costume and . . .)

Julian: I'll come back later.

(He turns to leave.)

Barb: Oh no you don't. We're going to have this out right now.

Hank: Barb, I think you'd better put something on.

Barb: The sweater can wait. I want to talk to Julian.

Hank: Barb, for heaven sake put some clothes on.

Barb: Julian, don't move.

(Barb goes back into the bedroom and closes the door.)

Hank: Julian, I'm sure you realise what an awkward position this places me in.

Julian: There's nothing to feel awkward about, Hank.

Hank: I'm not speaking of this. I'm speaking of tonight.

Julian: I'm not sure that I follow you.

Hank: Julian, when a man chooses to abandon his responsibilities, he has to be prepared to accept the consequences.

Julian: I didn't realise you had any responsibilities.

Hank: Julian, for heavens sake, I'm not talking about me. I'm talking about you!

(Barb comes out of the bedroom wearing a very plain dress.)

Barb: *(Dramatically)* Ah ha! So you came back, Julian Waterman.

Julian: I didn't see any reason to stay out all night.

Barb: All night! *(To Hank)* He was going to stay out all night.

Julian: I suppose I could have sat through the movie a second time.

Barb: *(To Hank)* What did I tell you. The back row of the balcony.

Julian: They didn't have a balcony.

Barb: Where did you sit?

Julian: Where we always sit. Half way down on the aisle.

Barb: That's where we always sit. Couldn't you pick someplace where you wouldn't be seen?

Julian: Why should I do that?

Barb: *(To Hank)* Do you hear that. He's not even ashamed.

Julian: Why should I be ashamed of a little nudity?

Barb: Nudity! My God, right there in front of the whole audience.

Julian: It was only half full.

Barb: He doesn't split hairs. He splits audiences. What kind of woman would do such a thing?

Julian: I have no idea why they do it.

Barb: They?

Julian: Yes.

Barb: *(To Hank)* He said **they**. *(To Julian)* You mean there's more than one?

(Hank starts for his room.)

Hank: Barb, I don't want to listen to this.

Barb: You stay right there. You're part of the family.

(Hank stops.)

Julian: I don't see why you're getting so upset. I only went there because there was nowhere else to go.

Barb: Couldn't you rent a hotel room?

Julian: For a couple of hours?

Barb: For fifteen minutes. What's the difference?

Julian: If I thought you were going to be fifteen minutes I wouldn't have gone to the movies.

Barb: What the hell has your going to the movies got to do with us?

Julian: I didn't want to disturb you.

Barb: When?

Julian: When I came home earlier and you were in the bedroom.

Barb: Who was in the bedroom?

Julian: You and Hank.

Hank: Now just a minute, Julian.

Barb: *(To Hank)* You keep out of this. *(To Julian)* You mean that you came home and thought we were in the bedroom?

Julian: Weren't you?

Hank: Certainly not.

Julian: Where were you?

Barb: Who?

Julian: You and Hank.

Barb: When?

Julian: When I came home.

Barb: Where were *you*?

Julian: Right here.

Barb: I mean after.

Julian: I went to an adult movie.

Barb: *(To Hank)* He went to an adult movie. *(To Julian)* Where were you when I phoned the office?

Julian: When?

Barb: Before you thought we were in the bedroom.

Julian: I must have been on my way home.

Barb: *(To Hank)* He was on his way home.

Hank: Julian, I'd like to apologise.

Julian: For what?

Barb: *(Quickly)* For not being here when you got home.

Julian: Why should you apologise?

Hank: We made a few mistakes here tonight.

Barb: *(Quickly)* That's right. We should have kept your dinner warm.

Julian: It wasn't necessary. I sent out for a sandwich.

Barb: And we shouldn't have got upset about the adult movie. After all, what's a little skin?

Julian: That's what I tried to tell you. By the way, where *were* you when I came home?

Barb* and Hank together:
We went for a walk.
*We went to a movie.

Barb: We walked to a movie.

Julian: That's nice. What did you see?

Barb* and Hank together:
Gone With The Wind.
*War and Peace.

Barb: On a double bill.

Julian: *(Incredulous)* In two hours?

Barb: They cut out all the good parts. Besides, we left early. We didn't want you to come home to an empty apartment.

Julian: That was very thoughtful of you.

Hank: Julian, about the incident with the sweater, I feel that I owe you an explanation.

Julian: Please. It's not necessary.

Barb: You'd better let him explain.

(She goes into the kitchen.)

Hank: I don't know whether you ever attended a high school dance or not.

Julian: Of course I did.

Hank: Then you must have some idea of the pleasant memories I have of them.

Julian: Not really. I usually ended up standing in the background.

Hank: Is that a fact.

Julian: The fellows on the football team seemed to do all the dancing in those days.

Hank: That was me! I tell you, Julian, we had our pick of the whole school.

Julian: I know you did.

Hank: Those little sawed-off, four-eyed bookworms didn't stand a chance.

Julian: You're telling me.

Hank: Those were the happiest days of my life, Julian.

Julian: I can believe it.

Hank: I guess you could say that I was dancing with my head in the clouds.

Julian: You probably were.

Hank: Life was so much simpler then.

Julian: Yes it was.

Hank: Just holding a girl in your arms could give you so much pleasure.

Julian: I can imagine.

Hank: Do you know, I could never figure out why those wallflowers bothered to come.

Julian: It was a good place to meet girls, I suppose.

Hank: What's the sense of meeting girls if you don't dance?

Julian: You could always take them out on the playing field.

Hank: At night? What would you do on the playing field at night? Surely you're not suggesting . . .

(Barb comes in from the kitchen with an extra setting for the table.)

Barb: Julian, there's a casserole in the oven and I'm making a salad. Did he tell you about the sweater?

Julian: I think he was just getting around to it. Right Hank?

Hank: It's really not that important, Julian.

Barb: What do you mean, it's not important. Julian, he's got a real thing about sweaters. It goes all the way back to high school.

Hank: Barb, please. It was just one of those things that doesn't seem to matter anymore.

Barb: I thought it was exciting.

(She crosses to the kitchen, and on her way out . . .)

Did Julian tell you he had his first experience in high school?

(She is gone.)

Hank: Now look here, Julian. Are you trying to tell me that all the time I was in there dancing, those guys were sneaking out on the playing field and, and . . .

Julian: Scoring goals?

Hank: *(Stunned)* I had no idea that sort of thing was going on.

Julian: You were dancing with your head in the clouds.

Hank: But that was twenty years ago. Before all this damned permissiveness.

Julian: That's right.

Hank: And on my football field! *(Enraged)* God damn it. Is there no decency left in the world?

(Barb rushes in.)

Barb: What happened?

Julian: We were just talking about high school days.

Hank: I'd rather we didn't discuss this in front

of Barb.

Barb: Why not?

Hank: In fact, I'd appreciate it if we just let the whole matter drop.

Julian: As you wish.

Barb: Why do you have to stop talking because of me?

Hank: Because there are certain things that a woman shouldn't hear.

Barb: What things?

Hank: Barb, I don't want to discuss this any further.

Barb: It's the sweater. Julian, he's upset about the sweater.

Hank: Will you stop talking about that God damned sweater! I'm sorry I ever mentioned it. In fact, I'm beginning to feel sorry that I ever came here. Excuse me.

(He goes into his room and closes the door.)

Barb: What did we do? What did we say? Julian go in and talk to him.

Julian: I think he'd rather be alone right now.

Barb: I don't understand what happened.

Julian: He's a little upset.

Barb: What the hell's he got to be upset about?

Julian: It was something that happened a long time ago. If we just give him a few moments to compose himself . . .

Barb: Julian, if he walks out of here I'll never speak to you again.

Julian: He's not going to walk out. A few moments of quiet reflection and I'm sure . . .

(There is a loud crash (golf clubs) from within.)

Barb: What kind of reflection is that?

Julian: He's probably just letting off a little steam.

(The sound of dresser drawers being opened and closed.)

Barb: Julian, that's not steam. That's packing. If you don't go in there, I will.

Julian: Alright, I'll see if I can reason with him.

(Julian goes to the door and knocks politely.)

Julian: Hank, it's Julian. May I come in for a moment?

Hank: *(Off)* I'd rather you didn't, Julian.

Julian: I hope you're not thinking of doing anything rash.

Hank: *(Off)* I'm only doing what I feel has to be done.

Julian: If we could just sit down and talk this out . . .

Hank: *(Off)* I'm sorry, but there's nothing to talk about.

Julian: *(To Barb)* He says there's nothing to talk about.

Barb: I heard. I heard.

(She comes to the door.)

Barb: Hank?

Hank: *(Off)* Yes.

Barb: I'd like to come in.

Hank: *(Off)* Please don't.

Barb: Just for a minute.

Hank: *(Off)* I'm sorry, but I'm right in the middle of something.

Barb: *(To Julian)* He says he's right in the mid-

dle of something.

Julian: Yes, I heard.

Barb: I don't care what the hell he's in the middle of. I'm going in.

(She tries to open the door, but it won't give.)

Barb: Julian, he's put something against the door.

Julian: Maybe it's stuck.

Barb: It's not stuck. I tell you, he's put something against the door.

(Julian tries it with the same results.)

Julian: You're right. He has.

Barb: Why would he do a thing like that?

Julian: I guess he doesn't want us to come in.

Barb: For heaven sake, why doesn't he just say

so. Who the hell goes around barricading doors. Julian, call the fire department.

Julian: I don't think that's necessary. He'll have to open it eventually. Why don't we just sit down and wait.
(Julian goes to the sofa.)

Barb: How can you sit while he's in there getting ready to leave?

Julian: He can't leave without opening the door.

Barb: *(Thinks about it)* You're right.

(She comes and sits beside Julian. The door to Hank's bedroom opens. Hank comes out and leans his golf clubs against a chair.)

Barb: *(Whispers to Julian)* Maybe he's going golfing.

Hank: I just came out to get my toothbrush.

(He goes into the bathroom and comes out holding a toothbrush.)

Barb: At a time like this you're going to brush your teeth?

Hank: I'm not brushing. I'm packing.

Barb: *(To Julian)* Do you hear that? He's packing. Julian, do something.

Julian: Hank, don't you think you're being a little hasty?

Hank: I've thought it over, Julian, and I feel it would be better if I left.

Barb: How could he think with all that packing? Julian, he's been in there two minutes.

Julian: She's right, Hank. You're not being fair to yourself.

Hank: Julian, I came here with certain memories and ideals which I have treasured for more years than I care to remember. In one evening, you people have either destroyed or distorted them beyond recognition.

Julian: We're sorry if we've been in any way responsible.

(Hank sinks into a chair.)
Hank: You've no idea how much those things meant to me.

Julian: Nobody likes to part with their illusions.

Hank: Illusions! These were not illusions. These were . . .

Barb: Illusions.

Hank: *(Mournfully)* All those years.

Julian. You can't live in the past, Hank. What's more important, a few sentimental boyhood memories, or a whole rich lifetime ahead of you?

Hank: I know that, Julian. It's just that no matter how fast the world and its values changed, I've always felt I had something I could count on. Now even that's gone.

Julian: It could be the best thing that ever happened to you.

Hank: What you're saying is that I haven't been facing up to reality.

Julian: If you like.

Hank: Maybe I have believed in something that didn't exist, but damn it all Julian, if it wasn't that way, it certainly should have been.

Julian: It's too late to change it now.

Hank: I just don't understand people anymore.

Julian: Working on your novel might help.

Hank: You mean by writing about it I might have a chance to thrash some of these things out?

Julian: That's right.

Hank: I never thought of it that way before. Say, I think you've really hit on something.

Barb: That's my Julian!

Hank: I'll bet I could get right to the core of this thing. That is if it's still alright with you people.

Barb: Oh for crying out loud. Of course it is.

Hank: I'm sorry if I sounded off at you just now.

Julian: It's perfectly understandable.

Hank: I hope I didn't say anything that was out of line.

Barb: Forget it.

Hank: To tell you the truth, I really didn't want to go. I know I've only been here a couple of days, but this has already begun to feel like home.

Barb: Did you hear that, Julian.

Hank: I haven't had a real home since I was a boy.

Barb: Well he's sure as hell got one now. Hasn't he, Julian.

Julian: He certainly has.
(Barb kisses Hank on the cheek.)

Barb: I'm going to put dinner on the table.

Hank: I'm hungry.

Julian: Shall I fix us all a drink?

Barb: No drinks. I've got a bottle of wine.

Julian: (Cheerfully) Wine! This is a real celebration.

Hank: I guess I can put this back now.
(He starts for the bathroom with his toothbrush. The phone rings.)

Barb: (Off) Julian, get the phone.

Julian: I've got it.

(He picks up the phone.)

Julian: Hello. Yes, he's right here. Hank, it's for you.
(Hank comes out of the bathroom and takes the phone.)

Hank: Thank you, Julian. (Into phone) Hank Grant. Hold on. I'll write it down. O.K. Let's have it.

(He writes on a pad which is beside the phone.)

Got it. Right. I'll be there. Thanks.
(He hangs up.)

Julian: Something important?

Hank: It was just the newspaper with my assignment for tomorrow.

Julian: The newspaper! In all this excitement I forgot to ask you about the newspaper. You must have got the job.

Hank: Yes, I did.

Julian: Isn't that wonderful. (He shakes Hank's hand) Congratulations. (Calling) Barb, Hank got a job on the newspaper.
(Barb comes in with the dinner.)

Barb: I know. Everything's ready. Sit down while it's hot.
(Hank and Julian approach the table.)

Julian: I think that's wonderful. (He indicates a chair for Hank) Hank.
(Hank sits.)

Hank: Thank you, Julian.

(Julian pulls out a chair for Barb and she sits.)

Barb: Thank you, Julian.

(Julian sits. He examines the bottle of wine.)

Julian: Hmmm. Very nice. (And now he pours) Well . . . here we are. Just the three of us, having a nice quiet dinner party in our own home. What more could anyone ask? Right, Hank?

Hank: You're right, Julian.

(Hank takes Barb's hand and looks lovingly at her.)

Julian: I would like to propose a toast . . . to Hank's new job.

Hank: If you don't mind, Julian, I'd rather you toast my novel.

Julian: Alright, to Hank's novel.

Hank: Thank you, Julian.
(They drink.)

Julian: By the way, what is your assignment for tomorrow? No, wait a minute. Let me guess. A ballgame!

Hank: No.

Julian: A tennis match?

Hank: No.

Julian: A swimming meet?

Hank: As a matter of fact, Julian. It happens to be an afternoon tea.

Curtain on Act two

As the curtain goes up, there is the sound of slow, thoughtful typewriting. Hank is seated at the desk, working on his novel. The desk has been repositioned so that it now dominates the room. A huge portrait of Papa Hemingway has replaced one of the paintings. Here and there are photos of Hank and the old school team, Hank and a fallen water buffalo, Hank with a giant fish.

It is evening and the drapes are drawn.

Julian enters from the dining area, goes to the windows, looks out and shakes his head.

Julian: It's getting worse.

Hank: *(Cheerfully)* Can't hurt us in here.

Julian: No, I suppose not.

(Julian pours a brandy and picks up a book.)

Julian: How is it coming?

Hank: Fine thank you, Julian. I'm almost finished the first chapter. Once I get that licked, I know I'm on my way.

Julian: *(Pleased)* Good.

(Julian settles down to read.)

(Barb enters, pulling off an apron. She is enormous.)

Julian: *(To Barb)* He's almost finished the first chapter.

Barb: *(Not impressed)* That's nice.

(She sits in a straightbacked chair, an exhausted hulk.)

Julian: How do you feel?

Barb: Pregnant. Very pregnant.

Julian: Why don't you go in and lie down?

Barb: Because I'm tired of lying down. Besides, I'm always afraid I won't be able to get up again.

Julian: Let's hope it doesn't come today. I don't know how in the world we'd get to the hospital in all that snow.

Barb: The way I feel we won't have to worry about snow. Tulips maybe, but no snow. I wonder if there's such a thing as a twelve months pregnancy?

Julian: I've never heard of one.

Barb: Today is the sixteenth. Now why the hell isn't it here?

Julian: It is possible for doctors to make mistakes, you know.

Barb: What if we'd made plans?

Julian: Why would we make plans with a baby coming?

Barb: That's not the point. We could have made plans.

(There is a great ripping sound as Hank tears a sheet from the typewriter.)

Julian: *(To Hank)* Is something wrong?

Hank: *(On the verge of a temper tantrum)* No, nothing's wrong. I just find it very difficult to concentrate with all the noise that's going on around here.

Barb: What noise?

Hank: All the chattering. It makes it very difficult.

Barb: We weren't chattering. We were talking.

Hank: Then would you mind talking more softly, please.

Barb: *(To Julian in a mock whisper)* Julian, he wants us to talk more softly.

Julian: We were a little loud.

Barb: *(Very loud)* Why the hell shouldn't we be loud? It's our apartment, isn't it?

(Hank drops a sheaf of paper in a nervous reaction.)

Hank: I happen to live here too. The arrangement was that I would be allowed to work on my novel.

Barb: What are we supposed to do while you work on your great novel?

Hank: You could be a little more considerate.

Barb: You could be a little more sensible and take the typewriter into your bedroom.

Hank: I cannot work and sleep in the same room.

Barb: I'll bet you Hemingway could.

(Hank gets up, turns his work over and puts a cover on the typewriter.)

Hank: This is impossible. I'm going out for a walk.

Julian: How can you walk in four feet of snow?

(Hank looks about helplessly.)

Hank: I'm trapped.

Julian: Why don't you pour a scotch and relax?

Hank: *(Nods)* I'm sorry. I'm all wound up. *(He proceeds to make himself a drink.)* I just can't believe that it's taken me this long. I've never missed a deadline in my life.

Julian: I don't think you have to look on this as a deadline.

Hank: I said six months, and it's six months. I haven't even got the first chapter done. Now if that isn't missing a deadline, I don't know what is.

Julian: Yes, but surely that date was an arbitrary one. There were only the three of us involved. It doesn't matter to us how long you take. *(Confidently)* Does it Barb?

Barb: Yes.

Julian: What?

Barb: He said he could write a novel in six months. I'd like to know why he hasn't written one.

Hank: You know why I haven't written one. I've had problems. For one thing, the newspaper took up more time than I'd counted on.

Julian: That's right. It did.

Hank: If they'd had room for me in the sports department it would have been different.

Barb: You're the one who said you'd be willing to cover garden parties.

Hank: Only because I didn't think they'd take me seriously. Who ever heard of a man with my background doing a social column?

Barb: The ladies didn't seem to mind.

Hank: Of course they didn't mind. That's what took up so much of my time. How could I get in and get the job done when I was expected to entertain the ladies with my tales of adventure? It was impossible for me to devote the proper attention to my novel. *(To Julian)* Julian, I just want you to know how grateful I am to you for allowing me to continue on here after I stopped working.

(Julian acknowledges this with a gracious nod.)

Barb: That was four months ago. Now why haven't you produced a novel?

Hank: You know why I haven't produced a novel.

Barb: Why?

Hank: Because I keep tearing it up!

Barb: *(To Julian)* He could have written the Encyclopedia Brittanica with all the paper he's stuffed down the incinerator. *(To Hank)* What I would like to know is, why do you keep tearing it up?

Hank: Because . . . *(This is painful)* because it isn't Hemingway.

Barb: What about this latest chapter? Is this Hemingway?

Hank: I . . . I don't know.

Barb: Why not? Haven't you read the damn thing?

Hank: I haven't had a chance to decide.

Barb: Then I suggest it's time you did.

Hank: You mean right now?

Barb: Yes now. I think you should read it over while we're all here and decide whether or not it measures up to 'The Snows Of Kilimanjaro.'

Hank: That was a short story.

Barb: I don't care if it was a note to the milkman. I just want to know how long this is going to go on.

(Hank goes to the desk, self-consciously picks up his manuscript and begins to study it.

In a very short time he reaches a terrible conclusion. He rips the manuscript in two, throws it in the waste basket, and sinks to his chair, holding his head in his hands.

Julian starts for the basket.)

Julian: Do you mind if I have a look at that?

Hank: *(Sharply)* Stay away from that!

(Julian stops.)

Julian: I thought perhaps a second opinion. . . .

Hank: I don't want any opinions. I know whether it's good enough or not.

Julian: You may be judging yourself too severely.

Hank: I will not lower my standards, Julian. I will not lower my standards for anyone.

Barb: You see what I mean. Julian, we could be grandparents by the time he finishes that novel.

Julian: I don't think we should discourage him while he's still willing to try.

Hank: Thank you, Julian. Sometimes I think you're the only one around here who understands me.

Barb: I understand you better than Julian. I understand that you're never going to finish the damn thing. You're going to sit here in our livingroom for the next thirty years, alternately typing and tearing, while Julian and I learn to communicate in sign language.

Hank: Now just a minute. If I've become a burden to you people, I'll leave right now.

(He stands.)

Julian: You can't. There's a snow storm.

Hank: I forgot.

(He sits.)

Julian: Of course I don't know too much about these things, but have you ever thought of modelling yourself after someone else?

Hank: You mean another writer?

Julian: Yes, maybe someone a little more contemporary. After all, it's some years now since Hemingway . . .

Barb: I heard that all those adventures were merely to prove to himself that he wasn't a coward.

Hank: *(Enraged)* That's a goddam, filthy lie. Anybody who says that is a vicious, emasculating, penis-envying gossip monger.

Barb: *(Calmly)* That's what I read.

Julian: I really don't think it's important.

Hank: It certainly is important. It's important to stop that sort of ugly rumour from spreading.

Julian: The point I'm trying to make is that perhaps you might have more success if you use another writer as your model.

Hank: I've thought of that, Julian, but the fact is that Hemingway has been my hero since I was a boy.

Julian: Now you take a writer like John Updike . . .

Barb: Oh for crying out loud, why does he have to copy anybody?

Julian: What was that?

Barb: The man is forty-one years old. Why the hell is he still trying to imitate people?

Julian: That's a good point, Hank.

Barb: If he can't say what he's got to say in his own damn way, he might as well give up right now.

Julian: I think she's hit it right on the head, Hank.

Hank: *(Interested)* What you're saying is that I should just be myself.

Barb: That's what I'm saying.

Hank: You mean that whatever comes out, I should stand by it because it represents me and nobody else.

Julian: Exactly.

Hank: That means that whatever I write, good or bad, it's at least unique and original.

Julian: Better to be first rate Hank Grant than second rate Hemingway.

Hank: By God I think you're right, the both of you. It's one of those simple truths that's so obvious.

Julian: Almost elementary.

Hank: The first rule of good writing. Why is it that for all these years I couldn't see something like that?

Julian: You were too close to it, I suppose.

Hank: The forest for the trees.

Julian: Absolutely.

Hank: I've certainly seen it now. Thanks to you two.

Julian: I think this calls for some sort of celebration.

(He starts for the liquor cabinet.)

Barb: I don't think he should waste any time.

Hank: She's right, Julian. I've got work to do, and I've got to keep a clear head.

(Hank starts for the typewriter.)

Julian: This is wonderful, isn't it Barb?

Hank: This has given me a terrific sense of release. I can feel the creative juices flowing right now, and they're my juices, Julian, my own original juices.

Barb: From now on I'd like you to get juiced in the bedroom, if you don't mind.

Hank: You mean you don't want me to work in here anymore?

Barb: I just think that Julian and I should be allowed to enjoy the comforts of our own living-room in our own apartment for a change.

Hank: Of course. It's been very selfish of me. You've been very kind and patient. A good writer should be able to work anywhere.

(He begins to gather up paper and typewriter.)

Julian: May I give you a hand?

Hank: No, no, Julian. You just sit down there with Barb and relax. I'll get out of your way in a minute. You probably won't be seeing very much of me. I'd appreciate it if you'd bring my meals in on a tray, Barb. I'm going in that room and I'm not coming out until I have my novel . . . except to go to the bathroom, of course.

Julian: Of course.

(Hank starts for his room.)

Hank: Here I go. I'll see you when it's done.

Barb: Don't be long. I won't stay this way forever.

(Hank stops in the doorway.)

Hank: I'm not sure I know what you mean.

Barb: You were going to finish your novel by the time I had the baby.

Hank: That was before I realised what I was doing wrong.

Barb: I don't see what that has to do with it.

Hank: You were expecting the baby on the sixteenth. That's today.

Julian: Don't you think you're being unreasonable, Barb?

Barb: Julian, I think it's quite obvious that the doctor has made a mistake.

Julian: Yes, but even if the doctor was out a few days, you can't expect the man to write a whole novel in that time.

Barb: He'll just have to type a little faster.

Julian: You're putting impossible demands on him.

Barb: Julian, either he can or he can't.

Julian: He's just reached a very important stage of his development. I don't think you're being fair.

Hank: It's alright, Julian. I think I know what's going on here. *(To Barb)* You're not going to crush me, Barb. I won't let that happen. You've tangled with the wrong person this time. The easiest thing for me to do would be to walk out that door and do this somewhere else.

Julian: It's still snowing.

Hank: *(Losing patience)* After it's stopped snowing! *(To Barb)* I could go elsewhere to write my novel and I could take all the time I want.

Barb: Not without Julian to support you.

Hank: *(Again losing patience)* I'd get a part-time job! *(Calmly)* The point is that I won't do that. I'll play the game your way, Barb. What's more, I'll beat you at it. You go ahead and have your baby. I'm going to write my novel, and I have a pretty good idea that I'll be finished before you will!

(Hank makes a dramatic exit, slamming the door behind him.)

Julian: He certainly means business.

Barb: He's got at least a month, Julian. I'm sure the doctor was out a month.

(Suddenly there is the sound of furious typing coming from Hank's room.)

Julian: Listen to that. I think he's really on to something.

Barb: Good luck to him.

Julian: I don't think there'll be any paper torn up this time. You can tell by the way he's typing that he knows exactly what he's doing. It must be stream-of-consciousness writing. I can't imagine anyone going that fast otherwise. I wonder what he's writing about in there?

Barb: To tell you the truth, I couldn't care . . . *(She straightens up)* . . . Oo!

Julian: What's wrong?

Barb: Nothing. Nothing at all.

Julian: You made a funny noise. There must be something wrong.

Barb: It's just the way I'm sitting.

(She shifts her weight in the chair.)

Barb: I'm fine now. Julian, I'll be so happy when he finishes that thing and gets the hell out.

Julian: I thought it was so important for you to have him here.

Barb: It was. At least I thought it was until he came. I thought he was going to bring some excitement into our lives.

Julian: *(Gently correcting her)* You mean into **your** life.

Barb: Alright, into **my** life.

Julian: I'm sorry. If I wasn't so dull, all this wouldn't have been necessary.

Barb: It's not your fault, Julian. It just happens to be your nature. Nobody expects you to be exciting.

Julian: I don't know why it is, but I always seem to see both sides of the story at once.

Barb: I know you do.

Julian: Three and four sides if there are more people involved. Sometimes I get so tired of being reasonable.

Barb: I don't think you should let it bother you.

Julian: I wish I could be a little more like Hank.

Barb: Julian, you are what you are, but there's a man who isn't what he's supposed to be.

Julian: How do you mean?

Barb: He makes promises he doesn't keep.

Julian: What kind of promises?

Barb: This whole experience was going to be so exciting, so completely open and free from conventional morality. After all, Julian, polygamy never did make much sense the way they used to practise it. One man can hardly satisfy one healthy female. Now how the hell is he going to manage two or three. The other way around makes sense.

Julian: It does make sense, I suppose.

Barb: Of course it does. Especially at your age,

Julian. Now is the time you have to worry about heart attacks. It's much easier on you. At least it would have been if he'd stuck to his half of the bargain.

Julian: I'm sure he would have if it wasn't for the baby.

Barb: I don't know what the baby has to do with it.

Julian: He just seemed to feel that he had to wait until after the baby was born. He didn't want to be responsible in case anything went wrong.

Barb: What the hell is to go wrong? The doctor says you can do it up to the last month. Not once! Not even once! It was all those women at the garden parites. That's what it was.

Julian: I don't think you're being fair. Besides, that was months ago.

Barb: Liaisons, Julian. He's managed to set up liaisons.

Julian: I don't see how he can. He's been sitting here all the time, working on his novel.

Barb: Then where the hell's he getting it?

Julian: It is possible to live without it, you know, especially when you're able to throw yourself into your work the way he has.

Barb: Well, all I can say is, thank God for you, Julian. You've certainly done more than your share.

Julian: And enjoyed every minute of it.

Barb: (Tenderly) Honestly, Julian?

Julian: I always have.

Barb: Do you know something. I think this has been very good for us. I think it's helped us to appreciate one another more. In many ways, it's been a very rewarding experience.

Julian: Yes, I suppose it has.

Barb: It's brought us much closer together.

Julian: In a way that's true.

(Barb stiffens.)

Barb: Oo!

Julian: What is it?

Barb: (Holding back) Nothing.

Julian: Don't say nothing. I distinctly heard you.

Barb: Oo!

Julian: My God. It's coming.

Barb: No it's not.

Julian: You're having pains.

Barb: False labour.

Julian: Are you sure?

Barb: Of course I'm sure. (She grimaces) Oo! Julian!

Julian: That's not false labour. You're having pains. We're going to have a baby.

Barb: Julian, will you stop getting excited. I'm sure it will go away. (She is hit by another.) Oo!

Julian: I'll call the doctor.

Barb: No you won't. You'll just sit down and everything will be fine.

Julian: What are you talking about?

Barb: Julian, he just got started.

Julian: I know, but sometimes they come very fast.

Barb: I don't mean him. I mean HIM.

(She points to Hank's room.)

Julian: What has he got to do with our baby?

Barb: I don't think we should interrupt him. If it wasn't for his coming here, we wouldn't have gotten to know one another better. Julian, we have to give him a chance. We owe it to him.

Julian: I don't think we're in any position to . . .

Barb: Ooo!

Julian: There, you see.

Barb: He needs time to finish.

Julian: He just got started.

Barb: Then I have no intention of being the one to make him stop.

Julian: You have no choice. There's nothing you can do about it.

Barb: I can exercise a little self-control.

Julian: I don't think you can do that.

Barb: Why not? It'll be like natural childbirth in reverse. If worse comes to worse, I'll sit on it.

(The typing has stopped. Hank comes out of his room. He is bathed in perspiration.)

Hank: Excuse me. I just came out for a glass of water.

(He goes towards the kitchen and stops.)

I want you people to know that I'm grateful to you for giving me this opportunity of truly finding myself.

Barb: (Aside to Julian) You see.

(Hank starts again for the kitchen.)

Barb: Oo!

(Hank stops.)

Hank: Pardon me?

Barb: Nothing.

Hank: I thought you said something.

(He is about to start again.)

Barb: Oo!

Hank: You did say something. It sounded like . . .

Julian: Hank, I think you'd better know that Barb is starting to have the baby.

Barb: Julian, you rat.

(Hank looks from one to the other in disbelief, in panic, in anger at their betrayal. He sets his jaw, hurries to his room and slams the door.

A second later there is the sound of furious typing.)

Julian: I don't think he understands.

(He starts for Hank's room.)

Barb: Julian, will you leave the man alone.

Julian: I certainly expected him to show some concern.

Barb: What difference does it make? The point is, he didn't stop. He went right back in there and went to work.

Julian: That's true. He did.

Barb: I think he's really got this thing under control.

Julian: He certainly seems determined.

Barb: I don't think we have to worry about him anymore. I feel much better about the baby already. Julian, call the doctor.

(Julian picks up the phone.)

Julian: I'll have him meet us at the hospital.

(The lights dim down . . . then come back again.)

Barb: Julian, what's happening to the lights?

Julian: I don't know. It must be the storm. They seem to be alright now.

(*The typing stops. Hank comes out of the bedroom, goes to the dining area, retrieves the dinner candles, and starts back to his room.*)

Julian: You'd better leave one of them for us, Hank. It looks as though we're having a power failure.

Hank: I'm sorry, but I'll need as much light as I can get.

(*He disappears into his room and the typing begins at once.*)

Barb: He's right, Julian. You can't expect the man to work in the dark.

Julian: I suppose not.

(*He finally gets an answer.*)

Hello. Is the doctor in, please? This is Julian Waterman. My wife is expecting a baby, and she's started having labour pains. I see. Oh, I see. Yes, I'll do that. Thank you very much.

(*He hangs up, looking a little worried.*)

Barb: What happened? Wasn't he in?

Julian: That was the answering service. They think he's snowed in somewhere up on the expressway. They haven't heard from him for hours. We'll have to go to the hospital anyway. I'll call a cab.

Barb: Why don't we just take the car?

Julian: I'd never get it up the driveway.

(*Julian dials.*
The lights dip down again.)

Barb: There they go again.

Julian: That's all we need.

(*The lights come back up.*)

Julian: These people aren't answering. I'll try another company.

B41

Barb: It'll be the same with all of them. How the hell is a cab going to get around in all that snow?

Julian: I'm sure something must be moving.

(He dials a new number.)

Barb: We'll end up walking. I know we will.

Julian: That's out of the question in your condition.

Barb: I don't know. What did people do before the telephone?

Julian: They ended up having them in their own . . .

Barb: *(Lets out a cry)* Oh! Julian!

Julian: What is it?

Barb: *(In pain)* Oh my God.

(Julian hangs up the phone.)

Julian: They don't answer either. What'll I do?

Barb: Call the emergency number.

Julian: The emergency number.

Barb: Yes. Oh Julian, it's killing me.

Julian: Where is the emergency number?

Barb: I stuck it under the phone. Julian, I can't stand this.

(Julian dials. He gets an answer almost immediately.)

Julian: This is Julian Waterman. My wife is going to have a baby, and I can't seem to get a cab to take her to the hospital. Yes, yes of course, I realise that. Yes, it certainly is coming down alright. I'm sure you're doing everything you can. Oh, I'm not blaming you one bit. I can see how difficult it would be.

Barb: Julian, stop being so considerate. It's an emergency.

Julian: *(With authority)* Yes, well surely there must be something you can do. This is an emergency. *(It gets results. Julian is surprised)* Our address? It's 560 Avenue Road, apartment 802. And please hurry. I think she's going to have it any minute.

(He hangs up.)

Barb: What did they say?

Julian: They said it was the biggest snowfall in sixty years.

Barb: We already know that. Are they sending an ambulance?

Julian: They're going to try, but they keep getting stuck in the snow. Meanwhile they're going to send someone over to help.

Barb: Who are they sending?

Julian: They didn't say.

Barb: Are they sending a doctor?

Julian: They didn't say.

Barb: Julian, you'd better get a doctor because I'm going to have the baby right now.

Julian: No you're not. Now just keep calm. The first thing we'd better do is get you lying down.

Barb: The first thing you'd better do is get me to a hospital, because I'm going to have it right here in the livingroom.

(Julian is about to guide her to the couch when he changes his mind.)

Julian: Maybe the bedroom would be better.

Barb: Alright, I'll have it in the bedroom.

(Julian helps her across the room.)

Julian: *(Reassuringly)* You'll have it in a nice bright delivery room just like every other woman in the city.

Barb: What city? We're living in the North Pole.

(The lights go down and up as . . .)

Julian: *(Off)* Now just lie down and rest until they get here.

Barb: *(Off)* I'm telling you right now, Julian. They're not going to get here in time. *(Strongly)* Oh. Oh. The pain. Julian, if you ever come near me again, I'll kill you. Oh. Oh Julian, do something.

Julian: *(Off)* I'll get Hank.

(He comes out of the bedroom and knocks on Hank's door.)

Julian: Hank, it's Julian.

(The typing goes on as Hank answers from within.)

Hank: *(Off)* What do you want?

Julian: Could you come out here for a moment.

Hank: *(Off)* I'm sorry, Julian. I'm too busy.

Julian: I think Barb's having the baby.

(The typing stops. Hank opens the door.)

Hank: Where?

Julian: In the bedroom.

(Hank goes to the bedroom and looks in.)

Hank: I don't see any baby.

Julian: It's not here yet.

(Hank starts back to his room.)

Hank: Then why are you interrupting me?

Julian: Because I need your help.

Hank: I'm sorry, Julian. I haven't got time. I have to finish my novel before the baby comes.

(He closes the door. Julian pulls it open.)

Julian: You don't understand. I can't get her to a hospital and I don't have a doctor.

Hank: I understand perfectly. You want me to help you deliver the baby.

Julian: If necessary, yes.

Hank: In case you've forgotten, Julian. I happen to be in a race, and that baby is my opponent. You don't win races by helping your opponent.

(He closes the door. The typing begins again. It is more frantic than ever.)

(Julian pulls open the door and shouts at Hank.)

Julian: How can he be an opponent when he's not even born yet?

Hank: *(Off)* That's his problem.

Julian: I appeal to you as a friend.

Hank: *(Still typing)* I'm sorry, Julian. This is between him and me.

Julian: He's just a helpless little baby.

Hank: *(Off)* He'll have to take it like a man.

Julian: You're being unreasonable.

Hank: *(Off)* That's right. That's how to survive in this world, Julian, by being unreasonable.

Julian: I have never been deliberately unreasonable in my life.

(Hank stops typing and comes to the door.)

Hank: Then it's about time you started. Excuse me, Julian. I've got work to do.

(He closes the door in Julian's face. The typing is heard almost immediately.)

Julian: *(To himself)* He slammed the door right in my face. I could never do a thing like that. He certainly made his point, though. Maybe he's right. Maybe there's a time when you have to be completely unreasonable in order to make yourself understood.

(He opens the door, walks in, and closes it behind him.

The typing stops. A moment later, Hank screams.

Julian comes out and closes the door behind him, wearing a little smile of satisfaction.

Barb screams.)

Barb: *(Off)* Oh Julian! Hurry. Hurry.

Julian: I'm coming.

(He rushes into their bedroom, closing the door behind him.

The door to Hank's room opens. Hank staggers into the livingroom, disheveled, a man numbed by tragedy.

The intercom buzzes.

Hank moves to it automatically, pushes the button, and sinks into a chair.

Julian rushes out of the bedroom.)

Julian: Heat up some water. Get some towels.

(He starts into the bedroom when he realises that Hank hasn't heard him.)

Julian: Water. Towels.

Hank: *(Drained)* How could you?

Julian: It was easy. Look, the baby is here. Now get moving.

Hank: Baby?

Julian: Yes, the baby.

(Hank gets to his feet in a slow, ominous rise.)

Hank: Your baby?

Julian: *(Apprehensive)* Yes.

Hank: An eye for an eye.

Julian: What are you talking about?

Hank: *(Stronger)* An eye for an eye.

Julian: Are you crazy?

Hank: You tore up my manuscript and threw it out the window. *(Like a maniac)* An eye for an eye!

(He charges the bedroom.)

Julian: He's crazy. Look out!

(As Hank hurtles by, Julian sticks out his foot. Hank sprawls on the floor. He starts to get up and Julian clobbers him with a statuette. Hank drops on his face and is still.

There is a knock on the door.

Julian goes to the door and opens it.

The young policeman steps into the apartment.)

Officer: We got a call from the emergency department. I'm here to help out until they can get through.

(He sees Hank on the floor.)

(Suspicious) I thought this was a maternity case.

(He approaches the body.)

Say, haven't I been here before?

(Julian starts to follow. The cop puts it all together and pulls his gun.)

Hold it right there, buddy. I thought you looked familiar.

(Julian struggles desperately with his phobia.)

Julian: Officer, my wife has just had a baby.

Officer: Don't pull that baby stuff on me again. I've got a long memory. Wow, you really clobbered him this time.

Julian: *(Still struggling)* I'm sorry, but I haven't got time to argue with you.

(*Julian starts for the bedroom.*)

(*The policeman levels his gun.*)

Officer: Don't move.

Julian: What will you do if I move?

Officer: I'll shoot you.

Julian: (*With all the dignity he can muster*) I am going to assist my wife.

Officer: (*Beginning to fluster*) You just killed a man.

(*Hank moans. The officer looks down at him. Julian slips into the bedroom like a thief.*)

Officer: Hey, you come back here.

(*He follows Julian into the bedroom. A moment later he comes out, his hand over his mouth, looking for the bathroom.*

Julian comes to the door and points the way.)

Julian: It's in there.

(*The officer rushes into the bathroom. Julian goes into the bedroom. Hank moans and sits up, holding his head.*)

Hank: Oh my head. What happened?

(*He struggles to his feet, and begins to remember.*)

My manuscript!

(*He rushes into his room to confirm the worst.*

The officer comes out of the bathroom looking wan and spent.

Hank comes out of his room in tears.)

Hank: How could a man be so unreasonable?

(*He sees the policeman.*)

Officer, (*Pointing to Julian's room*) There's a man in there who just killed my baby.

Officer: (*About to be sick again*) Please, don't mention babies.

(*Julian hurries out of the bedroom, crosses to the bathroom, comes out with an armful of towels and starts for the bedroom again.*)

Julian: (*To the officer*) Put some water on to boil.

Officer: Yes sir.

(*Julian closes the bedroom door behind him.*)

Hank: That's him! That's the man. Don't let him get away. Go after him.

Officer: You go after him. I'll just stick to heating up pots of water.

(*The policeman goes into the kitchen.*)

Hank: Pots of water? Officer, I don't think you fully understand what's happened here today.

(*He follows to the doorway as we hear the sound of cupboards, pots, and running water.*)

Officer: (*Off*) Mister, as far as you people are concerned, I'm not even going to try.

Hank: But don't you see, I've been working on this breakthrough for months. Finally, today, just when I came to a fresh understanding of my problem . . .

(*The policeman appears in the doorway.*)

Officer: Pardon me, but what is it you do around here?

Hank: I'm a novelist.

Officer: You don't write any of that porno stuff, do you?

Hank: Certainly not. I happen to be a serious writer.

Officer: Oh, you mean like Ernest Hemingway.

Hank: I mean like Hank Grant.

Officer: I don't think I ever read anything by him.

Hank: What I'm trying to tell you is that this man just tore up my manuscript and threw it out the window.

Officer: No kidding. What a lousy thing to do.

Hank: Yes, and I want him arrested for it.

Officer: (Thoughtfully) Well, I don't know about that.

Hank: Why not?

Officer: It's not as though it were a painting or a statue, now is it?

Hank: What's the difference? A work of art is a work of art.

Officer: Yes I know, but a painting or a statue, that's something that's irreplaceable.

Hank: My manuscript is irreplaceable.

Officer: You mean you can't remember what was in it?

Hank: Of course I can remember. Every word is indelibly inscribed on my mind.

Officer: There you go. All you have to do is type it over again.

(Hank thinks about it as Julian comes out of the bedroom.)

Julian: Where the hell is that water?

Officer: Give it a chance to boil, will you.

(Julian goes back into the bedroom.)

Officer: (To Hank) Tell me something. How do you manage to concentrate around here?

Hank: As a matter of fact, it's been very difficult lately.

Officer: I can believe it.

Hank: To tell you the truth, I don't think I can continue to work in this atmosphere.

Officer: No wonder.

Hank: What I need is a totally new environment, some place that's more conducive to creative thinking.

Officer: That makes sense.

Hank: A writer should have peace and quiet and complete contentment.

Officer: Say, my mother's a widow and she keeps a rooming house. It's very quiet. I'll bet you wouldn't have any trouble there.

Hank: Do you think she'd understand what I'm trying to do?

Officer: She's very fond of music and artistic things. Yes, I think she'd understand.

Hank: I've got to get out of here as soon as I can. When do you think I can move in?

Officer: The best thing to do is to go over and have a talk with her.

Hank: I'd appreciate that very much.

Officer: We'd better see how the water's coming.

(He starts for the kitchen. Hank follows.)

Hank: The point is that my whole life is wrapped up in this novel. The entire book is going to be about . . .

(He glances at the bedroom as though he were afraid of being overheard by Barb and Julian.)

Hank: (Whispers) The entire book is about this man and woman who invite another man to come and live with them. Well . . .

(Hank and the policeman disappear into the kitchen.

The empty stage fades quickly into darkness except for a shaft of light that comes from Julian and Barb's bedroom.)

Barb: *(Off)* Julian.

Julian: *(Off)* Yes dear.

Barb: *(Off)* Is everything alright?

Julian: *(Off)* Everything is fine.

Barb: *(Off)* A little girl?

Julian: *(Off)* A little boy.

Barb: *(Off)* It was the most fantastic experience.

Julian: *(Off)* I know.

Barb: *(Off)* You were magnificent.

Julian: *(Off)* So were you.

Barb: *(Off)* Julian.

Julian: *(Off)* Yes dear.

Barb: *(Off)* It was so exciting.

Curtain

The Twisted Loaf and Soft Voices

Aviva Ravel

Aviva Ravel is the first woman author in our collection. Normally this would be a point hardly worth mentioning, but in her case it deserves some consideration.

A famous conductor some time ago broke up a rehearsal with the somewhat mediocre orchestra he had been hired to lead with the words, "gentlemen, could we have more notes correctly and less music, please?" Emotion tends to take over, and emotion can sometimes lead to a very questionable result.

Aviva Ravel's emotional involvement, however, is of a different kind. She writes plays which are meant to be emotional; she relies heavily on her Jewish background in some instances — and is there a more emotional people in the world? And she relies heavily on her femininity — one hopes a status quo which will remain emotional.

In 1967, Aviva Ravel won the DDF Centennial Award for her first play, "Mendel Fish", which was produced in Toronto. In the same year, and for the same play, she also won the Canadian Women's Press Club Award for Humour. "Soft Voices", which appears in this volume, was produced at the Centre d'Art Canadien; her play, "Shoulder Pads" was produced by Instant Theatre and also published by The Book Society. Another stage play, "No More Ketchup", was a successful satire; and the play "Tuesday Games" was produced on Montreal television. She has had many short stories and poems published in "Canadian Forum", and several stories have appeared in "Viewpoint" magazine.

The current much more receptive climate for Canadian plays has assisted Aviva Ravel as much as it has many other Canadian authors. Nonetheless, it is noteworthy that two of her plays have been produced practically back to back within a very short time. And most recently, this gifted writer — who is also a full time teacher — has been awarded the Arts Medal by Loyola College, and has just received her B.A.

Max Tobin's photographs are used to illustrate "The Twisted Loaf". The lead picture in "Soft Voices" is that of Irene Balser and Mignon Elkins, who created the roles in the Montreal production. All other photographs in "Soft Voices" are from the recent Newfoundland mounting of the play, photo credit Richard Stoker.

Roy Higgins is a young man with considerable achievements, but with many more plans and ambitions. He started his career backstage at the Crest Theatre in Toronto at a rather tender age, and after some minor roles as an actor in Canada and the United States, decided that his main talent was in direction. It was quite a while before others agreed with him, — between the decision and the execution were many years of very hard work, which Roy Higgins used to become a proficient lighting man, make-up man, stage manager and ultimately technical director.

Finally those who do the hiring were convinced, and his first directing job was a full season at Belleville Theatre Guild's Pinnacle Playhouse. From there he went to Montreal International Theatre's La Poudrière.

The next step was directing plays at McGill University, including their Red and White Revue.

Roy Higgins directed "The Twisted Loaf" for the Saidye Bronfman Theatre in conjunction with "Elle", to create theatrical history in Montreal as the first English/French venture underwritten by the Secretary of State's office. It was at that time that he became involved with the writing of Aviva Ravel. The following spring he was sent to Newfoundland by Theatre Canada's professional training program, where he directed the St. John's Players in "Soft Voices". Following this, he directed the opening play, Noel Coward's "Private Lives" at North Hatley.

Currently Mr. Higgins is Artistic Director of the Playwrights' Workshop in Montreal, an organization which has a scope well beyond the local level.

Amongst their current programs are a theatre school and the provision of try-out facilities for playwrights in studio productions — but most important of all, they have created a bridge between English and French contributions to Canadian theatre, an area in which much remains to be done. This, we feel, is what gives Roy Higgins' efforts a national scope.

The Twisted Loaf

Aviva Ravel

Glossary of expressions in the play

Afikomèn — hidden piece of matsah children traditionally "steal"
chalè — Sabbath loaf
dee ferr kachès — the four questions
freilach — happy, joyful
geshmack — delicious, scrumptious
goldènè glicken — golden happiness, great prosperity
golem — statue
Gottenu — my God
goyim — Gentiles
gut yom-tov — good holiday
Haggadah — Passover prayer books
koyach — strength
meshugass — nonsense, craziness
nachès — satisfaction
nigun — melody, chant
nu shoin — well already?, come on now
seder — Passover meal
Shabbos — the Sabbath
sheinkeit — beauty
yom-tov — the holiday (the Holy days)
ziskeit — sweetness

Cast of Characters

Old Bessie — Age 65
Old Alex — Age 65
Auctioneer
Young Bessie — Age 25-35
Young Alex — Age 25-35
Sheila — Age 36
Judy — Age 35
Annie — Age 38
Nurse
Laibel — Age 30

Scene one

(A room in a hospital. On either side of the bed — a night table and chair. On the table, flowers, glass, tissues.

Bessie, a 65 year old woman lies in the bed. She stares at the ceiling.

Music: "We will build a little home" fades in. As she remembers the song, she sits up and smiles.

Suddenly, sound of drums, evokes a painful memory, she covers her ears with her hands and falls back.)

Scene two

(Auctioneer appears with his assistant, the drummer. The Auctioneer is a macabre figure who speaks to the crowd seductively, urging them to buy.

An older Man, Woman and their Daughter cling to their possessions, which are displayed on a table.)

Auctioneer: Ladies and gentlemen, the auction is about to begin! Come one, come all for the best bargain in town! Hurry, Igor, what's holding you up! Bring it all out, Igor, all of it!

(Igor, the drummer, hands the various articles to the Auctioneer.)

Auctioneer: What am I bid for this tablecloth?

A Woman: One ruble!

Auctioneer: One ruble? Are you mad? It's worth at least five!

A Woman: Two rubles!

Auctioneer: Ah, that's better. Take it away for two rubles! And for this soft warm blanket?!

A Woman: Fifty kopecks.

Auctioneer: Take it for fifty! And these candlesticks! Ah, such beauties. How much? How much?

A Woman: Three rubles.

Auctioneer: Three rubles?! I wouldn't give them to you for ten!

A Woman: Eight rubles.

Auctioneer: All right — give it away for eight rubles!

(The auction continues throughout the following dialogue — the buyers carry stuff off and return for more. The Auctioneer gloats.)

Daughter: *(Young Bessie as she sees the candlesticks being taken away)* Mama, they're taking everything we have!

Mother: *(Comforting her)* It could be worse . . .

Father: May the landlord rot in hell. May he die of the plague, may his children be cursed for generations!

Mother: Sha, papa, what's the use?

Father: I won't sha. Because a man can't pay his rent, they treat him like an animal? Worse than an animal. Who doesn't give a dog a shed to sleep in?

Daughter: Where will we go tonight?

Mother: To the auntie, and then, maybe a ticket to America.

Father: Who will send us a ticket, who?

Mother: My uncle. He's a good man.

Father: May I rot in my grave before I take charity!

Mother: We have no choice, papa. First we'll send Bessie, and then, God willing, we'll go . . .

Father: *(Going off)* The pogrom will get us first!

(The articles have been sold. The Auctioneer counts his money.)

Auctioneer: Not bad . . . and for me, fifteen per cent. *(Sneers at the Mother and Daughter)* Jews! If you believed in the True Prophet, this wouldn't happen to you. May He protect us from such evil. *(Throws a few kopecks at them)* There. And don't say I'm not a charitable man.

(The two women retrieve the kopecks. The Auctioneer laughs. Igor beats his drum. All Exit.)

Scene three

(Old Bessie opens her eyes.)

Bessie: Thank God I protected my children from that . . . ah my poor father. *(Reaches for a kleenex but the box falls.)* Ach, hospitals, they don't let a person be sick in peace.

(Enter Old Alex, her husband)

Alex: Nu, Bessie, how are you feeling today?

Bessie: My enemies shouldn't know from such pain. Give me the kleenex.

Alex: *(Patting her face with the tissue)* You don't worry about nothing. In a couple of days you'll be alright.

Bessie: Not in a couple of days and not in a couple of weeks. I know the truth, Alex, may God protect us from such truth.

Alex: What are you saying, Bessie? It was just a little operation. People get sick, they get well. You'll be home cooking me a good borscht in a couple of weeks. My stomach can't last from the restaurants.

Bessie: *(In disbelief)* Ach. *(Sees the book he is reading)* So what are you reading for a change?

Alex: They say that the brightest star of a constellation is called 'Alpha'. That's Greek, but it's like Hebrew — 'Alef'. Today we know eighty-eight constellations, but in those days . . .

Bessie: Ah Alex, your head is still in the stars.

Alex: That's where the future of the universe lies. Today they go to the moon, tomorrow to Mars, then to Jupiter . . .

Bessie: But what about the earth? For that you never cared much.

Alex: Sure I care, but what can I do about it?

Bessie: What can you do about the stars?

Alex: Nothing. But neither can anybody else. So, when it comes to stars, I'm not a loser, Bessie. (Warmly) You're my star.

Bessie: The one that gives the least light, the 'tav' one, uh?

Alex: No. You're the brightest, the 'Alef'.

Bessie: Ah, read your book, you foolish man.

(Nurse enters. Smiles at Bessie. Checks her pulse.)

Nurse: Hello, Mrs. Stein.

Bessie: How's your daughter today?

Nurse: She's better.

Bessie: Good. When she's better, you're better and I get better attention . . . Ah, never mind, you're the best nurse in the hospital, Angela. A regular angel. And look how pretty . . .

Alex: Nurse, I want you to tell Bessie she's getting well. Isn't she?

Nurse: Of course she is. You're doing very nicely, Mrs. Stein.

Bessie: (Patting nurse's hand) And you're a smart girl too.

(Exit nurse)

Alex: You see? The nurse said you'll be all right. And she should know.

Bessie: Did you hear from the children?

Alex: Yes. They're all coming to see you today.

Bessie: Sheila too?

Alex: Sure.

Bessie: Ach, I wish she'd find herself a husband.

Alex: Who's good enough for her?

Bessie: She's independent. I also wanted to be independent.

Alex: What's this? You're sorry you married me, Bessie?

Bessie: Now when my life is finished it helps to be sorry? . . . You're okay, Alex. You could have been worse . . . (Lies back) But Judy's all right, isn't she? (Looks to him for confirmation)

(Alex laughs)

Sure she is. With Arthur's money, who wouldn't be all right? . . . I'm trying all these years, I never mention a word, but I just can't get used.

Alex: To some things you don't get used.

Bessie: Oy, I can't lie on my back no more . . . Ah, the days are so long, I get all mixed up. Was Annie here yesterday?

Alex: Yes, but I don't know how she manages. She works, looks after the children, and what does Harry do? He sits around on his 'foorinten'. (behind)

Bessie: He studies. (Proudly) He'll be a lawyer.

Alex: What do I need a son-in-law a lawyer for? He can work by Arthur, be a salesman . . .

Bessie: She wants her husband to amount to something.

Alex: Annie's killing herself.

Bessie: She's okay.

Alex: She doesn't know if she's awake or sleeping, that's by you okay?

Bessie: Maybe you're right . . . ach, I'm tired.

Alex: (Rises) So you rest and I'll sit outside. The minute you want me, I'll be here . . . (Exit)

Bessie: Amount to something. In the end it all

amounts to the same thing.

Scene four

(Young Bessie speaks to Old Bessie.)

Young Bessie: What are you lying there for? You have to get the work out.

Old Bessie: I can't work no more.

Young Bessie: You thought you could go on forever.

Old Bessie: *(Tries to sit up)* Help me . . . *(Falls back)*

Young Bessie: Never mind, old woman, I'll manage. I always managed.

(Young Bessie sits at the sewing machine.)

Young Bessie: I have to get the work out. Annie and Sheila need shoes, and there's the grocery bill. Gottenu give me strength.

(Enter Young Alex)

Young Bessie: Where were you!

Young Alex: A little walk in the park.

Young Bessie: I sit by the machine and he sits in the park.

Young Alex: I was walking, Bessie, walking . . .

Young Bessie: Did you bring more work?

Young Alex: *(Picks up a newspaper)* No!

Young Bessie: What do you mean, no?

Young Alex: No is no. I'm finished with the factory.

Young Bessie: *(Rises)* So, you lost the job. And with what will I buy food? And how will we pay the rent? !

Young Alex: It's not my fault!

Young Bessie: Maybe it's my fault you can't make a living?

Young Alex: It's not my fault!

Young Bessie: Sure not. You fight with the foreman, it's his fault. You can't sew a straight seam, that's my fault. You work behind the counter and you can't be patient with the customers, that's their fault. I have exactly twenty-five cents in my purse. That's all I know.

Young Alex: I'm going out!

Young Bessie: No you're not! Sit down . . . now we'll talk. We have to do something.

Young Alex: So do, do! Call the Meshiach. What do you want from me? *(Reads paper)*

Young Bessie: I was thinking . . . We'll lend money from the Uncle and buy six machines. We'll put them in the house and get girls to sew. I'll manage everything. You'll just go to the manufacturers and get the work.

Young Alex: Bessie, here in the house? Where will we live?

Young Bessie: So we won't live. Who says we have to live? Who wants to live anyway? !

Young Alex: *(Skeptically)* You think the uncle will give us . . .

Young Bessie: *(Gets her coat)* I'm going right now to talk to him. When the baby wakes up give her the bottle. It's in the ice box. Warm it, but it shouldn't be too hot.

(Young Bessie bends to pick up his newspaper. Kneels beside him, to pacify him, to encourage him.)

Young Bessie: Alex, I know it's hard, but we got to try. Next week maybe, we'll have a few extra cents, we'll go see a Bette Davis . . . ah, does she act . . . we had some good times Alex. No? It's going to be good again. Maybe, if not for us, then for the children. I want to live to see them well off. That's all I care. *(Going out)* And have a look at Annie and Sheila. They always throw the blankets off. *(Exit)*

Young Alex: *(Reads from Talmud)* Ha-koynes tson la-dir v'noal b'foneho koroooi, v'yotsoh v'hiziko, posoor. Lo noal b'foneho korooiy v'yotsov'hiziko, chaov.

(Recite in Ashkenazi dialect from Baba Kama — Mishna 1)

(Translation — If a man brings sheep into a shed and locks the door, but the sheep get out and do damage, he is not liable. If he does not lock the door, he is liable.)

Scene five

(Annie and Sheila at a table in the hospital cafeteria.)

Sheila: So that's how it is . . .

Annie: Yes Sheila.

Sheila: Are you sure?

Annie: That's what the doctor said.

Sheila: Lousy coffee! *(Puts her cup down)* And **where** is the princess?

Annie: Judy'll soon be here.

Sheila: I hope we aren't disturbing her afternoon siesta, or does she see Pierre, her hairdresser, today?

Annie: I said she'll soon be here.

Sheila: Are you going to tell her?

Annie: Of course.

Sheila: I'm afraid the lady won't be able to take it.

Annie: Oh cut that crap already.

Sheila: The word is shit. Shit!

Annie: You're a big help.

Sheila: What do you want me to do? Make with the jokes? Ha, ha, that's a good one. Mama is dying . . . do you think she knows?

Annie: I'm not sure.

Sheila: What good will another operation do?

Annie: The doctor suggested . . .

Sheila: All that pain, it doesn't make sense. Nothing makes sense! Oh shit! *(Bends over)*

Annie: Are you all right?

Sheila: Sure I'm all right. Ask my psychiatrist. I'm the least fucked up of all his patients.

Annie: If you want to move in with us for a while . . .

Sheila: I can take care of myself!

Annie: At least you won't be alone . . .

Sheila: I like to be alone! I don't need your four little monsters driving me crazier than I am. And your husband, ugh, what a creep . . .

Annie: Your coffee's getting cold.

Sheila: *(Mimics)* 'Your coffee's getting cold.' You're a pain in the ass, Annie.

Annie: Thanks.

Sheila: Don't mention it.

Annie: When we see mama we'll smile, make her feel good, she's the one who's sick.

Sheila: *(Mock admiration)* Annie, Annie, how do you do it?

Annie: I had a good teacher.

Sheila: You know what I learned at home? To hate. Everything and everybody. Especially little Judy princess. *(Smiles)* Remember I tied her to a post and forced her to eat worms? And I cut off her curly locks . . . served mama right for calling her "Shirley Temple". And once I set a match to her crib and she almost burned . . . gee I was a rotten kid. Mama was so good to her and you know how she paid her back — by marrying a 'goy'. Mama never got over it.

Annie: A fat lot you ever cared for mama's feelings.

Sheila: She only married him for his money.

Annie: You don't know that.

Sheila: (Mimics Judy's husband) "Winters are so difficult in Canada. We must spend a month or two on the Riviera. My rheumatism you know . . ." And he's got these pudgy pink hands . . . ugh . . .

Annie: What do you want Sheila?

Sheila: I . . . don't know. I wish I knew . . . (Reaches out toward Annie) Annie . . .

Annie: (Taking her hand) You'll meet someone . . .

Sheila: (Withdraws) No! Some life mama had.

Annie: But she was happy with Papa.

Sheila: My ass.

Annie: Don't you realize that she loved him. All those hard years, she loved him.

Sheila: So what?

Annie: So she was happy. Maybe she didn't sound happy all the time, but there was peace inside her. I saw it in her eyes . . .

Sheila: Well I'll never . . . never . . .

(Annie sees Judy come in. She waves to her.)

Annie: We're here, Judy.

(Judy enters. She is elegant and very lovely.)

Sheila: (Looking Judy over) Look what the cat dragged in. Doesn't she look like hell? She ought to take better care of herself.

Judy: (Sitting) I'm terribly sorry I'm late.

Sheila: Don't tell me the maid broke a leg? Tut, tut, tut . . .

Judy: I had to . . . (Judy decides to keep silent. Then after an awkward pause) . . . Well . . .

Annie: Well . . .

Sheila: Well! Three wells make a river.

Judy: Is there something new? Mama isn't getting worse is she?

Sheila: Oh she's getting a hellova lot worse.

Annie: Sheila, for chrissake!

Sheila: Whatsamatter? The princess can't take it? Let's soften the blow then. Let's tell it to her slowly. Ma — ma . . . is . . . pass — ing . . . away.

Annie: Look Judy, it's like this. She won't get better, and the doctor wants to perform another operation.

Judy: (Pale) Then she has got . . .oh, my God . . .

Sheila: (Enjoying Judy's pain) Whose God do you think she's talking to, ours or Arthur's?

Annie: For godsake, Sheila, shut up!

Judy: You're disgusting!

Annie: That was a rotten thing to say.

Sheila: (Pauses and smiles) That's how it is. Everyone's always picking on me.

Annie: Judy, would you like some coffee?

Judy: (Shakes her head.)

Annie: We're going to see her now. And we'll be . . . cheerful. We'll talk about ourselves, the children. She wants to hear good things.

Sheila: (Bitterly) And what will I tell her?

Annie: Tell her . . . (Pause) . . . that your novel will be published. That you're going to be rich and famous! . . . (Breaking) . . . tell her anything! . . . it's impossible. She was so strong. Nothing could ever happen to her . . . (Cries softly)

Scene six

(The hospital room. Nurse enters humming. Old Bessie watches her.)

Old Bessie: You're so graceful, Angela.

Nurse: Thank you Mrs. Stein.

Old Bessie: Do you like to dance?

Nurse: *(Smiles)* Yes, I do.

Old Bessie: *(Remembering)* I used to be a good dancer.
(Music: Dancing Cheek To Cheek. Young Bessie wearing a dress in the style of the twenties, dances with Young Alex.)

Young Bessie: You're a good dancer, Alex.

Young Alex: You're not so bad yourself, Bessie.

Young Bessie: If only life could be one long dance.

Young Alex: So what have you decided, sweetheart?

Young Bessie: My uncle says I shouldn't marry you.

Young Alex: Maybe he's right. I can't promise you 'goldènè glicken', just that I'll always love you.

Young Bessie: If I was in the old country my mother would choose me a husband. Here it's different.

Young Alex: You're beautiful, Bessie.

Young Bessie: A girl has to have a family, a home . . .

Young Alex: So what do you say, Bessie?

Young Bessie: I say — yes, Alex — yes! !

(Young Alex and Young Bessie dance off.)

Scene seven

(Hospital room)

Old Bessie: *(To nurse)* Nowadays they don't know how to make music. In the old days, songs had melodies. Now it's all noise.

Old Alex: *(Enters)* Ah, you're awake, Bessie. How do you feel?

Old Bessie: If I didn't have good things to remember, it would be worse . . . Alex, when did we get old? It seems like we just got married?

Old Alex: When you get well, we'll go on a honeymoon. The sun shines in Miami all year round, they have beaches and sand . . .

Old Bessie: Miami? Why not the moon?

Old Alex: That's too far, Bessie.

Old Bessie: For me, Miami is just as far.

Old Alex: *(Bracing himself)* The doctor said . . . just one more operation and you'll be perfect.

Old Bessie: What! You talked to him?

Old Alex: Yes, just now, in the hall. Next week and you'll be perfect.

Old Bessie: Please, Alex, no more operations. Don't let them . . .

Old Alex: The doctor knows best.

Old Bessie: If I have to die, let me die in peace . . .

Old Alex: Don't talk like that! . . .

(Judy, Sheila, Annie enter)

Old Alex: Ah, my three million dollars. Did you ever see such beauties?

Annie: How are you ma?

Old Bessie: I'm getting better everyday. The nurse says I'm doing fine.

Annie: That's great, ma.

Old Bessie: Nu, and the children?

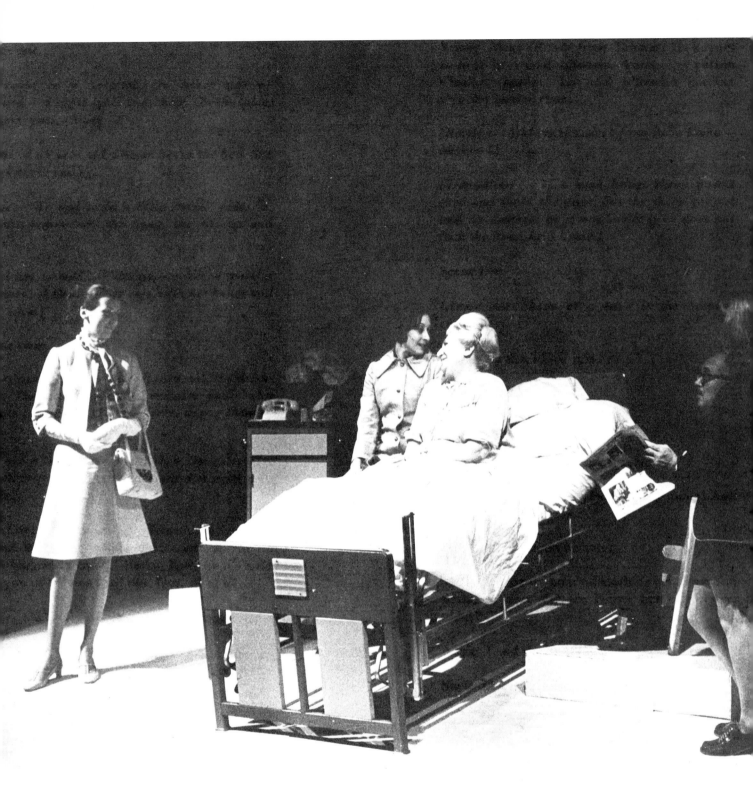

Annie: *(Enthusiastically)* Stevie's captain of the baseball team!

Old Alex: If he wants to know about baseball, you tell him to ask his Zaidè — also football, hockey, wrestling . . .

Old Bessie: He's an expert on everything, don't ask.

Annie: Alan is first in his class.

Old Bessie: But he's too skinny. Give him porridge in the morning. You never left the house without a hot cereal. And the baby, tell me about the baby.

Annie: He says 'candy', 'mummy' . . .

Old Bessie: Does he say 'bubby'?

Annie: Sure he says 'bubby' . . .

Old Bessie: Good! He's so 'geshmack' you can eat him up. And fat, like a child should be.

(All laugh lightly joining her in her pleasure.)

Judy: Mama, don't you want to know about my kids?

Old Bessie: Sure. Tell me. How are they?

Judy: . . . Fine.

Old Bessie: I'm glad to hear. Ah, too bad they go to that Catholic school. When they grow up, they'll think that Chanuka is a Japanese toy.

(Sheila stifles a giggle. Judy is hurt.)

No, no, Judy, I didn't mean it. I love all my grandchildren the same. Just promise me one thing, the younger one, he's named after my father, he should have a Bar-Mitsvah, a few Hebrew words, it can't hurt. Judy?

Judy: Yes, mama. I promise.

Old Bessie: *(To Judy)* Your Arthur's a good man. Look at the flowers. And he hires me a private nurse like I was a countess. Tell him, thank you. Alex, doesn't she look nice today?

Old Alex: What do you expect? She takes after my side of the family.

Old Bessie: And you, Sheila, what's new?

Sheila: Nothing.

(Annie catches her eye and stares at Sheila.)

Sheila: . . . well, there is something.

Old Bessie: Yes, yes?

Sheila: That book I'm writing . . . I sent it to a publisher . . .

Old Bessie: They're going to print it! And sell it in all the stores! You see, Alex, she's going to be all right. For that I give you a kiss, Sheila. *(Bessie kisses her)* That's all I want. My children should be settled and have 'nachès' from life. *(To Sheila)* You tell that publisher to send the book to Hollywood. Bette Davis would be perfect in your book. Ah, how she made me cry. *(Lies back in pain.)* Nowadays they don't know how to make movies.

Old Alex: *(To girls)* Your mother is tired. It's time to go . . . and how about a kiss for your father?

(Annie and Judy kiss their father. Sheila waits for her father to kiss her. Alex kisses her forehead lightly and sends her off. The three daughters exit.)

Old Bessie: Alex, listen, don't tell them about the second operation. They don't have to worry. *(Alex nods)* Good. If it'll keep me alive a little longer, let them do it. So I'll suffer, but at least I'll see them a bit more . . .

Old Alex: Bessie, you have to rest.

Old Bessie: Gottenu, I hope it's true about Sheila's book. I made like I believed her, she should feel good.

Old Alex: If you don't rest, I'm calling the nurse to give you a needle.

Old Bessie: Judy, my beauty, if I did the wrong thing, God forgive me . . . I'm resting Alex, I'm resting, soon I'll have all the time in the world to rest . . .

(Bessie closes her eyes.)

Scene eight

(Young Bessie sits at the sewing machine. Judy, about seventeen, enters excitedly.)

Judy: Ma, I want to talk to you.

Young Bessie: *(Sewing)* So talk.

Judy: You have to listen.

Young Bessie: *(Sewing)* I'm listening.

Judy: Mama, **please**!

Young Bessie: I have to get the work out. You want a new winter coat, no?

Judy: Mama!

Young Bessie: You had a fight with the new boyfriend?

Judy: No mama. I'm going away!

Young Bessie: You want to sleep by your friend, Elsie, go sleep there. You're a big girl . . .

Judy: I'm going to New York! You remember Michael Novack? He's a director.

Young Bessie: New York! What's this?

Judy: He has a job in a theatre. And he wants me to go with him.

Young Bessie: Are you crazy! A young girl to go off alone, God help us!

Judy: I'm not going **alone**. Michael will take care of me.

Young Bessie: He . . . wants to marry you?

Judy: He's only a friend.

Young Bessie: Judy, I don't want to hear no more 'meshugass'.

Judy: Everyone says I'm talented! Mama, there's nothing I want more in the world.

Young Bessie: Now you listen to me. You know how many beautiful talented girls walk the streets in New York? They become prostitutes, not actors! In one month, in one week, you'll be on the street, God forbid.

Judy: I won't fail, ma. I promise.

Young Bessie: So now you'll give me a written guarantee, uh? And let me tell you something else. Those theatre men want only thing from beautiful girls. I'm not going to let you ruin your life . . . Judy, pity me! You're my treasure. For **this** I work like a slave? For you to walk the streets in a strange city?

Judy: Mama, I want to **be** somebody!

Young Bessie: When you have bread on the table, you can afford to be somebody. You'll get married first, to a nice boy, with a good job, if he wants you to be an actress, you'll be an actress. In the meantime, you'll stay home.

(Returns to the machine. Switches it on. Her eyes mist over in aggravation, her finger is caught under the needle.)

Judy, the needle!

Judy: *(Runs to help her. Comforts her mother)* All right, mama, I won't go. The truth is, I'm a little scared myself.

(Auctioneer enters holding the silver candlesticks. Sound of drum under his words.)

Auctioneer: What am I bid for these silver candlesticks? Ten rubles? You're mad! They're worth at least fifty! Sold to the lady for fifty rubles! *(Exit)*

Scene nine

(Old Bessie in hospital bed.)

Old Bessie: That'll never happen to my chil-

C17

dren! Never!

Old Alex: Bessie, what's the matter?

Old Bessie: Such pain, Alex, such pain.

Old Alex: Nurse, nurse!

Old Bessie: Such pain . . . Gottenu haven't I had enough? What are you punishing me for? What did I do . . .

(Nurse enters. Gives Old Bessie a shot.)

Nurse: You'll be all right in a minute, Mrs. Stein.

Old Bessie: What did I do?

(Music: "Dancing Cheek to Cheek". Light on Young Bessie. She is at a party.)

Young Bessie: Don't you know?

Old Bessie: I don't remember.

Young Bessie: Then I'll remind you.

Old Bessie: Go away. Leave me alone. Go . . .

(Enter Laibel. Both he and Young Bessie are dressed in the style of the early thirties. Young Bessie has had a bit too much to drink. They dance during following dialogue.)

Laibel: So, Bessienu, we meet again. It's been a long time. What have you been doing all these years?

Young Bessie: Sh, Laibel, the old woman is very sick. Look what's become of her, poor thing.

Laibel: You'll never be old for me, Bessie. I'll always remember you like this. Come here, come, I don't bite. *(Kisses her.)*

Young Bessie: You're a terrible flirt, Laibel.

Laibel: I'm crazy for you Bessie. What good are all my riches, when I'm a lonely man.

Young Bessie: What about Alex?

Laibel: He can jump in the lake.

Young Bessie: That's not nice. This is a good party and you're cute.

Laibel: Come with me, Bessie, to California, the real land of milk and honey, with blue skies and beautiful palaces; you'll wear jewels and furs and . . .

Young Bessie: Go on, you don't mean it.

Laibel: But I do! *(Kisses her)*

Young Bessie: In front of all these people! I'm a married woman, Laibel, with a baby.

Laibel: Am I to blame that Alex met you first?

Young Bessie: *(Leans against him)* My head is turning round and round.

Laibel: Come Bessienu, we'll have a good time. I'll take you with me in the morning. You'll live like a queen . . .

Young Bessie: And my baby?

Laibel: Bring the baby. I love babies . . . I love you, Bessie.

(Laibel and Bessie dance off. Young Alex enters. He has been looking for Bessie.)

Young Alex: Bessie? Bessie!

(Young Bessie enters. She is dishevelled.)

Young Alex: You're here! Where were you?

Young Bessie: Nowhere.

Young Alex: It's five o'clock in the morning. I was looking all over the city for you. Where were you!

Young Bessie: *(Feebly)* I . . . fell asleep in the Uncle's house.

Young Alex: I went to the Uncle. You weren't there! You take me for a fool? I stay with the baby, so you can go out and what do you do? Where were you! Answer me!

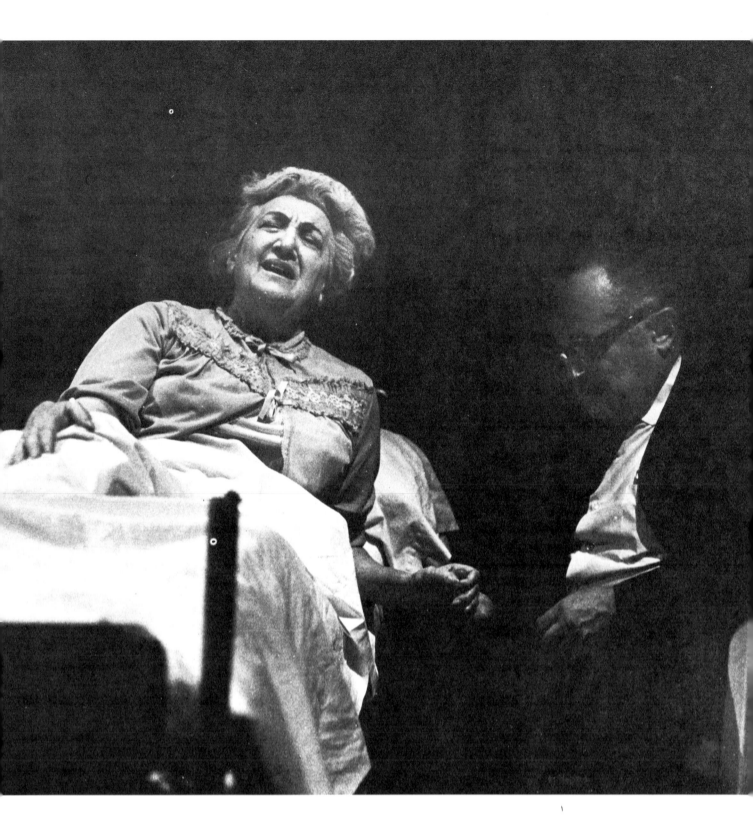

Young Bessie: Don't ask me, Alex. I'm back You see I'm back.

Young Alex: *(Pushes her off)* You could have stayed where you were!

Young Bessie: But . . . I love you, Alex. When it was over . . . I realized I love only you . . .

Young Alex: *(Horrified)* When it was over! Bessie! !

(Young Alex slaps Young Bessie and runs out.)

Young Bessie: *(Going after him)* Alex? Alex! Come back . . . Alex!

Scene ten

(In hospital room.)

Old Bessie: Alex! Alex!

Old Alex: I'm here, Bessie.

Old Bessie: You're not leaving me?

Old Alex: What an idea?

Old Bessie: You'll always stay with me, Alex?

Old Alex: Sure, my flower. I'm not going anywhere.

Old Bessie: You're not sore?

Old Alex: Why should I be sore?

Old Bessie: *(Lies back)* Tell me about the stars, Alex . . . tell me . . .

Old Alex: *(Covers her)* There's the Big Dipper, the Little Dipper, Orion, Leo, The Milky Way . . . over a hundred million stars . . . *(He looks over at Bessie)* It should have been me, Bessie, not you . . . it should have been me. *(Exit)*

Auctioneer: And for these beautiful silver candlesticks, how much am I bid? How much? How much?

(Auctioneer's drums fades into morning bells.)

Scene eleven

(Following morning. Nurse enters to look after Bessie.)

Nurse: How are you this morning, Mrs. Stein?

Old Bessie: *(Sighs)* You tell **me**.

Nurse: You look fine.

Old Bessie: Because I just took a walk in the fresh air.

Nurse: *(Smiles)* That must be it.

Old Bessie: Angela, not so long ago we were strangers, now we're good friends.

Nurse: That's right, Mrs. Stein.

Old Bessie: So I want to tell you something. Everything you live now, you'll live again when you're old. It'll only be in your head, but just as real as the first time. So do nice things, Angela, so your last days will be nice.

Nurse: Philosophy so early in the morning?!

Old Bessie: Even I'll be with you when it's your turn to live on memories . . . Angela, you're not listening to me.

Nurse: *(Busy with her work)* I am, Mrs. Stein, I am.

Old Bessie: Nu, that's the way of the world. Everyone's got to find out for himself . . . Is my husband here yet?

Nurse: No, but your daughter is waiting in the hall.

Old Bessie: Which one? The blonde one?

Nurse: She's wearing a beige coat.

Old Bessie: Ah Annie. But it's so early . . . Please tell her to come in.

Nurse: *(Inserts thermometer into Bessie's mouth)* Just as soon as we're ready, Mrs. Stein.

Old Bessie: Enough already. Please tell my daughter to come in . . . *(As Nurse leaves)* We'll talk more philosophy later.

(Nurse smiles and exits. Annie enters.)

Old Bessie: What's the matter, Annie?

Annie: I just dropped in before going to work.

Old Bessie: Harry's all right? The children?

Annie: Sure ma.

Old Bessie: I don't like the way you look.

Annie: That's your fault. If I had different parents I'd have been prettier.

Old Bessie: Ah, Jack Benny . . .

Annie: Can I get you something?

Old Bessie: Sit down. Just look at yourself! You work all day in the office, you come home and cook and clean and wash . . . you're all worn out. I don't like it.

Annie: In two years Harry will graduate. Then everything will be fine.

Old Bessie: Ah Annie, we live every day worrying about the future. But what happens to today, to now? The years go in the garbage and there's nothing left but a bundle of garbage . . . If you don't watch out, Harry's going to find a young girl with red cheeks and lots of 'koyach'.

Annie: Mama!

Old Bessie: Give me my purse. Don't stand there like a 'golem' — my purse is in the drawer . . .

Annie: Your purse? *(Gets it)*

Old Bessie: *(Opens purse)* I want to put some lipstick. Clark Gable is visiting me today.

(Old Bessie writes cheque.)

Annie: What are you doing, ma?

Old Bessie: You stop working today, you hear?

Go to the beauty parlour; buy a few dresses. It's a shame the way you go round in that coat.

Annie: Mama, are you out of your mind? !

Old Bessie: Listen the way a daughter talks to her mother! And take that baby home from the neighbour, you hear?

Annie: Mama, I don't need it, I manage.

Old Bessie: I saved this from working in the factory. You think I'm going to take it with me to the grave. And don't worry about Papa — Arthur will look after him and the hospital bills . . . I'm sorry I don't have no more.

Annie: Mama, I can't.

Old Bessie: All my life I worked, not for myself. When you grew up, to buy the grandchildren presents, to dress nice you shouldn't be ashamed of me. Now, it's all finished . . .

Annie: Mama, don't talk like that.

Old Bessie: *(Presses cheque into Annie's hand.)* Please, make me happy. And go with Harry to a show tonight. See a Bette Davis . . .

Annie: Mama . . .

Old Bessie: Okay, see the Beatles. But have a good time. Enjoy, before it's too . . . *(Lies down)*

Annie: Mama are you all right?

Old Bessie: Go already. I can't listen to you no more.

Annie: Bye ma.

Old Bessie: *(Sits up)* And don't broadcast it on the radio. Your father doesn't have to know . . . and one more thing . . . please Annie . . . look after Sheila, she's all alone . . .

Annie: Sure ma.

Old Bessie: So go, go . . . *(Lies down)*

(Old Alex enters.)

C21

Annie: Hello, pa.

Old Alex: So early, Annie?

Annie: I was lonesome for you. (*Hugs her father and exits.*)

Old Alex: (*To Bessie*) What did she want?

Old Bessie: These modern mothers don't know what to do when a baby has a cold. I told her, put a mustard plaster.

Old Alex: The children still come to you for advice?

Old Bessie: To who, then, to **you**?

Scene twelve

(*Young Bessie at the sewing machine speaks to Old Bessie.*)

Old Bessie: The children need you like a hole in the head.

Young Bessie: They'll always need me.

Old Bessie: They never did what they wanted.

Young Bessie: This country gave us a home, a place to live in peace, as Jews. What more could they want?

Old Bessie: You know what I mean.

Young Bessie: Annie has a good husband, she's all right.

Old Bessie: All right is not enough.

Young Bessie: Don't bother me! I have to get the work out. The children need shoes . . .

(*Enter Young Alex absorbed in a newspaper.*)

Young Bessie: Alex?

Young Alex: Bessie, it says here that next week there'll be an eclipse of the sun. Imagine . . .

Young Bessie: Did you being more work!

Young Alex: I didn't know what to do.

Young Bessie: What do you mean?

Young Alex: They're making muffs this season. Do you know how?

Young Bessie: Sure I know how!

Young Alex: But you never made muffs before . . .

Young Bessie: You bring them home, and I'll know how.

(*Young Bessie puts some work before him to finish — cut the threads off the garments, — and goes to the bread-board where her dough has been rising. She braids the dough into a chale. Judy plays on the floor with a deck of cards. She is about 12. Sheila writes poetry. She is 14.*)

Sheila: "Stars are little buttercups
worn in the lapel
of the night's coat . . .
They are the angels' flashlights
turned on to see in the dark . . .

(*Annie, 16, enters excitedly, waving her report card.*)

Annie: Look mama, my report card!

Old Bessie: (*Glancing at it*) Very nice.

Annie: You see? 96 in chemistry, 95 in algebra and 97 in geometry!

Old Alex: If you made 97 already, why not 100?

Annie: Papa!

Old Bessie: 97 is excellent. That one (*Sheila*) couldn't even make a 50 to pass.

(*Judy giggles.*)

Annie: Mama, I spoke to the principal today. He can arrange a scholarship for me.

Old Bessie: (*Busy working*) A what?

Annie: So I can go to university free! I want to

be a scientist.

Old Bessie: And what does a scientist do, for instance?

Annie: He can . . . invent drugs to save people's lives.

Old Bessie: *(Motions to pail)* Go, Annie, bring more coal for the stove.

(Exit Annie. Young Bessie turns to Sheila.)

Young Bessie: Sheila, wash your face already. I can't stand looking at you!

Sheila: If you don't like it, you can lump it.

Young Alex: Listen how she talks to her mother. Go wash your face!

Young Bessie: Leave her, leave her . . .

(Annie enters with a pail of coal.)

Annie: So what do you say, ma?

Young Bessie: About what.

Annie: University.

Young Bessie: You see your father over there? He can hardly make a living.

(Young Alex glowers, handles the garments agitatedly.)

And look at that one. *(Sheila)* She's not worth nothing. She quit school, sits home all day, reads books. Should I throw her out on the street?

Sheila: *(Saucily)* Anytime you say ma.

Young Bessie: I'm hoping you should get a job and bring a few cents into the house.

Annie: But my schooling won't cost you anything!

Young Bessie: And books and pencils? You should start thinking about a husband.

Annie: Mama!

Young Bessie: You'll go to business college, then work in an office . . .

Annie: I'd rather die.

Young Bessie: I wish I had the education to work in an office. You don't break your back, nice men come in, maybe the boss's son . . .

Annie: Mama, I want to study!

Young Bessie: You **want**, I also want lots of things. Maybe if you were a boy, it would be different. Now we'll save up some money, get a nice place for you and Judy to bring your boyfriends . . .

Annie: *(Runs out crying)* Mama, you make me sick!

Young Alex: Maybe Annie should . . .

Young Bessie: Should what? !

Young Alex: Never mind.

Young Bessie: She'll cry a little, she'll get over it.

Sheila: And what about **my** boyfriends?

Young Bessie: First you have to learn to wash your face! Come help me put the chalè in the stove.

Sheila: I don't feel like it.

Young Alex: *(Letting it out on Sheila.)* Sheila, go help your mother!

Young Bessie: Leave her, leave her. Juda'le, come . . .

(Judy rises obediently.)

My 'ziskeit, my sheinkeit' . . . then you'll go next door and buy a jar of pickles by Mrs. Finkelshtein.

(Judy exits with 'chalè'.)

(To Alex) And **you,** take those bundles to the factory. It's Shabbos in a few hours. Go already! *(Exit)*

Young Alex: I'm going, I'm going . . . *(Exit)*

(Shiela looks up from the book and rises.)

Sheila: I wish they were all dead. Then I'd be an orphan. A kind lady would adopt me. She'd have beautiful gardens with fountains and golden fish swimming in clear streams. A handsome prince would come along . . .

(Sheila exits dreamily.)

Auctioneer: Ladies and gentlemen! Who will buy these magnificent candlesticks? A pair of rare beauties. Their value goes up every day. Sold to that lucky gentleman for one hundred rubles!

Scene thirteen

(In the hospital.)

Old Bessie: A scientist she wanted to be, that's no life for a girl.

Old Alex: What are you talking about, Bessie?

Old Bessie: In my town girls were lucky if they learned to read and write . . . If I had the chance, I wonder what I could have been . . . a teacher, a bookkeeper . . .

(Nurse enters with tray.)

a nurse . . .

Nurse: Here we are, Mrs. Stein.

Old Bessie: I'm not hungry.

Old Alex: Bessie, you have to eat something.

Old Bessie: Ach . . .

Old Alex: Don't make trouble, Bessie, eat . . .

Old Bessie: *(Takes toast and bites into it)* This toast is dry like last year's matsah . . . matsah, I won't be here for the next 'seder'.

Old Alex: Bessie eat, and don't talk crazy.

Old Bessie: *(Smiles)* You think they have a 'seder' up there, Alex? I wonder what 'nigun' the angels sing. Yours or my father's . . .

Old Alex: *(Aggravatedly buries himself in his paper.)* Bessie!

Old Bessie: The children looked so nice sitting around the table.

Scene fourteen

(A table, covered with white cloth, is set for Passover. Matsah, white matsah cover, silver tray, wine glasses, Haggadah books, candlesticks are on the table.
(Passover music)
Young Bessie covers her head with white kerchief, lights the candles, and says the holiday prayer. The children and Alex stand around the table.)

Young Bessie: Boruch ato adonoy èlohaynu mèlèch ho-olom ashèr kidshonu b'mitsvosov v'tsivonu l'hadlēek nayr shel yom toiv.

Young Alex: *(Kisses Bessie)* Gut yom-tov Bessie. Gut yom-tov children.

(All are seated. Alex, standing recites prayer for wine.)

Young Alex: Boruch ato adonoy èlohaynu boyray pree ha-gofèn.

(All sip wine. Alex continues reading from "Haggadah".)

Sheila: This year I'm stealing the 'afikomèn'.

Annie: You got it last year. It's my turn.

Judy: No, it's mine.

Sheila: Shut up stupid.

Judy: *(Cries softly.)*

Annie: Don't make her cry.

Sheila: Don't boss me around.

C26

Young Bessie: Children, children.

Young Alex: So, can we begin already?

Young Bessie: Sure, Alex, we're ready.

Young Alex: Ho lachmo anyo di acholu avhatono d'aro b'mitroyim . . .

Sheila: I want matsah.

Young Bessie: Not yet, Sheila, soon.

Sheila: I want it now.

Young Bessie: Soon, soon.

Young Alex: *(To Judy)* Now, my 'sheinkeit', 'dee feer kashès' . . .

Sheila: Why does **she** always get to say them?

Judy: Because I'm the youngest.

Sheila: *(Sticks her tongue out at her.)*

Judy: *(Sings looking into the haggadah.)*
'Ma nishtana ha-layla ha-zè
Mee kol ha-laylot
Shè-b'chol ha-laylot
Anoo ochleem: chmaetz u-matsa
Ha-laila ha-ze
Koo-lo matza

Sheila: I'm hungry. I want to eat.

Young Bessie: Sh . . . later.

Sheila: I can't wait.

Young Bessie: Soon, soon.

Sheila: I want to eat right now.

Young Bessie: Listen how nice your sister sings.

Sheila: *(Mimics Judy's melody.)*

Young Alex: Sheila, quiet!

Judy: I lost the place.

Annie: *(Shows her)* Here, here . . .

(Judy continues singing.)

Annie: *(Gets the "Afikomen" which is under the tablecloth.)* I got it, I got it! What will you buy me, papa? I want skates.

Sheila: That's not fair. I never get anything.

Young Alex: Bessie, keep that child quiet.

Sheila: *(Blurts)* Shit!

(All fall silent, gasp. Sheila tightens up, expecting the worst.)

Young Alex: *(To Sheila)* Get away from the table.

Sheila: *(Protesting)* Papa!

Young Alex: Out I said!

(Sheila runs out. Bessie goes after her.)

Young Alex: Bessie!

Young Bessie: *(Torn, reluctantly returns to her place.)*

Annie: I'll get her later, mama.

Young Alex: *(Begins the reading)* Avodim ho-eenu l'Phoroh B'Mitsroyim . . . *(To Bessie, inviting her to sing.)* Nu, Bessie?

Young Bessie: *(Sings)* Avodim ho-eenu l'Pharoh B'Mitsroyim . . .
(Passover music.)

Scene fifteen

(In the hospital. Sheila enters Bessie's room.)

Old Bessie: Ah, the middle one is here.

Sheila: Hi ma.

Old Bessie: You're not working today, Sheila?

Sheila: I had to see you. I want to tell you . . .

Old Bessie: Your book, it's not going to be printed.

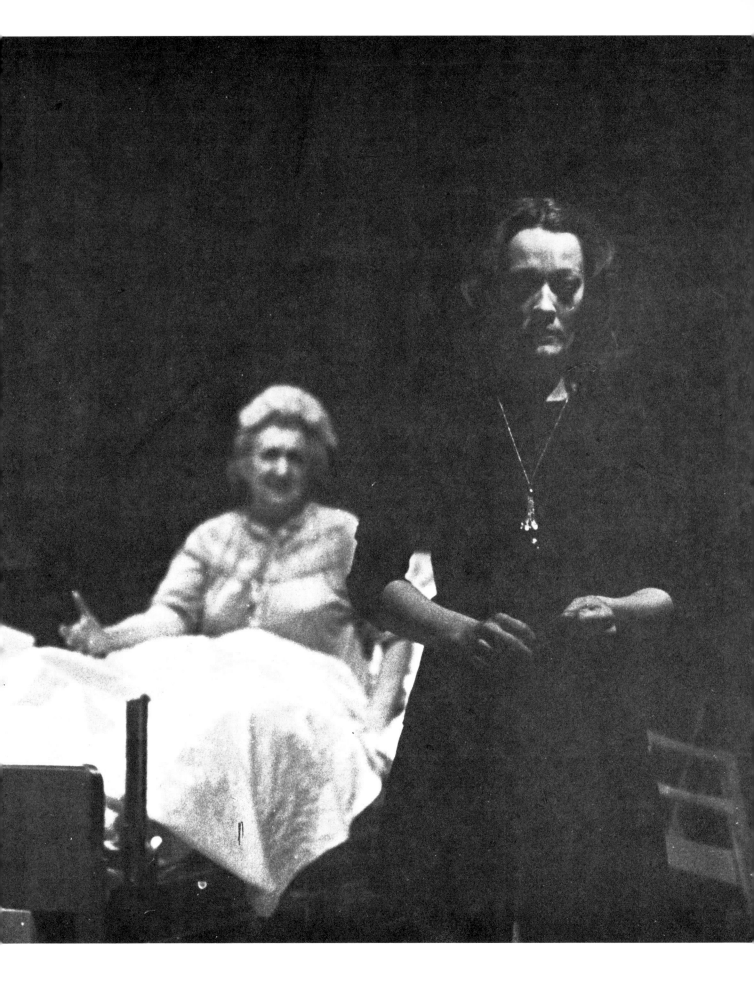

C28

Sheila: That's not what I want to tell you.

Old Bessie: It doesn't matter child, it's not important.

Sheila: Of course it is. Face it mama. I'm a complete and total failure.

Old Bessie: It's not **you** that's the failure, child.

Sheila: Don't blame yourself. **I** don't want to succeed. I never wanted to give you the pleasure . . .

Old Bessie: Gottenu, what are you saying?

Sheila: Mama, my life is full of shit.

Old Bessie: So whose isn't?

Sheila: I'm going away. I hate my job, I hate everything . . . I want to go to Europe, maybe in another place . . .

Old Bessie: You'll meet new people, make new friends . . .

Sheila: You don't mind?

Old Bessie: Since when do you ask me permission to do something?

Sheila: I have to go **now**. I don't sleep nights. I stuff myself so full of pills I feel like a walking nightmare.

Old Bessie: So go, child. Maybe it'll do you good.

Sheila: You've got to understand. I can't bear to see you sick like this!

Old Bessie: You don't have to explain me . . . go . . . enjoy . . .

Sheila: You don't mean it.

Old Bessie: I do. Judy and Annie are here, your father . . .

Sheila: You don't mean it . . .

(Sound: Sheila remembers: "Papa, do you love me? So kiss me. You don't really mean it? So kiss me. You don't mean it!"

Sound: echoes and re-echoes. Sheila covers her ears.)

Sheila: No one ever means what they say to me!

Old Bessie: You're still a child . . .

Sheila: Mama, I'm going today. And I don't care what you think.

Old Bessie: Take a warm sweater. And send me a postcard.

Sheila: You're not angry?

Old Bessie: If going away will make you happy, **I'm** happy.

Sheila: *(Moving toward exit)* Good-bye ma . . .

Old Bessie: Sheila, try to remember me like when I was well. Busy, working, not like this . . .

Sheila: *(Running out)* Mama, I love you! *(Exit)*

Old Bessie: *(Holds up her hand)* You see this hand? No matter which finger you cut off, they all hurt the same . . . the trouble is, child, you won't find what you want, not in Europe, not in Africa, and that's why I cry, not for myself, Gottenu, not for myself . . .

Scene sixteen

(A younger Sheila stumbles into the house. She is crying. Her clothes are torn, her face bruised. Young Bessie runs to her.)

Young Bessie: Sheila! Gottenu! What happened? What happened? !

Sheila: Two boys . . . in the lane . . . I . . .

Young Bessie: Sheila, my baby! *(Reaches for her)*

Sheila: Don't touch me! Don't anybody . . . ever touch . . . me . . . again . . . *(She is faint)*

Young Bessie: Judy, Annie, help me!

(Judy and Annie take Sheila off.)

(Young Bessie speaks to Old Bessie. Drums roll under the following dialogue.)

Young Bessie: That wasn't my fault.

Old Bessie: She had no business being out on the street at night.

Young Bessie: She had a fight with Alex. She tore his book. He yelled and she ran out. I was too busy to go after her. How was I to know that . . .

Old Bessie: You also loved the others more.

Young Bessie: No! I had to keep peace in the house. The two of them always shouting at each other. I had to keep peace!

(Drum and Old Bessie fade.)

Old Bessie: Sh . . . Bessie, soon you'll have peace, lots and lots of peace.

Scene seventeen

(In the hospital.)

(Nurse enters with small tray.)

Nurse: Are you all right, Mrs. Stein?

Old Bessie: Sure, sure.

Nurse: I brought you some nice cold juice.

Old Bessie: Thank you, Angela, thank you.

(Exit Nurse.)

Old Bessie: My enemies should have such an all right.

(Enter Old Alex.)

Old Alex: Hello, Bessie.

Old Bessie: Alex . . . how are things outside?

Old Alex: *(Sits, opens newspaper)* It's cloudy, maybe it'll rain.

Old Bessie: Is everything still the same? The busses, the stores? . . .

Old Alex: Of course.

Old Bessie: Then I'm not so important after all.

Old Alex: What are you saying? Of course you're important, the most . . .

Old Bessie: No matter who comes or goes, the world still goes on. Day and night, summer — winter. People are born, they get married . . . yes, they get married . . .

(Old Bessie remembers Judy's wedding.)

Scene eighteen

(Music: The Anniversary Waltz.)

(Judy wears a wedding veil, carries a bouquet of flowers. She looks radiant. Young Bessie and Young Alex look on at her.)

Young Bessie: Such a beautiful wedding.

Young Alex: What's there to be so 'freilach' about?

Young Bessie: My child, she has so much.

Young Alex: In a couple of years, he'll call her 'dirty Jew'.

Young Bessie: God forbid. They love each other. You see the way he looks at her, the presents he brings . . .

Young Alex: You bring a child up in a Jewish home and . . .

Young Bessie: Times are different. It's not so bad.

Young Alex: By you, whatever the children do, is not so bad.

Young Bessie: You want to spoil me the wedding? You want me to go home? Alex, we have to make the best. The more you complain, the worse it will be. You want to lose her altogether?

Young Alex: *(Slight pause)* Ah never mind. You, Bessie, were a lot more beautiful at our wedding.

Young Bessie: Now that's what I like to hear.

Young Alex: I saw your Uncle. I'll go bring him a drink.

(Exit Young Alex. Young Bessie goes to Judy.)

Young Bessie: *(Embraces Judy)* Have a good life, child, go now, go to your husband.

Judy: Then you like him, mama?

Young Bessie: Sure I like him, I like him.

(Judy exits.)

Young Bessie: By me, whenever something good happens, it has to have a little bad too. Nu, maybe it'll be all right. And if not, she can always come home to Mama.

(Auctioneer appears with candlesticks.)

Auctioneer: Step right up ladies and gentlemen. What am I bid for these silver candlesticks? One hundred rubles? You're mad! They're worth at least five hundred. Sold to the gentleman for five hundred rubles!

Scene nineteen

(Drums roll under the Auctioneer's speech. Sound of telephone ringing dispels the drums. Old Bessie tosses her head on the pillow, covers her ear with her hand.

Old Alex rises to pick up the receiver.)

Old Alex: Hello? . . . yeah, it's papa, who else? . . . She's sleeping.

Old Bessie: *(Mumbles)* I'm not sleeping. Who is it?

Old Alex: Judy.

Old Bessie: Give me the phone . . . "nu shoin",

give it to me . . . Judy? Why aren't you here yet?

(Judy at the other end of the line, is at home. She is upset. She smokes a cigarette. Music: Piano softly under the dialogue: 'Paper Doll'.)

Judy: . . . Cathy . . . ran away.

Old Bessie: Ran where, when?

Judy: She left school this morning.

Old Bessie: Ah she's by a friend. Remember when you were lost and we found you . . .

Judy: We called her friends. She told one she was going to hitchhike to Vancouver.

Judy: Yes . . . to get as far away from the "phoniness" as possible.

Old Bessie: Hitchhike? A 15-year old girl alone on the road! You don't worry. The police will find her. You called the police?

Judy: Yes mama.

Old Bessie: What does that mean — the "phoniness".

Judy: It's when things aren't real. Everything is like a song without music. You want to sing, but there are no notes.

Old Bessie: What's this? By you it's not real?

Judy: It's crazy, ma, but I'm a little jealous.

Old Bessie: So get yourself a knapsack and start hitchhiking.

Judy: I don't mean that, ma.

Old Bessie: You don't sound good. You come over here right away, you hear?

Judy: Sure, ma, I'll be there . . . later.

(Judy hangs up. Old Alex returns the receiver tp place.)

Old Bessie: She doesn't sound good. Maybe

she's bored. She should do charity work, open a home for old people. I'll tell her . . .

Old Alex: Bessie, you have **ideas** . . .

Old Bessie: At least the **ideas** by me are still working.

Old Bessie: And **such** ideas. If you knew what I'm thinking . . . You see, the children have their own troubles, and you and I Alex, are left by ourselves . . . it's funny, it really is funny . . . *(Smiles)* I mustn't laugh, my stomach will hurt, but it **is** funny. *(Begins to laugh)* I just found out why people get married!

Old Alex: Bessie, quiet!

Old Bessie: It took me forty years to find out. Now I know! *(Laughs)*

Old Alex: Bessie, stop!

Old Bessie: I mustn't laugh . . . but I can't help it . . . you want to know why? So when you're dying, you won't die alone! That's what it's all about!

Old Alex: Bessie, I beg you . . .

Old Bessie: *(Hysterical)* I can't . . . stop . . . it's so funny . . . live a whole life together so you don't die alone!

Old Alex: Bessie!

Old Bessie: I can't stop . . . the pain . . . I can't . . .

Old Alex: Nurse! Nurse!

(Nurse enters. Bessie continues bobbing up and down. Nurse gives her a shot.)

Nurse: There, there, Mrs. Stein . . . try to rest . . . there, there . . .

Old Alex: *(Helplessly)* Why did it have to be you, Bessie, why not me?

Scene twenty

(Sound: Nightmare quality. Music: "Paper Doll" to accompany Judy.)

Auctioneer: *(To Judy)* So, what can you do, Miss Stein?

Judy: Sing, dance, act . . .

Auctioneer: Very nice. There **is** something, but out of town.

Judy: I'll go anywhere.

Auctioneer: Good. Come. Come . . .

Old Bessie: I mean the best for you.

Judy: I have to make my own life, mama . . .

(Auctioneer announces.)

Auctioneer: Ladies and Gentlemen! The Silver Dollar Club proudly presents — Miss Judy Lee!

(Applause. Music: 'Paper Doll')

Judy: *(Sings)* "I want to buy a paper doll
that I can call my own,
A doll that other fellahs
cannot steal.
And then the flirty flirty guys
with the flirty flirty eyes
Will have to flirt with dollies
that are real . . ."

Annie: *(Recites letter she has typed. Sound of typewriter.)*

"In reply to your letter of the fifteenth
we will be glad to ship your order
as soon as possible. We regret the delay . . ."

Sheila: *(Recites as patient in mental institution.)*

"The walls are covered with thick slime.
I touch them accidentally and my fingers
are caught in the mess. I pull with
all my might but the stuff drips from
my hand, like from a leaky faucet.
There is no place to run, for my legs
sink in the sewage . . ."

Judy: *(Overlapping)* . . . I want to buy a paper doll . . .

Annie: *(Overlapping)* . . . We hope we didn't

inconvenience you, but due to the trucking strike . . .

Sheila: *(Overlapping)* Sink, sink, sink . . .

Young Bessie: They're taking everything we have!

(Their voices blend into a single sound. Halt. Nightmare sound is repeated.)

Sheila: You loved me least, but now I love you best . . .

Annie: We have no choices . . .

Judy: I want to be somebody . . .

Old Alex: Why didn't you leave me, Bessie . . .

Annie: No choices, no choices . . .

Sheila: I love you best . . .

Annie: No choices . . .

Judy: Be somebody . . .

Old Alex: Leave me, Bessie, leave me . . .

(Young Bessie dances in with Young Alex.)

Young Bessie: If only life were one long dance.

Young Alex: I can't promise you 'goldènè glicken', just that I'll always love you.

Old Alex: Leave me, Bessie, leave me.

Annie: No choices . . .

(Their voices overlap.)

Old Bessie: Stop!

(Sound halts)

I did everything for you! Where would you have been without me? . . . but I forgot to live myself.

Young Bessie: Why does life end just when you begin to understand? Gottenu, that's a dirty

trick you play on us. Let her live a little longer. She has things to fix up. So much to do!

Old Bessie: *(To Young Bessie)* Tell them to come back!

Young Bessie: I can't. Too late . . . too late . . .

Young Alex: I wanted you to have an easy life, Bessie. But I was afraid of rich men, politicians, goyim. When I was a little boy, the soldiers came into our village. They burned the houses. Then they came to our house. They stabbed my mother six times, she fell on the floor and died. My older brother ran out in the street to fight them with his bare hands. They shot him. I hid in the cupboard. At night I ran away. A man took me across the border in a wagon of straw . . . Since then I've been afraid.

Judy: *(Begins to laugh)*

Sheila: *(Joins in laughter)*

Annie: *(Laughs louder)*

(Sound of laughter grows. Auctioneer appears and laughs grotesquely.)

(Bessie screams and wakes up. The Nurse enters. Bessie is alone.)

Scene twenty-one

(Nurse enters to prepare Bessie for the operation.)

Old Bessie: Listen to me nurse. I was a young girl in a strange country. I didn't know the language. My little town had only three streets. I knew everybody. I never understood America. Too many people, too much work. I did my best. I made Shabbos for the family. 'Yom-Tov' was 'Yom-Tov'. I was a good Jewish daughter. I did my best!

Nurse: Of course you did Mrs. Stein. You're a good girl. Now lie back and we'll get you ready.

Old Bessie: Ready?

Nurse: *(Puts up side of bed)* Today is the operation. Have you forgotten?

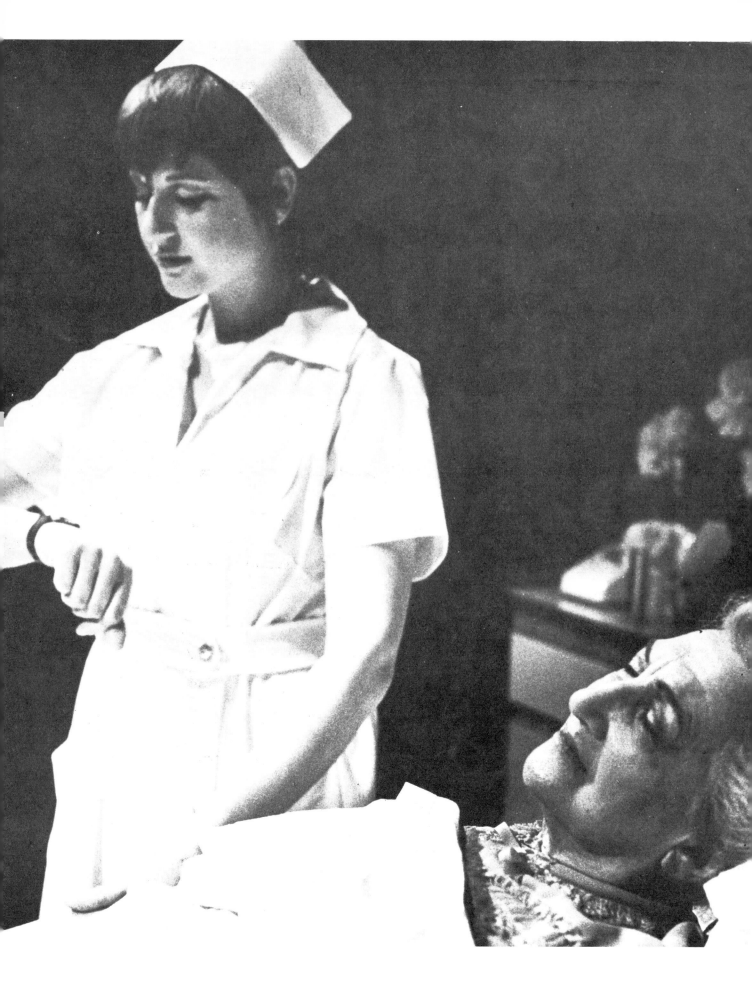

C34

Old Bessie: Today . . .

Nurse: You'll be back in your room in just a few hours.

Old Bessie: Where is Alex, my children? !

Nurse: *(Puts up other side of bed)* They'll be here.

Old Bessie: Alex? Judy? Sheila, Annie? Tell me where they are?

Come help me!

Nurse: You must relax Mrs. Stein. It'll be all right.

(Nurse exits holding pillows.)

Old Bessie: Then it doesn't matter in the end. You're alone anyway. The pain, the fear, everything is lived alone.

(Music: We Will Build a Little Home)

Old Bessie: My little house. I understand now. With buttercups and clover. That's the grave, Alex, the only house I'll ever have. And all our troubles will be over . . . *(Lies back)*

(Auctioneer appears with the silver candlesticks)

Auctioneer: What am I bid for these beautiful candlesticks? What? ! Only one hundred thousand rubles? They're worth at least a million. Sold to the lucky· gentleman for one million rubles!

The end

Soft Voices

Aviva Ravel

Characters in the play

Carol
Toby
Both women are in their mid-thirties

Time: The present

Place: A bachelor apartment in Montreal

(The scene is a bachelor apartment. At first glance this apartment resembles thousands of others like it, yet on closer examination one sees an unreal quality about the room — as though the present surroundings were part of another sphere of reality.

The living room contains many objects and pictures collected over the years as though the owner could not part with keepsakes of the past. The room displays trophies, albums, class photos, diplomas, souvenirs of other countries. There are books on shelves and piles of magazines on a rack. A child's painting hangs on the wall — a mountain scene, two little girl figures in the background.

A couch, small round dining table, hassock, hi-fi, make up the furniture in the room. On the credenza stands a large photograph of three young children. A toy-box takes a place in a corner. A window looks out on to the street facing the audience. (The actresses speak at the window from time to time when they reminisce.)

Off the living room a little kitchenette with a frigidaire, stove, sink, etc. The living room leads into a bedroom which we do not see. Props referred to in the play: man's hat, coat, ladies' hats, pipe.

Carol lives here.

Musical themes: Referred to in the play: "The Lady in Red." "Someone to Watch Over Me." Music Box: Oranges and Lemons.

Lighting Effects: Change from present to past; from reality to illusion according to indications in the text.

Toby is anxious to leave. As Carol speaks she looks about the room uneasily, glances at her watch.)

Carol: . . . Then this elegant, handsome stranger comes up to me and says: *(In French accent)* Pardon the audacity, Mlle, but I have two tickets to the Opera. Would you do me the honour? " "Which opera? " I asked. "La Bohème" he says. So I said, "I adore La Bohème," which isn't true, but the gentleman looked so . . . promising.

Anyhow it turned out that it was the French Ambassador! After the opera I met a Duke, a Count and a roomful of millionaires. What a night that was!

Toby: *(Rises)* I can imagine . . . well, I think I'll go now, Carol.

Carol: No, not yet. I want to show you something . . .

(Toby gathers her shopping bags, parcels, as Carol brings a photograph album. Carol flips the pages.)

Ah, here it is. *(Shows Toby)* This is you, Toby, in your red dress. Look how beautiful you were. "The Belle of Mount Royal" . . . and there's nothing wrong with you now.

Toby: Why . . . thanks.

Carol: *(Points out photo in album)* And here am I, skinny, with mousy, straight hair . . . ugh, what a sight.

Toby: I lost all the old pictures.

Carol: I kept everything. *(Points out another photo)* Here's Miss Johnson. *(Mimics the teacher)* 'Attention class, no talking please' . . .

Toby: *(Gets her purse)* I better go . . .

Carol: *(Goes after her with album)* Not yet . . . Have a cigarette.

Toby: No thanks.

Carol: Oh, I understand. It must be dear Henry. He won't find you at home and he'll wonder where his Toby has been all afternoon. We don't want to upset Henry, do we? *(Takes Toby's purse from her hand.)*

Toby: For heaven's sake, I have to go.

Carol: Of course you do. You were on parole this afternoon but now it's time to return to the cell. "Hurry up please, it's time . . . "

Toby: Don't be ridiculous, Carol.

Carol: Your prison is a well-furnished bungalow, twice-mortgaged, surrounded by barbed wire in the shape of a green hedge. But it's not all that bad, honey, they let you out once in a while.

Toby: *(Asking for her purse)* Carol, please . . .

Carol: Don't you want to know what it's like to be free? To do exactly what you like, **when** you feel like it? Free to come and go at any old hour with no one in the world to watch over you with **love** — tender, sweet, and suffocating love. *(Shoves the purse into Toby's hand.)*

Toby: We'll get together again. It was nice seeing you after all these years.

Carol: *(Trying to entice her to stay.)* But we hardly **talked**! Say, can you still sing? You stood up on the bandstand in that red dress, like a star. *(Sings)* "The lady in red, the fellahs are crazy about the lady in red . . . " that's it, isn't it?

(Toby is drawn to Carol now. Carol takes her hand.)

Carol: Please stay, for old time's sake . . .

Toby: I'd like to, but I have to feed my family . . .

Carol: Oh, if you won't put the roast in the oven, someone else will. There's always someone to put that damn roast in the oven.

Toby: I'm terribly sorry, Carol, but I must go.

Carol: *(Pursuing her)* You were my "best friend." We never have "best friends" when we grow up. You were the most popular kid on the block, yet I could make you do what I wanted. Now, **I want** you to stay and have dinner with me . . . or, are you still afraid of me?

Toby: For one, Betty's waiting for me at ballet school, and Henry must be home by now.

Carol: So call a cab for Betty, then phone Henry and tell him you're eating out with an old friend. Be sure to say **girl**friend or he'll get the wrong idea. Are you afraid of him too?

Toby: *(Angry)* I'm not afraid of anyone! Good-bye, Carol.

(Toby grabs her parcels, hurries toward the door, trips and hurts her foot.)

Carol: Toby, you hurt yourself. I'm sorry . . .

(Carol bends to touch Toby's leg. Toby inches away.)

Toby: It's nothing, Carol, really . . .

Carol: *(Making one last stab at it.)* Please don't leave. After we eat, I'll call my friends. If you want a poet, I'll get Simon. And if it's a singer, I'll phone Lawrence. You used to **like** Lawrence.

(Toby shows interest.)

We'll have fun. We'll dance and sing all night. We'll hike up the mountain and stand on the chalet on top of the whole city . . .

(Carol takes Toby's things from her.)

Toby: *(Hesitating)* I suppose there's nothing wrong with a few old friends getting together. Henry **could** bathe the children.

Carol: He must be the sort of husband my Gilbert was. Generous and devoted. I bet you can put anything over on Henry and he wouldn't know the difference.

Toby: *(Annoyed)* I never put anything over on him.

Carol: A marriage of heavenly bliss.

Toby: Henry and I are perfectly happy.

Carol: Of course you are. So, phone him.

Toby: Henry worked hard all day. It's not fair to . . .

Carol: *(Irony)* You have **your** job, he has his.

Toby: That's right.

Carol: How about a few old friends getting together?

Toby: Another time.

Carol: Lawrence is leaving town this week. There won't **be** another time.

Toby: Oh . . .

Carol: Oh.

Toby: All right. I'll stay, but just to say 'hello'.

Carol: *(She goes to phone)* Good . . . what's your number?

Toby: *(Takes the phone from her)* I'll dial.

Carol: *(Hands phone to Toby)* With pleasure.

(Toby dials. Carol begins to get dinner ready. Sets the table, hums happily.)

Toby: Hello dear . . . I'm with an old friend I met downtown this afternoon. A **girlfriend** . . . shopping . . . there was a sale on children's clothes . . . Carol Forrest, Sherbrooke West . . . I'd like to stay for dinner . . . she invited me . . . no, don't bother picking me up . . . *(Loudly)* can't I go out with an old friend? ! . . . I'm sorry, I didn't realize I was shouting . . . she's at ballet, I'll call a cab . . . there's jello for dessert . . . no, there's nothing wrong . . . please give the kids some cough medicine before they go to bed . . . see you later . . . bye now. *(Henry has hung up)* Henry? Henry . . .

Carol: *(Takes receiver and replaces it)* Nice work, honey. Miss Johnson would have given you an excellent for that.

Toby: *(Uncomfortable)* It's not right . . .

Carol: First we're afraid of our mummys and daddys, then our hubbies take over.

Toby: I told you I'm not afraid! . . . it's just . . . that I left the house in such a mess.

(Carol continues preparing dinner.)

Carol: You think he can't handle it, uh?

Toby: Of course he can. He often helps me.

Carol: Isn't that just jolly nice of him.

Toby: He happens to be a good person! !

Carol: So who said he isn't? . . . oh, don't worry, Toby, he won't divorce you for this.

Toby: I'm not worried.

Carol: After we eat, I'll call the boys. Lawrence mentions you from time to time.

Toby: (Trying to be nonchalant) Does he? How is he?

Carol: Fine.

Toby: What does he do?

Carol: Strums a guitar and sings in nightclubs. I ran across him several times in Europe. He often works for the National Film Board, Hollywood too.

Toby: Really? !

Carol: He's still single and handsome. I wouldn't be a bit surprised if you fall in love with him . . .

Toby: Oh go on.

Carol: How many times have you been in love with another man since you're married? And I don't mean Paul Newman either.

Toby: (Taken aback) Never.

Carol: Honestly?

Toby: Sure.

Carol: Liar.

Toby: Believe what you like.

Carol: You can tell me the truth. I won't tell. Come on, sit down.

Toby: It is the truth.

(Carol and Toby sit at table. Carol serves.)

Carol: I used to fall in love every six months when I was married. A new pair of blue eyes, a sweet low voice. There's nothing like being in love. You bloom, kid, you bloom. You float and sing with the birds. You can't even see the dirty laundry on the bathroom floor and yesterday's leftover potatoes. All you see is your beloved, as he grows taller and more handsome every hour. You meet him secretly in the moonlight and . . .

(Pause)

Toby: And what?

Carol: You get caught. (Sits to eat) But, dear Gilbert always forgave me, until one day . . . he didn't.

Toby: I see.

Carol: It's the masculine perogative to be hurt. I insulted his precious virility.

Toby: But didn't you consider his feelings?

Carol: What feelings?

Toby: He's a person too . . .

Carol: The only important person is yourself. Live today, tomorrow you'll be bent and wrinkled. When you see Lawrence you'll fall, and it'll be worth every minute.

Toby: I'm not going to fall for anyone.

Carol: Then why did you stay with me? Why didn't you go home like a good little wifey-wifey?

Toby: You begged me to stay. It had nothing to do with . . . Lawrence.

Carol: Whatever gave me that idea? I won't even mention his name again. I won't even call him.

Toby: (Quickly) I didn't tell you . . . not to call him.

Carol: Look at these faithful wives. Give them a chance and they'll become streetwalkers.

Toby: Carol!

Carol: I'm sorry, honey. You're probably a cold fish anyhow.

Toby: I am not!

Carol: Okay, okay. "I save it all for hubby."

Toby: Look, I'm happy with Henry. I don't **need** anyone else. I'm not a . . . nymphomaniac.

Carol: Neither am I! **I'm** honest. When I want a man I say so. Men boast about all the women they've had, but just catch a woman talking like that and they say she's sick.

Toby: I'd never let myself get involved with anyone. My family . . .

Carol: *(Mocking her)* Your family? ! . . . I know for a fact that Henry hasn't been all that faithful.

Toby: What do you mean?

Carol: Why aren't you eating? This was catered by the finest restaurant in town.

Toby: Carol, **what** do you know?

Carol: Well, if I must, I must. *(Eats heartily)* Last summer you were in the country, weren't you?

(Toby nods. Looks anxiously at Carol who is enjoying herself.)

All good husbands send their wives to the country. And Henry was a free bird. He visited a girl in this apartment. Henry Willis, that's what she said.

Toby: I don't believe it.

Carol: So don't.

Toby: You're making it up.

Carol: Why should I? *(Eats)* This stuff's good. Try some . . .

Toby: I know you're making it up.

Carol: Could be another Henry Willis. It's a big city.

Toby: Henry wouldn't do that to me.

Carol: Who knows?

Toby: Tell me . . .

Carol: *(Bursts into laughter)* I'm still mean to you, honey. I was only kidding.

Toby: You were?

Carol: Sure. I'm an old hand at lying. I'd lie to God if he'd believe me.

Toby: I should have known better . . . *(Smiles, amused now)* I don't know how I even suspected, Henry is so — straight . . .

Carol: Gilbert is still as beautiful . . . as ever. I used to say, "If you weren't my husband I'd have an affair with you." He didn't like that. Men have no sense of humour.

Toby: I need some coffee . . .

Carol: I'll get it. *(Rises)* The best part of eating out is being served. At home you can get indigestion — stand up, sit down. I haven't forgotten those meals.

Toby: Someday . . . *(Wistfully)* We'll afford a cook and a maid . . .

Carol: And a butler. But by that time Henry will have knocked himself out and died of a heart attack. *(Dabs her eyes with napkin, playing a lady at a funeral)* "The poor man, so young, and very devoted to his family. Worked 15 hours a day so that she would live well. How sad." *(Removes napkin)* But don't worry, you'll remarry and have your maids and a young husband on the insurance. All devoted husbands carry lots of insurance.

(Carol pours coffee and gives cup to Toby. Toby is partly confused, partly amused by Carol. She does not know whether or not to take her seriously.)

(Carol shows photo of her children.)

Carol: There's nothing about the family institution I don't know. There's mummy, daddy and all their little parasites. I don't bother with mine much. Let their stepmother worry about their measles and I play with them on weekends. You should see them gorge themselves on ice cream and cake. Come, I'll show you their toys.

(Lights go down slow — toy box area accented.)

(Music in Oranges and Lemons toy piano effect.)

(Carol goes to a toy box. As she lifts the lid we hear the sound of a music box. She pulls out a large, beautiful doll. Carol picks her up and holds her tenderly.)

Carol: Toby, let's play house, like we used to.

(Amused, Toby rises and stares at Carol.)

This is my baby. Isn't she lovely! Her skin is so soft and smooth — and look at the dimples in her legs. See her blue eyes, her curly blonde hair . . . *(Proudly)* Don't you think she looks like her mother? Give me her bottle, Toby. Come on.

(Toby hands her an imaginary bottle.)

Pick out something nice for her to wear. Her wardrobe comes from Japan, Italy, France. I spared no expense. One's child should be properly dressed. I embroidered the nightie myself.

(Carol 'feeds' the 'baby'.)

Carol: There, baby, isn't that good? Don't cry, mama is right here. Sh . . . *(To Toby)* She's not used to strangers. This lady's not a stranger. She's my best friend. Oh, she's crying again. Give me that diaper.

(Toby gives Carol a napkin. Carol puts the 'baby' over her shoulder to burp her.)

There, that's better. She'll be all right now.

(Carol puts the doll down, and admires her.)

Isn't she a beautiful baby?

Toby: She . . . must have cost a fortune.

Carol: Sh . . . you'll wake her. I don't know what to do with her. She eats so poorly. Her bowel movements aren't too good. I have so many problems. My washing machine broke down last week. Repairs came to seventy dollars. I'd love to take a job but Gilbert says I must be with my three babies all the time. First it's tonsils, then the flu. Every three months a new pair of shoes. I'm always short. Gilbert just can't seem to get a raise.

Toby: It was hard for us too in the beginning, but now Henry is doing well. He's an accountant for a big firm.

Carol: *(As though she hadn't heard Toby.)* And one can't wear the same dress every Saturday night.

Toby: We still have to budget. There are so many things we need.

(Stops playing.)

Carol: I don't need **anything** anymore. *(Carol gets a drink)*

(Music out. Lights to normal. Carol raises her glass.)

Carol: *(Music up — Bach Brandenberg Concerto.)* To my freedom, and my kingdom!
'My name is Ozymandias, king of kings,
Look on my works, ye mighty and despair . . . "

Toby: *(Remembering)* Shelley!

Carol: Our poet.

Toby: Our love.

(Carol plays a seventeenth century courtier. Music up.)

Carol: "Wilt thou accept not
The worship the heart lifts above
And the heavens reject not . . . "

(Toby plays the coy Lady. Moves about graciously.)

Toby: "The desire of the moth for the star,
Of the night for the morrow."

Carol: (*Kissing Toby's hand*) "The devotion to something afar
From the sphere of our sorrow."

Toby: (*Her hand outstretched*) Shelley?

Carol: (*Carol leads Toby about as in a garden.*) "My highborn maiden in a palace tower . . ."

Toby: Oh poet hidden in the light of thought . . .

(*Toby bursts out laughing and the game is finished.*)

Toby: What crazy girls we were. You know I fell asleep in his arms every night. I sailed with him under Mediterranean skies . . .

Carol: I drowned with him in the sea . . . (*Pause*) Look at us now Shelley and despair. Do you see the wrinkles under our eyes? Have you noticed I colour my hair of late? You haven't made a pass at me in years. Old men look at me, but young poets don't notice.

Toby: No, Carol, you look wonderful.

Carol: True. I'm a lovely lady and you're just a plain matron. Shelley wouldn't be interested in **you**.

Toby: (*Accepts drink from Carol*) Is that so?

Carol: But where **is** he now? Hiding in the freezer under the fish? Among the soiled diapers in the laundry bin? Where are you poet-lover whom we stroked till dawn? Fifteen years we've gone our separate ways and left him alone, neglected and forgotten.

Toby: (*Drinks*) From now on we'll see each other often. You'll visit us.

Carol: Nothing doing. In a few weeks you'll think I'm after Henry . . .

Toby: (*Smiles*) Oh, he's not your type.

Carol: (*Acting the gossip*) "Isn't she **nice**, your friend Carol. She always remembers to bring something for the children. She **does** dress well, but uses a **trifle** too much eye shadow, don't

you think? She probably has **other** motives for visiting . . . you know these divorcees . . ." Thanks Toby, but no thanks. (*Finishes off her drink.*) What we need are a couple of men around here. (*Goes to table*) After we clear this away, I'll call them.

(*Music out. Toby begins to bring dish to sink. Carol takes it from her.*)

Toby: I don't mind, really.

Carol: In my house no one does the dishes. I break them.

Toby: What? !

Carol: (*Smashes dish on floor*) Can you think of a better way of getting rid of dishes? Well, go on . . . (*Hands her a dish*) try it.

Toby: I . . . can't . . .

Carol: Aren't you tired of washing those damn dishes every day? Pots, frying pans, greasy plates! Don't you want to smash them?

Toby: . . . But this is a good dish . . .

Carol: I'm rich. I'll get another. Go on, smash!

Toby: Okay, here goes . . . (*Throws plate to floor.*)

(*Carol hands her several dishes. Toby smashes them and laughs like a child. Carol then gets broom and sweeps up pieces.*)

Toby: (*Finishes her drink*) That was fun . . . oh Carol, you're really something.

Carol: Stick around, kid, there'll be lots more fun . . .

Toby: (*Pause*) Do you . . . see Lawrence often?

Carol: Oh no. He's only been in town a couple of weeks. (*Then looks straight at her*) But there's no telling how much can be accomplished in a week or two.

Toby: (*Bites her lips*) Oh . . .

C46

Carol: Don't worry, honey. He's all yours. Tonight I'll save my charms for poor Simon. I've been neglecting him lately. Let's swear on it . . . *(Like a child)* "Two fingers up to God . . ."

(Music box up. They go into child's game now. Sound: Children's voices in background.)

Toby: Cross your heart and hope to die?

Carol: I'll never hurt my best friend.

Toby: We'll be friends forever and ever?

Carol: *(Gets ball from toy box bounces it, singing.)* "Don't you think that I'll look cute? In my father's bathing suit." *(Throws the ball to Toby.)*

Toby: *(Bounces)* "My name is Toby
And my husband's name is Tom,
And we come from Toronto . . . ".

Carol: *(Takes ball. Then makes fists for counting game. Toby follows suit.)* "One potato, two potato
Three potato four . . .

Toby: Five potato, six potato
Seven potato more! "

Carol: You're out! I'm the man.

Toby: I'm the lady.

Carol: *(They dance)* I'm the father.

Toby: I'm the mother.

(Carol and Toby listen to the music against background of children's voices.)

Carol: *(As adult)* Music when soft voices die,
Vibrates in the memory . . .

(Music box out.)

Carol: I never played the mother.

Toby: You were strong . . .

Carol: I had to be with those brothers of mine . . .

Toby: I was jealous that you . . . had a big family and I was an only child.

Carol: Jealous! **Your** mother was such a . . . lady. Mine was a bitch. *(Bossy)* "Go to the baby, he's crying! Then get your father a cold drink and his slippers. *(Harrassed)* Peel the vegetables and I'll put up the soup." *(As child)* "When I grow up I'm going to be a daddy. I won't be a fat old cow like you! " *(Pause)* My father was a king then, when I grew up I saw a little nobody. What a disappointment!

Toby: Like when we marry, we think our husbands are the greatest and then . . . they turn out to be . . .

(Cutting off Toby.)

Carol: Selfish and inconsiderate. There I was, stuck in the house, with three screaming brats. I was going crazy! So I went to work. I found housekeepers for them, but they kept coming and going like common trains. Gilbert begged me to stay home until the kids were older and I said: 'You stay home.' And he just stood there and laughed at me.

Toby: You can't expect a father to be a mother.

Carol: You silly brainwashed dunce. Their propaganda has really got to you.

Toby: I can just see Henry in the kitchen — what a mess. And I could never earn a decent living for my family.

Carol: But I can. I took a job and went back to school. Did everything I wanted. *(Shows Toby certificate)* See this? Outstanding scholar. First class honours. Took three or four credits a year. You should have seen me. I was out every night of the week. Brought home A's in every paper.

Toby: You were always a good student.

Carol: Good? I was a monster! *(To Gilbert)* Another 'A'. Bet you don't like that? To hell with the housework. I want to live in **your** world.

Toby: (Plays Gilbert) But the children need you.

Carol: Anyone can give them a glass of juice.

Toby: Tommy still wets his bed. His teacher says he's not learning well. Debbie has measles; who will stay with Peter when he has his tonsils out?

Carol: You will!

Toby: I have my job!

Carol: I also have a job!

Toby: The children will grow up . . .

Carol: I can't wait. I can't wait!

Toby: You don't love me.

Carol: It's not enough for me to be a wife and mother.

Toby: Our mothers look back on the days when their children were young as the nicest time of all.

Carol: Our mothers were stupid and old-fashioned. Down with swollen bellies and vari-cose viens. Down with nursing and bottles and wasting precious hours pushing a stroller in the park! I want to live!

Toby: Why did you marry me?

Carol: To . . . prove to everyone and myself that I'm . . . normal. Well I don't need you and the kids to make a woman out of me! First and foremost I'm a human being! Good-bye Gilbert and good riddance!

(Carol begins to weep softly.)

I never really knew him when we were married. He wasn't real . . . After I left I realized he loved me . . . (Surprised) Yes, he loved me.

Toby: Carol, are you all right?

Carol: Sure, I am. (Takes Toby's hand) You like me, Toby?

Toby: Of course I do. You're wonderful.

Carol: I'm glad you stayed.

Toby: Me too.

Carol: (Offers Toby a candy) Here, have one . . .

Toby: My favorite kind!

Carol: Didn't I write in your autograph book — "when I grow up and I'll feel blue: I'll eat cherry chocolates and think of you."

(Carol pours drink for herself and Toby.)

To us. (Both drink) You were such a pretty kid. I was so proud of you. I helped you put on that red dress, the red hat, the red gloves and I paraded you up to the mountain. (Moving to toy box)

(Sound: Brass band — tiny toy box effect, lights down to toy box.)

I pulled you up on the bandstand.

(They play as children.)

Carol: (As child) Come on, Toby, here. Hold your hands to one side, like this. Don't forget to sing into the mike. Are you very nervous?

Toby: I'm not sure I remember the words.

Carol: Of course you do. They'll love you.

Toby: You think so, Carol?

Carol: Sure. You'll win first prize again.

Toby: Is my dress all right?

Carol: Just perfect. Oh, there's Mr. Murphy. He wants to introduce you. "Ladies and gentle-men! Attention please. We have with us tonight our talented Belle of Mount Royal. Miss Toby Livingstone! And she's ready to sing "The Lady in Red". (Like child) Listen to them applaud, Toby. The summer stars twinkle over the moun-tain. The night air is fresh and sweet with wild clover. The whole city is at your feet. Sing,

Toby, sing. Sing for me, for Mr. Murphy, for the crowd . . . *(Applause)* You were wonderful! Listen to them!

Toby: They liked me.

Carol: They loved you *(Like Mr. Murphy)* First prize goes to the Lady in Red!

Toby: Thank you, thank you everybody.

Carol: Someday you'll be a great movie actress!

Toby: You think so, Carol?

Carol: Sure. And I'll be your agent, promise?

Toby: I promise.

Carol: We'll live in a mansion with two dozen servants and we'll have all the ice cream we can eat.

Toby: And peanut butter and strawberry jam

Carol: A limousine and a chauffeur.

Toby: And handsome men to take us about.

Carol: I'll have many suitors, like Queen Elizabeth the First. Who wants to have kids and get old and fat.

Toby: Not me . . .

Carol: Not me . . .

(Music out lights to normal. They continue saying 'Not Me' as their voices become adult.)

Carol: Look at yourself Toby. Where is your talent. What have you done with your life?

Toby: Nothing much I suppose.

Carol: Well little Mrs. Nothing, how come you gave up singing?

Toby: *(Remembering)* It happened so fast. Lawrence suddenly left town, and I never heard from him again. Then I met Henry. We both thought that my so-called singing career was . . . kid-stuff. *(Directly to Carol)* He's such a solid, stable person. I was lucky.

(Carol smirks.)

What was I supposed to do? Sit around and mope? Maybe **you** can live in fairy tales, but **I** can't. Anyhow I wasn't such a hot singer. I wouldn't trade my children and husband for all the fame in the world!

Carol: Poor, unhappy Toby.

Toby: *(Shouts)* I'm very happy! I'm happy!

Carol: *(Raises her glass)* I drink to your happiness. May your cup of soapsuds bubble over and your marriage bed triumph in ecstatic orgasms once a week!

Toby: *(Furiously slaps Carol.)* Shut up!

(Carol is taken aback. Holds her cheek and looks at Toby.)

I'm sorry . . .

Carol: *(Slowly going into her number)* Good for you. The lady in red is made of fire and flame.

Toby: *(A little frightened)* I . . . can take care of myself.

Carol: Can you?

(Carol now plays tough little girl. She pins Toby's arm behind her back. Toby screams.)

Carol: Quiet. The needle-man will hear you. Now, say 'uncle'.

Toby: Uncle.

Carol: Say: 'I am a dunce.'

Toby: I am a dunce.

Carol: Carol is my lord and master.

Toby: Carol is my lord and master.

Carol: I will obey her forever.

Toby: I will obey forever.

C51

Carol: I am unhappy.

Toby: I am not . . . I am not . . . I am not . . .

(Carol tightens her grip. Toby is in pain. Toby cries.)

Toby: Let me go! I am unhappy. Let me go!

Carol: *(Releases her.)*

Toby: Why do you always hurt me, Carol?

Carol: (Puzzled) I don't know. Maybe it's . . . because of that party we're going to at Millie's house. Her parents won't be home. *(Softly, almost painfully)* The boys will choose partners and we'll go into the bedrooms. A plain, skinny girl always goes to the bedroom when she's asked. How else will she be popular? *(To Toby)* But you, princess, you'll sit in the living room twiddling your thumbs until the rest of us come out all messed up. You're so pretty, the boys will take you out in any case. You don't have to go to the bedroom!

Toby: I'm afraid to.

Carol: So am I. But even more scared to refuse. I want to show them I'm a **real** girl, like you.

Toby: I hate those parties.

Carol: And the boys with their bony fingers poking away at me. I want to scream. I want to run home with you.

Toby: Let's never grow up.

Carol: Let's be children forever.

Toby: Even if we have Miss Johnson for a million years! *(Play-acts Miss Johnson)* 'Stop giggling, stop that at once. You sound like a laughing hyena, doesn't she, class. I'll have to send you out of the room. Out! Such nonsense, intolerable. Now where were we. X minus Y is the sum of 2a plus b. Sit down Carol and listen. You have a good mind. Pay attention and you will go places.'

Carol: Where will I go, Miss Johnson?

Toby: 'That all depends on you, Carol. Carol! Toby must learn to think for herself. You must not tell her the answers. Well, Toby, beauty and brains never did go together, did they? Toby, you're cheating again! Go to the back of the room. Yes, Carol, **you** will go places . . .'

(Sound: Echoes . . . 'places . . . places . . .' Game ends.)

Carol: And I did. I went all over the world.

Toby: Really?

Carol: Miss Johnson was right. I made it.

Toby: What do you mean?

Carol: I'm Caroline Fitzgerald, the most popular feature story writer for over a decade. Haven't you heard of me?

Toby: *(Dumbfounded)* **Caroline Fitzgerald?**

Carol: How do you like the 'Fitzgerald' bit? Classy uh?

Toby: I read your articles for years . . . about Greece, Spain . . .

Carol: Been everywhere, seen everything.

Toby: Imagine . . . my best friend is famous.

Carol: But what is that compared with one day of our childhood. Come let's go back!

(Carol starts making a pile of the magazines on the floor.)

I'm the King of the Castle and you're the dirty rascal. Jump!

(Carol jumps.)

Your turn, now, Toby. Come on, it's fun. *(Carol pulls Toby on the pile and pushes her off.)* Jump!

(Carol jumps off again. She sits on the magazines.)

Wasn't it fun to play at life. Everything we did

never counted. I could say: 'go to hell, tell the teacher to jump in the well,' and the world didn't collapse. 'Let's climb the moon tomorrow' and we don't climb, but no one is sorry, and down we fall on our roller skates and we have fresh cuts on our knees, so what? We cry for a moment and get up laughing! *(Pause)* Now everything counts, everything is for real.

Toby: Yes. But if I have problems, Henry helps me.

Carol: Why don't you help yourself?

Toby: Henry is smarter than I. He's always right about everything. I . . . I like to be taken care of.

Carol: You're so feminine, you make me sick!

Toby: I make you sick? And you say you like me. Well let me tell you something. I don't like you. You make **me** sick. You're not normal! I don't care if you **are** the famous Caroline Fitzgerald. You frighten me. You're not like any woman I know! And I'm getting out of here!

Carol: No Toby! Please. I didn't mean that **you** make me sick. It's the whole damn system . . . *(Pleading)* Don't go, not yet . . . please . . .

Toby: *(Looks away)* Actually I'm jealous. I wish I could be like you. *(Fondles the doll)* I'm nothing without Henry and the children . . . my house, my garden. I never wanted anything else. *(Laughing at herself)* You won't believe this . . . but I **play** housewife. I **am** the ladies in the women's magazines, the soap operas. I wear a pretty starched apron, I decorate my home, I pack lunches for the cubs . . . and I think that soon the producer will pay me for my appearance and I'll go home . . . but I have no other home.

Carol: *(Delighted)* You're catching on Toby! You're beginning to understand . . .

Toby: *(Drinks again)* You see, I'm not such a dunce after all . . .

Carol: Toby, you're fantastic. I . . .

(Telephone rings. Picks up the receiver)

Hello? . . . yes . . . yes I'll be in all evening. When? Good. I'll be expecting you . . . Sure. Bye now . . . bye . . . *(Replaces receiver and grins)* Guess who **that** was.

Toby: *(Excitedly)* No!

Carol: Oh yes. Lawrence is coming over.

Toby: Oh, what's he like now?

(Carol puts an old record on. She beckons Toby to come and dance with her.)

Carol: Come, I'll tell you. Close your eyes. He's tall and broad. His face is chiselled into perfect features like a Greek god. His curly hair falls in soft waves on his forehead. And you are sixteen again. *(Now they walk hand in hand.)* Your golden hair gleams in the sun. You walk with him, hand in hand, the tall grass clings to your thighs. Then you lie down among the wild flowers, his strong arms hold you under a clear blue sky . . .

(Toby's face registers delight. Carol seems happy for the first time in their encounter . . . Telephone rings.)

Carol: *(Mumbles a swear word and picks up receiver.)* Yes? ! Yes, speaking . . . Just a moment please. *(Motions to Toby)* For you, honey.

Toby: Me? Who in the . . . oh, it must be Henry. What does he want? *(Picks up receiver)* Hello. Yes, I'm fine . . . is everything all right at home? *(Louder)* So why did you call? . . . *(Awkwardly)* No, no objections at all . . . *(Firmer)* I told you I'm all right. I don't know when . . . for godssake, no one **else** is here . . .

Carol: Yet.

Toby: *(Louder)* If you don't believe me, come up and see for yourself. *(She swallows some of her drink)*

Carol: How cosy.

Toby: . . . *(Sheepishly)* Oh, I forgot . . . She got home all right didn't she? A person **can** forget. I told you I'm perfectly all right! Yes. Good-bye. *(Replaces the receiver)* I forgot to send a cab for

Betty. He took her home. Still, it's no reason to call. He just won't leave me alone for two minutes! *(Drinks)* You should have heard him, my Master. *(Holds the drink)* Henry doesn't **let** me drink. Boy is he square. If I **talk** to another man at a party, he has to know exactly what we said just in case we make an appointment to meet. "These things happen, you know". Well, they don't happen to **me**.

Carol: *(Listening comfortably)* That's awful.

Toby: It's dreadful the way he inhibits me. He even watches the clock when I'm out playing bridge with the girls. If I come in after midnight, he has a fit! But I never say anything to him when **he** gets in late. And you know something else. He won't let me wear short skirts. No more than one inch above the knee. He's a medieval fanatic.

Carol: He's arrogant, selfish and conceited. They're all like that.

Toby: He says it's his duty to protect me. Well I'm old enough to protect myself. Oh . . . I'm so humiliated! He didn't have to call . . . well don't just sit there, get me another drink!

Carol: *(Obliges)* At your service.

Toby: I want to have a good time. You call Lawrence right away and tell him to come over now . . . wait, **I'll** call . . . *(Picks up the phone and winks at Carol)* I need a little practice first.

(Picks up the receiver. Crosses her legs in a seductive position. Holds her drink in one hand and pretends to speak to Lawrence.)

Toby: Guess who? No, guess again . . . Your first sweetheart . . . yes, it **is** Toby . . . how are you dear? Have you really? I've thought about you too. Often. Why don't you come up and have a look. Bring your guitar . . . hurry . . . I'm waiting for you. *(Replaces the receiver)*

(Toby kicks off her shoes and begins to dance about, the drink in her hand.)

(Sings) "Come, come, I love you only,
My heart is true . . . "
What's so great about being true, Henry? I'm

not your property. I've got a right to have some fun too. You go away when you feel like — to Chicago, Detroit . . . is it always **business**. I bet Carol **wasn't** kidding about the girl in this apartment. **I'm** always stuck in the house. Now, I'll do anything I please. So there . . .

(Toby laughs. Carol joins in.)

Boy it's hot in here. *(She removes her blouse throws up her arms and goes into the Lady in Red number.)*

"The lady in red, the fellahs are crazy about the lady in red . . . "

(Affecting a pose) You think the fellahs will be crazy about me?

Carol: Absolutely.

Toby: *(Throwing herself around)* Not bad after three kids, uh?

Carol: Perfect, I'd say.

Toby: *(A sudden inspiration)* Carol! Let's change places. You go home to Henry and I'll have this apartment all to myself!

Carol: You really mean that?

Toby: Of course. I drink to it. *(Drinks)*

Carol: But Henry will belong to **me** . . .

Toby: You can have him.

Carol: You'll be sorry.

Toby: Oh, he's not such hot stuff. 'Finders keepers, losers weepers, if he won't like it, he can lump it and take his head and bump it' . . . *(She is quite tipsy now.)*

(Toasts herself)

Here's to not getting up to the baby in the middle of the night, here's to all the meals I won't have to prepare, to the loads of washing may they stay dirty wherever they are. Here's to the ironing, the dishes and the whole works! Long may they reign under Carol's rule. *(To*

Carol) But you won't agree, not even for your best friend.

Carol: I'd do anything for you, Toby.

Toby: Good. And you can also go with him to the hockey games, the football games — **all** the games. *(Giggles)* And don't stick up for the Alouettes.

Carol: Why not?

Toby: It makes him angry when I support the other side. *(Laughs)* Does he get mad! Well, who cares which team wins anyhow?

Carol: I'll be on Henry's side.

Toby: Always agree with him. Say: "yes, yes, yes!" even when you're bursting with "no, no, no!"

Carol: Yes, yes, yes!

Toby: Now I want to give you a few pointers about the kids. *(Holds doll)* If they don't behave, give them a few swats on the bottom.

Never mind the psychology stuff. If you feel like screaming, scream! That frightens 'em. Tears also help. They feel sorry for their mother and calm down. Oh, I can't **wait** to get them out of my hair. I had three kids in seven years and it wasn't easy. I was in labour for thirty-nine hours, fourteen minutes and seventy-four seconds. I'll never go through it again. Never!

Carol: I could have had a dozen, like that, *(Snaps her fingers)* and nursed them for years.

Toby: I tried to nurse, but I couldn't. And Henry, one hundred per cent perfect Henry said, 'you just don't want to hard enough'. 'Why don't **you** nurse them. I'm not a cow. But you're only a bull, and you haven't got an udder. Well neither have I. So there.' *(Laughs)* He didn't talk to me for a week after that. That's what he does when he's angry, he doesn't talk. It can go on for days. I get so nervous, I have to ask **him** to forgive **me** even though he was wrong in the first place. I get what is known as . . . *(Drinks)* . . . the silent treatment.

Carol: I bet you're as good a mother as he'll find in all suburbia.

Toby: I'm excellent. Super-duper special. I could be displayed with their model-houses. Step right up and see me, the model mother. I even sew frilly kitchen curtains and bake bread. If you need the recipe, give me a call some day. *(Toby throws the key at Carol.)* Here, take the key, it's all yours!

Carol: *(Holding it)* The key to home.

Toby: And **I'm** free. *(She pulls off her skirt and throws it on the floor)*

Carol: After twelve years of drudgery.

Toby: I'm still young and beautiful.

Carol: And foolish.

Toby: But I'm doing exactly what **you** do.

Carol: I don't do anything.

Toby: Oh come now, you have orgies going on here every night of the week.

Carol: Nothing happens here, ever!

Toby: I'm broadminded now, Carol. You don't have to lie to me. I think it's going to be fun sleeping with all those men. *(Laughs giddily)*

Carol: You're stupid.

Toby: You were always jealous of me, you funny kid with your boney knock-knees. Lawrence will come in and sweep me into his arms and you'll be left hugging the wall, a wall-flower.

Carol: Shut up . . .

Toby: *(Teases)* I'm going to steal all your boyfriends. You're just like Henry, like a jealous man.

Carol: *(Slaps Toby)*

Toby: *(Backs away)* Carol!

Carol: Everything will be all right now. *(Taunting)* I'm going home to Henry! I'll say: 'take up your newspaper and relax, Henry. I'll feed the baby, I'll wash Betty's hair and give Sandra her

cough medicine. I'll be good to you. Toby and I were best friends. We were like one person. It makes no difference which one of us you take. Toby's left you. Take me. Take **me**.'

(Toby sits, dishevelled. The laughter has gone out of her. She watches Carol. Quite drunk by now, Toby slurs her words. She is very confused.)

Toby: Hey, you can't go to Henry. He's **my** husband.

Carol: Anyone can be Mrs. Willis. It doesn't have to be you. *(Like Mr. Murphy)* 'Ladies and gentlemen, I wish to introduce you to the lady who lost her name. Mrs. Henry Willis! '

Toby: I am Toby Livingstone.

Carol: Right! You gave me your children and Henry. No one needs you anymore.

Toby: I am needed. I **am**.

Carol: She's worthless, she's garbage. Janitor! Come collect this pile of scrap.

Toby: No, I'm pretty and talented.

Carol: Just a plaything for the boys and when they're through with you, we'll throw what's left down the incinerator.

Toby: No . . .

Carol: You're like a lump of soft clay. I pull you here, you go here. I pull you there, you're there. I can make you long and thin and flat and square.

Toby: *(Protesting like a child)* I'm not a lump of clay. I'm not.

Carol: *(Like Miss Johnson)* Then what are you, Toby. Answer me? Put your palm out, dunces get the ruler when they don't answer correctly. Well, what are you?

Toby: *(Cannot mouth the words)* I'm a . . . I'm a . . .

Carol: We haven't got all day. The class is waiting, the principal is waiting. I am waiting.

Toby: I'm a . . . m . . . mother.

Carol: A mother who wants to give her children away? I'm afraid we'll have to give you the ruler after all, Mrs. Willis.

Toby: *(Hides her palms)* No! It was a game, a joke!

Carol: Life is one big joke, but the laugh's on us. We're in this together now.

Toby: I don't want to play anymore. My head is spinning.

Carol: *(Teases)* Toby is a poor loser. Toby is a poor sport.

Toby: *(Quickly)* "Sticks and stones will break my bones but names will never harm me . . ."

Carol: *(Goes after her)* "Come out, come out wherever you are."

(Toby faces Carol)

Toby: You can't have Henry. He's **my** husband. I've loved him for twelve years.

Carol: **What** is love? *(Like teacher)* Answer me Toby!

Toby: *(Remembering)* "The . . . desire of the moth for the star . . ."

Henry is the moth and **you** are the star.

(Repeats) Henry is the moth and I am the

Then you must step on him. He clouds arlight.

Toby: I can't . . .

Carol: You must. And we will go back. Steady now. Pick the spot and play it right. We'll escape, to roller skates and skipping ropes. To sidewalks with cracks at calculated intervals . . . "Don't step on the crack or you'll break your

grandmother's back . . . "
(They play jumping over the sidewalk cracks.)

Toby: *(Rises and walks dizzily)* "Don't step on the crack, or you'll break your grandmother's back."

Carol: "Don't step on the crack or you'll break your grandmother's back."

(This is repeated rhythmically several times. Music in toy box — Oranges and Lemons.)

Carol: Look, dandelions, let's pick them.

Toby: If we do we'll wet our beds.

Carol: Let's pick daisies instead. 'He loves me, he loves me not. He loves me, he loves me not.'

Toby: He loves me . . .

Carol: He loves me too!

Toby: Careful, do not crush the pretty maple leaves.

Carol: Red, blue, yellow.

Toby: Purple brown green.

Carol: Light lilac.

Toby: Deep indigo.

Carol: Roaring rust.

Toby: Laughing lilly.

Both: Red, orange, yellow, green, blue, purple . . .

Carol: Sh . . . a robin. Let's see how close we can get before he flies away . . .

Toby: We're so close, he doesn't mind. He's our very own robin. Oh . . . *(Watch him fly away)* . . . he flew away . . . he's gone.

Carol: We'll chase squirrels.

Toby: Let's build castles in the clouds. I'm the princess.

Carol: I'm the charming prince.

Toby: (Pointing upward) That's my castle.

Carol: Let's ride away on my white horse, racing with the skylark, up to our mountain . . .

Toby: There's Shelley, and the skylark . . .

Carol: "The devotion to something afar from the sphere of our sorrow."

Toby: There, on the mountain . . .

Carol: The mountain . . .

(Music out. "Mountain" overlapping and then resume adult roles.)

Carol: Where is the mountain now?

Toby: It's still there, but it's not the same.

Carol: We forgot how to see and feel and breathe. The shades fell softly over our eyes, imperceptibly, like the lines on our faces. There are other little girls chasing the squirrels now. They don't wait for us.

Toby: No moth, no star, no white horse, no skylark . . . what is real?

Carol: Nothing. My children, are a paper photograph. My stories, forgotten; things I've seen and heard and lived — really happened. (Takes Toby's hand) You're the only real thing I have. I put my hand in yours and I feel life throbbing in me again. Toby, stay with me, forever.

Toby: I can't, Carol.

Carol: You promised. A long time ago, you promised.

Toby: We were children. We can't go back.

Carol: Then we have nowhere to go. They ought to display us in a freak show. "Step right up and see formless women. They ran away from home and now they float in the land of nowhere."

Toby: (Dizzy) I have a place. There is a bed and a garden. But I gave them to Carol. She's my best friend.

Carol: (Holds the key to Toby's home) She gave you three children, Henry, and she left you. That's what I did to Gilbert. He cried when I left. I never saw a man cry before. Then he told the kids I died. He said it would be better that way. How right he was. No, I can't go to Gilbert anymore . . . only this morning, his new wife had a baby. So Carol's life ends with . . . the whimper of a little baby. (Referring to the doll) The only baby I have is a toy, and I'm tired of breathing life into her. I, too, am a lump of clay. (Carol throws doll at Toby)

(The doorbell rings. The women sit up tensely.)

Toby: Who is that?

Carol: I don't know.

Toby: It's Lawrence! How do I look, Carol?

Carol: Quiet. I want to see who's there.

Toby: Who else can it be?

Carol: (Peers through keyhole) I get many callers . . . (Faces Toby) It's someone I don't recognize. It must be Henry. What shall I do?

Toby: Don't answer. Let's pretend no one's here. The nerve . . .

Carol: Sh . . .

Toby: The nerve, the nerve . . .

Carol: Listen. I hear his footsteps. He's going away. (Looks through peephole) He's gone.

Toby: Good.

Carol: Well, that's that. He's gone.

Toby: Isn't it like him to chase after me! You're lucky, Carol, you don't have anyone following you around.

Carol: Yes, I'm lucky.

Toby: You think I should have let him go like that?

Carol: I'll call him back, and you can save him for company in your old age?

Toby: No! I'll never go home now, never. Carol, help me be like you.

Carol: All right. Then let me tell you who that was . . . it was Simon.

Toby: Not Henry?!

Carol: No. Simon's my poet with a flaming red beard and fiery eyes.

Toby: I want Lawrence.

Carol: Simon's much better. You'll sail with him like a seagull, the earth will disappear and you and he will be the only people left in the whole world. Then down you'll float into a sinking sieve, down, down, down, into the sea.

Toby: Where is Lawrence?!

Carol: I don't know. I haven't seen him in years.

Maybe he's dead.

Toby: (Hits wildly at Carol) Liar!

Carol: I don't think my Simon would be interested in a little girl.

Toby: Little girl? We'll see about that . . .

Carol: Then you want Simon?

Toby: Maybe.

Carol: Let me tell you about him. He's all mine!! A nice, respectable school teacher. But I sent him away. I'm looking for Shelley, just like you're looking for Lawrence, on a white stallion soaring into the clouds . . .

Toby: I can see right through you now! You brought me here to make a fool of me! You're cruel. I was your only friend, because you were mean to everyone else. I'll never forgive you for this, never! (Cries)

Carol: (Goes to her. Tries to touch her.)

Toby: Leave me alone!

Carol: Good-bye, Shelley, there are no dreams left for us.

(Toby falls asleep.)

I love you my little lost kitten. I'll show you the way home as I find it myself. Today I'll play the last game of all.

(Carol goes to toy box, opens lid. Music is Oranges and Lemons, counterplayed with Brandenberg Concerto.)

(Toby dreams)

Toby: Gilbert? Henry! Don't go away! Get off your roller skates and come home. Look out! There's a giant coming toward you. It's Lawrence! Run. (She can't move) I can't help you. Run. No Lawrence, please don't do it. Your guitar is a gun (Screams) You killed him! (Bends over) What has he done to you Henry? I'll get the janitor. Come and take them away. I have a funeral on the mountain . . . no flowers, squirrels, birds, or trees. Only bare brown sand and scattered maple leaves. No, Carol! I don't want to sing. I'm too sad. Our husbands are dead. I don't remember the words! (Sings faintly) 'The lady in red, the fellahs . . . ' I can't remember. I lost my name. I'm the lady who lost her name. Leave me alone! (Sound: Audience boos) Don't push me! Where are you taking me? Betty, Sandra, Jimmy my baby, you too? I want to go home. Please let me go home. Not to the ship. It's full of holes. Don't make me go there. The ship is sinking! Where's the captain? Oh . . . Henry is the captain, my Henry. But he's dead. Henry? . . . Henry!

(Music out sharp. Toby comes out of her dream.)

Toby: . . . Oh, Carol . . . what happened . . . oh my head . . .

Carol: My poor Toby.

Toby: What time is it?

Carol: Only ten.

Toby: I must call home. (Goes to phone. Dials) Hello? Hello? . . . who's speaking? . . . oh . . . where is Mr. Willis . . . I see, yes . . . This is Mrs. Willis. Is everything all right? . . . I'll be there soon . . . good-bye. (To Carol) Henry went out. He hired a babysitter. I better go. (She sways as she attempts to gather her clothes.)

Carol: First you'll have a nice hot cup of coffee.

Toby: (Starts dressing) Why didn't he tell me? . . .

Carol: (Smiles) I hope he doesn't find out what you've been up to tonight.

Toby: I didn't do anything.

Carol: Not much you didn't.

Toby: What did I do?

Carol: Look how innocent . . .

Toby: What do you mean?

Carol: Lawrence and Simon were here. They were so impressed with you. They said you don't look a day over twenty-one. (Gives her coffee) It was hilarious. Lawrence wanted you all to himself, but you preferred my chubby, bald Simon, who carried you to the bedroom and you thought he was adorable.

Toby: What are you talking about? !

Carol: Don't you remember?

Toby: No! You're lying.

Carol: Toby's gone and lost her memory. Soon I'll be as lucky as you. I'll hold your hand in that sinking sieve and down we'll go and where we'll land no one will know.

Toby: (Takes a sip of coffee) Carol, I don't want to play anymore. (Rises) I'm leaving.

Carol: You're not ready yet.

Toby: (Frightened) Let me go . . . (Softer) You

said you liked me. *(Getting dressed)* You're going to be nice to me. You're my best friend, aren't you? And I want to go home.

Carol: You were always home, but I looked for you everywhere. In strange cities, in libraries, in . . . *(Gets hats out of toy box)* hat shops. *(Puts on hat)* Let's play Ladies. I'm the Queen of England, what are you?

Toby: I don't know if I'm awake or asleep.

Carol: It's all the same. Time is in the imagination. We are what we want to be. *(Puts hat on Toby)* Well, what are you — Cinderella?

Toby: *(Pulls hat off her head)* I want to be **me**.

Carol: And who is that?

Toby: I am Toby. Henry and the children love me.

Carol: I love you too.

Toby: You must forget me, Carol.

Carol: Forget my little kitten. You're all I have.

Toby: Call . . . Simon, go to him. He needs you.

Carol: But I have nothing to give. I'll weave his body into my web, and eat him up alive. I did that to Gilbert and the others.

Toby: It doesn't have to be that way. Let me help you.

Carol: I can hardly help myself.

Toby: I'll help you. I care about you, Carol.

Carol: No one cares! I walked a million streets past a million people and no one cared. And I don't care about anyone either.

Toby: You cared about me.

Carol: Yes, only about you. I brought you home so we would be together again . . . *(Warmly)* But, I'll let you be. I'll go back alone.

Toby: You can't remain alone . . .

Carol: I know. Did you ever wake in the middle of the night and walk miles to share your terror with the empty streets? Then fall into bed cold and trembling, the loneliest prison in the world, with no guard to assure your safety.

Toby: Simon will be with you.

Carol: Simon: I despise you when you agree. I despise you more when you forbid. I despise you for bloating me with your seed. I despise you more for letting me be barren. Any way you look at it, I'm wrong. If I can't live at peace with one man, how can I be at peace with the world?

(Carol takes articles and drops them in a heap on the floor, suggesting a funeral pyre.)

Simon's pipe, his hat, his sweater. They all belong to my late, loving Simon. Farewell.

Toby: What are you doing?

Carol: Saying good-bye. My articles *(Music box in, distorted. Makes pile of magazines)* the photo of my children, the toys and . . . your lady in red costume. See?

Toby: Oh my God, it is . . .

Carol: I kept it all these years. I waited for the right moment and it has finally come. Isn't it adorable, Toby? I had a friend. She was beautiful. *(Puts dress on pile)* Gilbert and Simon are dead. Now Toby will die too.

Toby: Carol, you mustn't play anymore!

Carol: *(Gets skipping rope from box)* I will play forever.
'I should worry I should care
I should marry a millionaire . . .
He should die and I should cry . . . '
Want to skip with me, Toby?

Toby: Carol!

(Music getting louder.)

Carol: Only five minutes till the bell rings. Five more minutes to skip. Look, there's Miss Johnson. She's waiting for me in the yard. Line up everybody, line up.

Toby: Miss Johnson's not here. No one's here!

Carol: Poor Miss Johnson. I was her favorite pupil, yet I wasn't with her when she died. But I'm not alone now. You're with me, Toby . . . (*Hugs the costume*)

Toby: (*Takes costume from her*) See, it doesn't fit! You can't go back, ever!

(*Music louder*)

Carol: Sing! I want to hear you sing again.

Toby: I can't.

Carol: Please, one last time!

Toby: (*Sings through tears, weakly*) 'The lady in red, the fellahs are crazy about the lady in red . . .' (*Cries*)

Carol: Yes, that's it, the voices, they're still with me . . .

Toby: (*Afraid for Carol*) Come home with me, Carol.

Carol: Where is home? A new age that made a monster out of me and left my Shelley alone and lost. I breathe fumes instead of mountain flowers. I'm intoxicated with my prowess. I am the new woman, and I destroy everything I touch.

(*Refers to articles on the floor.*)

Set a match to this heap of rags and let it rise in flame. And I shall leap into the fire and set myself free.

(*Toby goes to toy box and slams lid. Music out. Turns to Toby. Hands her a bag. Pause.*)

Carol: Toby, you're free to go now. Go!

Toby: You'll be all right?

Carol: Yes, I'll be fine. Go, Toby, go home.

(*Toby hesitates for a moment, she is afraid for Carol, but she is anxious to leave. Toby whispers 'good-bye' and runs out.*)

(*Music: Brandenberg Concerto — softly*)

(*Carol stands looking over the heap of articles, picking up red dress goes to toy box, drops dress in toy box.*)

Carol: "The lone and level sands stretch far away."

(*Sound: Musical theme interspersed with children's voices. Grows louder.*)

Blackout.

C63

Vicky

Grahame
Woods

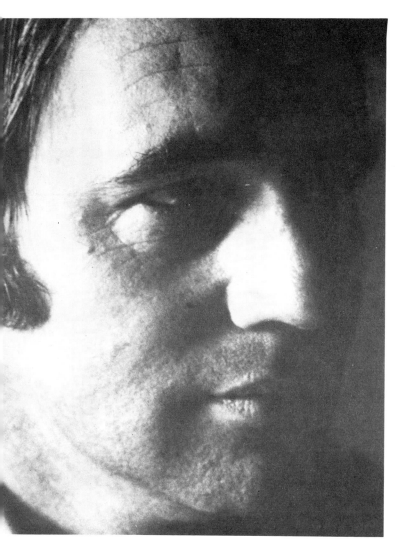

Grahame Woods was born in England in 1934 and came to Canada in 1955, where he joined the Film Production Department of the Canadian Broadcasting Corporation. There are few people who would argue with the fact that, for the next ten years at least, he was best known in Canada as a cinematographer, — a reputation which quickly spread to other parts of the world as he began to bring home prizes for such works as "The Chief", a portrait of John Diefenbaker; the controversial "The Open Grave", a thought-provoking modern parable which paralleled the story of the Resurrection; "40 Million Shoes", filmed in Brazil; and perhaps his most beautiful work of all, "The Gift", set in Japan.

In 1966 he was appointed Director of Photography for the well-known and phenomenally successful "Wojeck" series and later, the "Corwin" series, "Anthologies" and "To See Ourselves" — all for the CBC. During his term as cinematographer on "Wojeck", he wrote an episode for that series — "After All, Who's Art Morrison?" — which was the CBC's official entry in the Monte Carlo Film Festival. During his years at the CBC, Mr. Woods also won three Wilderness Award medals and a Canadian Film Award for cinematography. In 1970 he decided to pursue his writing and directing career on a full-time basis, and left the CBC to take up freelance work.

All his writing to date has been for television — "The Mercenaries", which critic Patrick Scott called "the best drama of the year"; "12-1/2 Cents" which was nominated for a Canadian Film Award; "Kalinski's Justice"; "The Disposable Man"; and the highly controversial "Strike", a finalist in 1973 ACTRA awards for dramatic writing.

We are proud to present Grahame Woods' latest work "Vicky" — originally written for television as a sequel to "12-1/2 Cents", and now adapted by him for the stage.

Karen Liggins was born in 1948 in Chatham, Ontario. Short and dimpled, full of life and a great giggler, she is also very sensitive and deeply thoughtful, — one has to be prepared for long silences while she gives careful and intelligent consideration to her replies.

She is also enormously talented. Her studies began at the Schneider School of Art in Actinolite, Ontario, and continued in New York, where she studied painting at The Museum of Modern Art, art therapy at The New School for Social Research (working with disturbed children) and psychology at New York University.

Subsequently, Karen taught at the Robert McLaughlin Gallery in Oshawa, The Senior Citizen Centre — also in Oshawa, where she taught print-making — and Sheridan College where she taught painting and drawing.

She has never given in to the temptation to take on a "regular" job which was not related some-how to art, — very unusual in a female artist. Amongst other things, she once earned herself $1.80 an hour painting blue stripes on running shoes — not what one would call great art, but still painting!

Her family background, in her own words:

"1 parachutist father with the (then) R.C.A.F.
 1 nurse mother who was always up to some creative endeavour or another — creative needlework, like designing her own patterns.
4 children in family:
1 dancer sister
1 musician brother (rock group variety)
1 pianist/athlete star brother
"Favourite Canadian artist — Tom Thomson, for no reason at all — or perhaps there are a million reasons why — who knows? "

This is Karen Liggins . . .

D4

Cast of characters

Vicky
Therapist (woman)
Father of Vicky
Gord — husband of Vicky
Ruth — hospital inmate
Lillian — hospital inmate
June — hospital inmate
Ben — a roomer
Mrs. Kroyt — landlady
Other inmates, roomers, etc.

Act one scene one

(The play is set in Toronto in the early seventies with time moving freely about . . . into the past and, eventually, up to the present.

The main part of the set represents a mental health hospital with a slightly curved cyc at the back of the stage, flanked by a platform on each side. The centre of the stage is kept bare except for the requirements mentioned as the play progresses.
Downstage left is Vicky's room which has an old hospital bed, bedside table, chair and, on the wall, a blow up poster of Steve McQueen.

Downstage right is a cheap, wooden table with four chairs. For scene five a sideboard is added, dressed with mementos of two marriages and two life styles.

At the back of the stage a large set of prison like bars, hang from the flies . . . something that is always present during act one . . . even when a single spot is lighting a character there is just enough light on the bars to make their presence felt.

The lights come up on the cyc, silhouetting the hanging bars . . . then a group of people, moving slowly and restlessly. In the background we hear an eerie, flute like instrument, echoing. As the music fades slightly, we hear the disembodied voice of a man . . . and the group of people move slowly off stage as the lights go down and we crossfade to a single spotlight on Vicky, sitting in the chair at center stage . . . lost and alone. The music finishes at the end of the first speech.)

Man: In the fall of 1968, shortly after Labour day, Vicky Adams . . . the Lieutenant Governor's Warrant called her Victoria Elizabeth Adams . . . was transferred from the jail in Toronto to a provincial mental health hospital, her illness being duly certified pursuant to and in accordance with the statute in that behalf. The warrant, signed by and with the seal of the Lieutenant Governor, charged the hospital to " . . . safely keep her until I order such person back to imprisonment, or until her discharge is directed by me or other lawful authority."

Therapist: *(In shadow)* Do you know why you're here?

D6

Vicky: (Blankly) No.

Therapist: Are you sure?

Vicky: No.

Therapist: You had a letter today.

Vicky: A Christmas card.

Therapist: Who from?

Vicky: My father.

Therapist: He sent one last year.

Vicky: And the year before.

Therapist: But never comes to see you?

Vicky: He did last year . . . at Christmas.

Therapist: Why doesn't he come more often?

Vicky: I don't know.

Therapist: Are you sure?

Vicky: No.

Therapist: How do you get along with him?

Vicky: Ah . . . all right I 'spose.

Therapist: Always?

Vicky: Same as any other kids, I guess.

(Spotlight up on platform, stage right, on father.)

Father: I've bin looking at your report card.

Vicky: (Turning to him) I know.

Father: Your mother and me don't think it's very good. Three C's, two D's . . . and you told me you got a B-Plus for history. You didn't, did you?

Vicky: No . . . I thought I might . . .

Father: (Taking off thick, leather belt) You lied, eh?

Vicky: No . . . I just thought . . .

Father: I don't like my kid to lie . . . and you gotta be taught . . .

(He raises the belt and swishes it through the air. Blackout.)

Therapist: Is that why you ran away?

Vicky: No . . . it was after my mum died . . . I was seventeen then . . . working . . . I missed her. I mean, I could talk to her and she'd understand.

Therapist: What would you talk about?

Vicky: Oh . . . things . . . nothin' special . . .

Therapist: So you ran away . . .

Vicky: Yeh . . . I mean, after she died . . . I used to go and sit in her room . . . like I did when she was sick . . . there was a picture of her . . .

(Spotlight up on father. On platform. Stage right.)

Father: (Looking down to Vicky) You shouldn't be in here . . . I've told you that. It won't help. Anyway . . . this was mine and your mother's room. (Gently) Listen . . . crying won't do any good. She's been gone for two months and we gotta get used to it.

Vicky: She was very sad . . . and she looked so peaceful lying there with those roses.

Father: How d'you think I feel? For God's sake stop blubbering. We couldn't do anything. (Piously) We must be thankful for those years we had together, however short. We never realise how close it is until it comes, and then we wish we'd . . . we'd done all those things we wanted to and never got round to.

Vicky: I loved my mum . . .

Father: (Nodding agreement) Yeah . . . we were just unlucky that . . . you know, that bit in the paper was pretty good. "Gone from this life, but never forgotten, a loving mother and a wonderful wife." I couldn't get anything to rhyme with 'forgotten'.

Vicky: It was nice . . .

Father: They're smart though, those ad people. They wanted to know if I'd like a reminder on the anniversary for another announcement. I'll tell you something. They'll bleed you for every penny . . . have no consideration for a person's grief. They take advantage . . . just like the mortician. Because you're grieving doesn't mean you don't know when you're being taken . . . *(Pause, staring at Vicky)* . . . you know something Vicky? Until this very minute . . . I din' realize . . . well, how much you've grown up . . . I mean, you know, filled out a little bit . . . I mean, in that nightgown you look a bit like the movie magazines you read . . .

Vicky: D-a-d . . .

Father: I just hadn't noticed . . . Vicky . . . take it off, let me look at you . . .

Vicky: D-a-d . . .

Father: Vicky . . . we gotta get to know each other . . . all those years . . . switch that light out me love . . .

(Blackout on father)

Therapist: So you ran away . . .

Vicky: *(Upset)* Yeh . . . wouldn't you? Sure I ran away. An' I met this guy . . . thumbing a ride . . . an' he stopped . . . he was driving this fifty-five convertible and we just hit it off . . . he was nice to me and understood me . . . and we just drove and drove . . . the top was down . . . I thought, "Vicky . . . this is what you've bin missing, living in that shitty house and doing that dumb job . . ."

Therapist: And?

Vicky: *(Laughing)* D'you wanna hear something funny? He left me in a motel in Sarnia . . . went out to buy some booze . . . an' I never saw him again. I'll tell you something else . . . I was well

and truly knocked up . . . one way an another . . . *(Becoming relaxed and suddenly enjoying a memory)* . . . an' I got this job back in Toronna . . . a factory . . . an' I met Gord . . .

(Spotlight up on Gord, on the platform, stage left. Vicky spins in her chair to see him.)
Gord: I don't care about the baby. It's you I want to marry.

Vicky: I know . . . but it doesn't seem right.

Gord: So I'm not the father? What the hell does it matter? If I were that worried I wouldn't be asking you to marry me. You and the baby sorta come as a package deal . . . eh? *(Laughing)* You like that? Listen . . . we'll quit our jobs at the factory and find a small place. You can stay at home and look after the baby and I'll play snooker. I'm pretty good . . . hundred a week . . . **minimum.**

Vicky: It sounds . . . great . . .

Gord: *(Enthused)* Then, when the baby's old enough, we'll get a car and tour. I'll play the pool halls from here to Vancouver. The snazzy hotels . . . steaks. We got it made kid . . .

Vicky: *(Eager)* Let's do it Gord . . . get married and all those things . . .

(Blackout on Gord.)

Therapist: But he's never been in to see you?

Vicky: Nah . . .

Therapist: What about touring from here to Vancouver and snazzy hotels *(Vicky shakes her head "No")* . . . steaks? But you got married? *(Shakes head "Yes")*

(Spotlight up on table as Gord walks in and sits, flipping a pack of cards. He talks to an unseen person beside him.)

Gord: Eh . . . you haven't met Jennie. Nice kid. She's not mine though . . . Eh, Vicky? I was telling him, she's not mine. Some other guy got there first. A tumble in the backseat wasn't it? What the hell, if it wasn't him it would have bin me . . . *(Laughing)* Eh, Vicky?

(Vicky suddenly leaves the chair and hurries across into Gord's light.)

Vicky: You din' have to say that.

Gord: Come on . . . I was just kidding.

Vicky: But not in front of Jenny.

Gord: Forget it.

Vicky: I felt like a tramp. I mean, in front of a stranger.

Gord: It's true isn't it? It happens to a lot of people. Anyway, he could care less. He thought I was kidding. Who'd believe a story like that anyway?

Vicky: It just wasn't nice . . . that's all . . .

Gord: Well, at least the other one's mine . . . we know that, don't we . . . *(Laughing)* . . . or maybe, you bin getting something on the side . . . that'd be the day . . . eh, Vicky?

(But she has left him and wandered back to the chair where she stands, limp, facing the audience. For the first time we see the Therapist as she moves into Vicky's light and starts to massage her shoulders. Blackout on Gord as his words trail off.)

Therapist: What happened then Vicky?

Vicky: *(Agitated)* I dunno . . . it was after that . . . Gord was at the pool hall . . . my little girl . . . Jenny . . . she was the oldest . . . the baby was in her crib . . . *(She starts to relive her own hell)* Jenny . . . was bouncing a ball in the kitchen . . . an' the radio was going. You know, all that rock and roll stuff . . . *(Nervous laugh)* I even remember the tune . . . Twelve O'clock Rock . . . loud . . . I had a headache. I always seemed to get headaches . . . aspirin never did a thing for me . . . except make me throw up . . . she was bouncing this ball with one hand 'cause her other arm was busted and in a cast. She bounced it and bounced it . . . an' it got louder . . . the radio . . . the ball . . . an' I screamed at her to stop and the baby woke up and started crying . . . an' the radio was going and I couldn't stand it. I hit her and she yelled at me . . . *(Long pause)* . . . and I grabbed something to hit her with and she screamed and the baby screamed . . . *(Long pause)* . . . and suddenly it's all very peaceful and quiet. I had a carving knife in my hands and . . . Jenny was on the floor covered in blood . . . an' the baby was covered in blood. The radio was smashed . . . an' . . . they were dead . . . I didn't mean it . . . but the noise . . . *(Tears start to stream freely, not convulsive crying, just tears that have never streamed since she was a child.)* There they were . . . on the floor . . . dead.

Blackout

D9

D10

Scene two *(The lights come up on the hospital bed. Vicky is sitting on the bed smoking a cigarette and flipping through some true romance magazines. Ruth is sitting on the chair. Both are wearing bathrobes. On a table are two mugs of coffee.)*

Ruth: You don't really believe all that stuff you read?

Vicky: Sometimes . . . when I feel like crying.

Ruth: You never cry . . . except that day in therapy. You really cried then. You never talked like that before.

Vicky: No.

Ruth: It's tough, eh? Spilling your guts. I mean, you feel like a fool afterward.

Vicky: Yeah . . .

Ruth: I know I did . . . it was the first time I ever talked to anyone about it.

Vicky: I wasn't there. *(Lighting another cigarette.)*

Ruth: You were new . . . I cried just like you did. I could see him like it was real . . . on the bed with all that blood coming from his head . . . *(Indicating cigarettes)* Can I have one of those? I left mine in the lounge. *(Vicky throws them)* Thanks . . . *(She lights up)* . . . I could see myself standing there with the gun and I could hear it echoing around the room . . . I've never cried since.

Vicky: They say it happens.

Ruth: Yeah . . . now it's like he never existed.

Vicky: Did he?

Ruth: I'spose . . . *(Laughing)* . . . that's why I'm here isn't it? But it doesn't seem real.

Vicky: They say it's good when it gets like that . . . not being real.

Ruth: They do?

Vicky: Yeah . . . I heard that somewhere.

Ruth: Is it real for you?

Vicky: It was . . . that day . . . but not anymore. It's like I left one world and started in a new one. Sometimes I dream . . .

Ruth: But not very much?

Vicky: No . . . not anymore . . . *(She looks away, sad.)*

Ruth: What's the matter? *(She knows what the matter is and goes and sits beside Vicky.)*

Vicky: Nothing.

Ruth: You heard?

Vicky: Yeah. They turned me down . . .

Ruth: They . . .

Vicky: I know . . . when you going out?

Ruth: A couple of weeks . . .

Vicky: *(Trying to lighten it)* You won't get to stay in that new section they're building . . . pretty fancy they say. The cans have doors and modern showers and things . . .

Ruth: It won't be the same . . . sittin' with three others all cozy while they fart away.

Vicky: Won't have to hum so loud . . . *(They laugh but it fades.)* What will you do?

Ruth: I dunno . . . *(She starts to massage Vicky's back and Vicky lays flat to help her.)*

Vicky: That's the problem isn't it? What do you do? Everyone used to say that life would get better.

Ruth: It doesn't though.

Vicky: No.

Ruth: Will you miss me?

Vicky: Of course stupid.

Ruth: You'll be lonely.

Vicky: I know . . .

Ruth: You gonna have a bath tonight?

Vicky: Don't think so . . . *(Laughing)* . . . I still feel funny . . . having a bath in front of all those people . . . all that ugly, fat flesh . . .

Ruth: And Rita stinking . . . *(Getting up to go)*

Vicky: Yeah . . . and me skinny with my tiny tits. I used to send away for all those creams you can buy . . . and stand in front of the mirror and rub it in to watch 'em grow . . .

Ruth: What happened?

Vicky: All I did was get horny . . . I should have asked for my money back.

Ruth: You look all right to me.

Vicky: Yeah?

Ruth: Yeah . . . d'you want me to come back tonight?

Vicky: *(Shaking her head, "No")* Not to-night . . .
(The Therapist enters, nodding to Ruth as she leaves.)

Therapist: May I come in?

Vicky: Sure . . . cigarette?

Therapist: I just stopped by to say . . . well, I'm sorry that they turned you down . . . but I'm sure, next time . . .

Vicky: It's not surprising though . . . is it? I mean . . . these things take time, don't they? Anyway, I like it in here . . . no worries . . . I might never leave . . . you'd be stuck with me.

Therapist: *(Smiling)* I'll see you tomorrow.

Vicky: I didn't mean that . . . about you being stuck with me.

Therapist: I know . . .

Blackout

Scene three	*(Lights come up on the full stage. Down at the front, centre, is a small table with three chairs. In the background a group of people move silently, others are sitting. We see the Therapist and Ruth among them. Gord enters from stage right, dressed in outdoor, winter clothing. He looks around confused and ignored. Finally the Therapist sees him and goes over. We don't hear what they say. Somewhere in the background, Vicky appears, wearing a blouse and skirt. She freezes, a panic setting in . . . then runs off. Gord goes to move after her but the Therapist stops him and directs him to the chairs. Vicky appears in her room, very upset. The Therapist follows her off and appears in the room.)*

Vicky: I don't want to see him.

Therapist: You don't have to. We had no idea he was coming. I guess we get used to . . .

Vicky: Me never having visitors?

Therapist: Yes.

Vicky: *(Defending him)* He came once . . . after the trial.

Therapist: That was over three years ago . . . *(Gently)* . . . he's still your husband . . . you used to love him. You told me that once.

Vicky: That was then . . . a long time ago . . . not any more.

Therapist: When you go back outside . . .

Vicky: "When" is what we always talk about. Another year . . . another review board.

Therapist: When you go back outside . . . you'll have to face up to situations that are unpleasant.

Vicky: That'll be then . . . not now.

Therapist: He says it's very important that he sees you. He's moving out west and won't be back . . .
(This hits Vicky like a bomb.)

Vicky: Out . . . west? Is that what you . . .

Therapist: Yes . . .

D14

Vicky: *(Fighting back tears)* That's funny . . . I mean, we always talked about going out west . . . he was gonna play snooker . . . and . . .

Therapist: I can tell him you won't see him . . . you don't have to . . . but if you do . . . we can do it in my office . . .

Vicky: *(Long pause)* Jean . . . in the lounge . . . sit with him in the lounge . . . I'd like to do it where everyone else sees **their** visitors . . .

Therapist: Why don't we go together? . . .

Vicky: Okay . . . do I look all right . . . I mean, my hair . . . *(Straightening blouse)* . . . it's not too creased?

Therapist: You look fine . . .

(They exit . . . and Gord lights a cigarette, watching the inmates, but feeling self conscious.)

(Vicky and the Therapist appear in the background and Vicky stops the Therapist from coming any further as she and Gord see each other. He gets up as she comes down to him. It is an awkward moment, full of memories, of being watched by the other inmates. They don't know what to say as Gord nervously puts out his cigarette. Finally:)

Vicky: Hello Gord . . . *(Nervous laugh)* . . . you've put on weight . . .

Gord: Yeah . . . too much beer . . . you know how I like my . . . *(Long pause)*

Vicky: Let's . . . sit down . . .

Gord: Yeah . . .

Vicky: Mrs. Grove says . . . you're going out west . . .

Gord: Yeah . . . in a few weeks . . .

Vicky: Nice . . . *(Eager)* . . . we always used to talk about that. Going out west . . . you playing snooker and me looking after the . . .

Gord: We did?

Vicky: *(Stung)* Yeah . . . we did . . . once . . . *(Bouncing back)* . . . d'you still play . . . I mean, for money?

Gord: Now and then . . . when I need some extra bread. You're looking good.

Vicky: *(Pleased)* I am?

Gord: Yeah . . . you're not so skinny either . . .

Vicky: D'you remember what you used to say about me . . . *(Embarrassed laugh)* . . . a big ass and no boobs? . . .

Gord: *(Embarrassed)* Yeah . . . that's right . . . hey, I gotta job you know.

Vicky: You're kidding?

Gord: Seriously . . . I drive a truck . . . one of them big mothers . . . ten gears and all that.

Vicky: Must be interesting.

Gord: Yeah.

Vicky: Mrs. Grove said you had something . . .

Gord: Important to see you about . . . you like a cigarette?

Vicky: Yes . . . thanks . . .

(He gives her one and offers a light. She takes his hand to pull the match closer and for her it is a traumatic moment: Just touching him, feeling that skin. For him . . . he is offering her a light. Nothing. No feeling except for a little guilt about having only seen her twice in four years. Ruth is watching them closely.)

Gord: You must smoke a lot . . . you've got nicotine on your fingers . . .

Vicky: *(Coming back to reality)* I use bleach to get it off . . . *(She doesn't take her eyes off him which makes him uncomfortable)* . . . I have my own room now . . . I thought maybe you'd like to see it . . .

Gord: *(Suddenly)* I wanna get divorced . . . I mean, we should have done it sooner but . . .

well, we didn't. What with you in here and things . . . and Mrs. Grove said you might be out within a year . . .

Vicky: You said . . . me in here . . . and **things**.

Gord: Just things.

Vicky: A woman?

Gord: Look . . . I wanted to make this easy for you . . .

Vicky: Do I know her?

Gord: No.

Vicky: Have you bin . . . living with her?

Gord: Yes . . . Jesus Vicky . . . what d'you expect? I'm gonna live like a monk waitin' for you to get out of this place? . . . And, anyway, that's nothing to do with it. You're confusing me.

Vicky: Couldn't we try to . . .

Gord: No.

Vicky: *(A whisper)* Are you gonna marry her?

Gord: Yeah . . . we've gotta kid . . . two years old.

Vicky: *(Pause)* Is it . . . a boy or a girl?

Gord: It doesn't matter.

Vicky: I'd like to know.

Gord: It's none of your business . . .

Vicky: Please Gord . . . *(He looks away)* . . . I guess that's it then.

Gord: I guess.

Vicky: *(Sliding her hand to touch his, but he pulls it away)* You'll look after things . . . I mean . . . it's difficult for me *(Fighting back tears)* . . .

Gord: Yeah . . . I'll look after things . . .

(Vicky stands, takes a last look at Gord, and runs off.)

Blackout

Scene four   *(The lights come up on centre stage . . . back-lights on two bathtubs, up stage, left. Two female inmates are having a bath and, around them, mill a group of women of all sizes, some naked, others wearing bath robes. Downstage, right, are some wash basins, the only part of the set with a front light. Vicky's room is in darkness. We find Lillian, facing the audience, using one of the wash basins. It is an impersonal and de-humanizing scene.)*

Lillian: The lazy bitch who used the tub before me didn't clean it.

Woman: So?

Lillian: So where were you dragged up? D'you live that way at home?

Woman: Ah . . . drop dead . . . you don't like it . . . complain . . .

Lillian: Listen to her . . . *(Vicky enters at second wash basin, wearing a robe. Her face is drawn and strained.)* . . . you don't look good dear. Crying?

Vicky: Just a headache.

Lillian: What you need is a massage . . . the neck . . . *(She starts to massage Vicky's neck.)*

Woman: Watch her Vicky . . . she's all hot to trot . . .

Lillian: *(To Woman)* Bugger off . . . *(To Vicky)* . . . I'm going to put her in her place one of these days. I think you're much better off keeping to yourself like you do. That's the way it should be in here . . . you can do what you like and no one minds . . . except that noisy bitch over there . . . how's that?

Vicky: Much better . . . thanks . . .

Lillian: You're welcome . . . *(June enters at third wash basin. To Vicky.)* . . . you haven't met June. She came in today . . . Lieutenant Governor's warrant.

Vicky: Hi . . . join the club . . .

Lillian: . . . and these gorgeous specimens of women's lib that surround you . . .

D18

June: *(Nervous)* I'm June Rogers . . . *(They look at each other briefly and smile.)*

Woman: Someone stole my soap . . . who's got my soap. It was a new Avon lemon . . . nothing's sacred around here . . .

Vicky: *(To June)* I was about to tell you . . . watch your soap . . . it'll be lifted.

Lillian: I wouldn't mind being the Lieutenant Governor's pleasure . . . *(Belly laugh)* . . . but we're both too old . . . him and me . . . eh, Vicky?

June: I think I'll come back later . . .

Lillian: It's more private then . . . you don't have to put up with . . .

Woman: Whatsa matter with her . . . too stuck up to take her clothes off? Come over here sweetie and use my water. Let's all have a look at you *(June hurries off)* . . . my, my . . . d'you all get a look at her . . . stacked . . . and that fancy, new robe. What she think this is . . . the Hilton? *(Ruth enters, coming to the wash basin as Lillian leaves)*

Ruth: *(To Woman)* Knock it off . . .

Woman: Whatsa matter . . . you staked a claim already?

Ruth: I said knock it off . . . Christ, I'm not surprised you're in here . . . *(To Vicky)* . . . so that was him, eh? Good looking . . .

Vicky: Yeah . . . *(Burying her head in a towel.)*

Ruth: He really got to you . . . listen, crying's gettin' to be a habit. It's no good worrying about it. I s'pose he's shacked up with someone. I mean, you really didn't expect him to be waiting . . . did you? *(Vicky ignores her)* . . . I know it's a long time. But you suddenly discover you don't need 'em . . . after you get rid of that ache in your stomach. You remember that guy Stan? Nervous breakdown? Well we got very friendly . . . *(Smiling to reassure Vicky)* . . . it was two years ago . . . anyway, **nothing**. Like brushing your teeth. Maybe I'll feel different outside . . .

D20

(They exit and the lights go down on centre stage and come up on Vicky's room, as they enter.)

Ruth: D'you want a drink? My sister smuggled me in a mickey . . . rye. *(Producing the bottle from her robe pocket, she takes a drink and passes it to Vicky)* I'm gonna stay with her . . . my sister . . . till I get a job. I don't think her husband approves. I mean, he and Brad got to quite like each other. They even went to football games together . . . *(Bottle continues to pass between them)* It's funny how we seem to always talk about them . . . I talk . . . you haven't said a bloody word.

Vicky: Some days you don't feel like talking.

Ruth: Yeah . . . they say the new rooms are better than these pissers . . .

Vicky: I'm gonna get a job.

Ruth: Great.

Vicky: Grove knows a place . . . a restaurant.

Ruth: Waitress?

Vicky: Yeah.

Ruth: Ever done it before?

Vicky: When I was a kid . . . a drive-in and at the Ex . . . hot dogs.

Ruth: You'll be out every day.

Vicky: Get to find it all out again.

Ruth: I'll come and see you and get a free coffee.

(She moves over and starts to rub Vicky's back.)

Vicky: *(Relaxing)* Sure . . . an' a hot pork with french fries . . . I always liked hot pork and french fries with lots of gravy soaking the bread.

Ruth: Would you call me . . . the nervous type?

Vicky: Hardly . . . you come on like gangbusters.

Ruth: Yeah . . . well I'm nervous about going outside. I mean . . . people . . . when I get a place of my own . . . what d'you do . . . all by yourself?

Vicky: I dunno . . . never thought about it.

Ruth: You'll come and see me, eh? You know, for old times sake?

Vicky: Sure . . .

(Ruth stands and takes off her robe and lets it drop to the floor as she moves toward Vicky.)

Blackout

D21

D22

Scene five   *(A spotlight comes up on two chairs at centre stage. We find the Therapist and Vicky facing each other.)*

Therapist: So how'd it go today?

Vicky: I made four fifty in tips . . . an' my adding up's getting better . . . an' after work I walked around looking at all those new buildings. I mean, when I came in . . . they were all old, crummy places . . . and now . . . *(Like a child discovering the world)* . . . and the new busses. An' all those clothes in the windows . . . I don't think I could wear them. My legs aren't good enough. Some of 'em are like not having clothes at all. *(Laughing)* I'm not a prude . . . but I don't think . . .

Therapist: *(Pause)* So . . . you ready for the news?

Vicky: *(Eager)* They're gonna let me out?

Therapist: We got the word today . . . you can leave any time.

Vicky: *(Sitting there not quite able to comprehend the full meaning. Finally, quietly:)* That's great . . . I mean, isn't it?

Therapist: Yes . . . I think so.

Vicky: It makes me all nervous.

Therapist: There's nothing to be nervous about. You do just fine. *(Vicky starts to tense up)* What's the matter?

Vicky: *(Nervous laugh)* Nothin' . . . **really** . . .

Therapist: Did something go wrong today?

Vicky: *(Long pause)* I went back.

Therapist: To the house?

Vicky: Yeah . . . and it wasn't there . . . *(It hits her as being very funny and she starts to laugh in an uncontrolled manner)* . . . it wasn't there. Just a bloody great hole in the ground . . . a big hole of nothing. I mean, there's nothing left, is there? Gord has gone . . . and the house. There's just me left . . . even Ruth has gone.

D24

Therapist: Did she ever come back and see you?

Vicky: Nah . . . they never do. Once they get out they don't want anything to do with this place or the people.

Therapist: That's good.

Vicky: It is?

Therapist: Yes . . . and you'll be the same.

Vicky: I will? You know . . . people always leave . . . no one ever stays anywhere . . . *(Smiling)* . . . imagine, me going out . . . it'll be spooky . . . I think I'll go and see my dad . . . phone him outa the blue. Why not? It's like starting all over again.

Therapist: Why not.

(The lights come up on the table and we see Father, all dressed up, nervously pacing. Vicky leaves the spotlight and walks down to him. Spotlight goes.)

Father: *(Seeing her)* Well . . . look who it is . . . *(Forced laugh)* . . . Don't just stand there . . . come on in before you get pneumonia . . . w-e-l-l . . . you haven't put any weight on . . . what they feed you in there?

Vicky: The food's good . . . I always was . . .

Father: Skinny . . . like your mother . . . I always said you never had any ribs for the porridge to stick to . . . eh? Remember that? The stodgy porridge yer old mum used to make?

Vicky: Yeah . . . that's going back some.

Father: How about a little shot of something to warm yer up . . . you do still drink?

Vicky: Yes.

Father: Yer never know . . . I mean, they don't allow booze in there do they?

Vicky: No.

Father: Well then . . . what'll it be? Rye and ginger?

Vicky: Straight.

Father: Straight? You have grown up. *(Looking her over)* I s'pose you have filled out a little. Bit more of a woman if you know what I mean.

Vicky: I was when I was seventeen . . . after mum died. Unless you've forgotten.

Father: *(Embarrassed)* You didn't have to bring that up. We all do things that we . . . anyway, we got your letter . . . *(Fixing the drinks)* . . . you should have let us know when you came out.

Vicky: I meant to . . . but I was busy looking for a place to live.

Father: What d'you get?

Vicky: A room . . . near the park . . . High Park.

Father: Pretty swanky area.

Vicky: They're all the same.

Father: Yeah . . . four walls and a bed. If you'd have let us know when you were coming out . . . we got a room upstairs you could have had for a while. Saved some money.

Vicky: You keep saying "we" and "us" . . . who's "we"?

Father: W-e-l-l . . . things got pretty lonely after your mum died . . .

Vicky: And you got married again?

Father: Not exactly . . . we have an arrangement.

Vicky: You're shacked up?

Father: I wouldn't put it that way exactly . . . but yes. What are you smiling at?

Vicky: What do the neighbours think?

Father: To hell with the neighbours.

Vicky: *(Laughing)* But you were always so straight laced. It was always important that we didn't do anything wrong in case the neighbours thought something.

Father: Don't you start preaching morals to me, my girl. I haven't forgotten you got knocked up when you did. So let him who casts the first stone or something . . .

Vicky: Yeah . . . and who did it?

Father: What d'you mean?

Vicky: You know goddamn well what I mean.

Father: Come on . . . what you trying to pull? You know that's not true . . . listen my girl, if you've come here just to haul out old skeletons, then you can leave. I made a gesture by asking you out here and I don't expect to get my face rubbed in the dirt. We all make mistakes. You included. It was that punk you hitched a ride from and you know it.

Vicky: I don't . . . but still . . .

Father: Anyway . . . I took precautions . . . after all . . .

Vicky: I was your daughter . . .

Father: That's it. You can go . . . right now.

Vicky: I'm sorry . . . I didn't mean to bring it up. It just happened . . . I've had a long time to think about things . . . and . . .

Father: And I didn't come to see you . . . just that once . . . and I should have . . . but it's all past . . . forgotten . . . let's have another drink.

Vicky: *(Picking up photograph of Flo)* Is this her?

Father: Yes. Flo's her name . . . a lovely lady. Left her husband for me. So you see . . . the old man still has a bit of charm.

Vicky: Didn't he have something to say about it?

Father: Nah . . . he was something of a stunned bastard. I mean, while he was having an afternoon sleep once . . . *(Thinking better of it)* . . . anyway, talking about stunned bastards, I wasn't surprised to hear about you and Gord.

Vicky: Yeah.

Father: I mean . . . it had to happen eh?

Vicky: Yes.

Father: D'e treat you right? You know, a settlement. Bread and things?

Vicky: Five hundred dollars and some of the furniture.

Father: You mean those old orange crates?

Vicky: And the fridge . . . *(Laughing)* . . . I gave them away to the Salvation Army . . . that's a switch, eh?

Father: Yeah . . . that's very funny . . . I s'pose you'll be thinking of getting married again?

Vicky: I don't know.

Father: Shouldn't rush it . . . that's what Flo and me think. What's a bit of paper mean anyway I always say. You'll like Flo . . . different from your Mum . . . I think it was her who was straight laced.

Vicky: *(Smiling)* That wasn't the way it sounded to me.

Father: *(Embarrassed again)* I always knew you were a sneaky bitch. Pretending to be asleep . . . snea-ky . . . *(Pouring himself another drink)* So how's the job going?

Vicky: Great . . . fifty a week plus tips an' extra if I work weekends.

Father: Well . . . you know how to look after yourself . . . I always like a person to be self sufficient. Like I was. The army stood me in good stead. That's **really** going back some . . . I mean, over thirty years . . . I remember coming back from the war and you met me at Union Station with your mum. The whole family. *(Chuckling at the memory)* And when you saw me you burst into tears and hid behind mum's skirt . . . oh, we've some good memories as well Vicky my love. Have another belt.

Vicky: You're getting pissed Dad.

Father: So what? It's a special day . . . I always thought of the day I could sit and talk with my

D27

own daughter . . . like adults . . . equals . . . oh, I know I did some shitty things in my time. To you . . . and mum . . .

Vicky: When's Flo coming home?

Father: She went out so we could have some time together . . . I mean, if you want to know the truth . . . your mum and me never did hit it off after the war. I was gone all that time and it changed me. It had to for Chrissakes . . . me, a kid from Bleeker Street who'd never bin further than Wasaga Beach . . . and there I was . . . killin' and living it up in London and Paris . . . booze, babes . . . oh, I'm being honest. Don't ever say your old man wasn't honest. I was a Sergeant with men under me and I come back to that shitty little house and a rotten job . . . and a wife that was old. **Old** before her time I always said. Wrinkles . . . sagging everywhere. It wasn't the same . . . so you see . . . we all have our cross to bear or something. But let me tell you . . . it's good to see my little girl though. Back where she belongs.

Vicky: Maybe I should make some coffee.

Father: Nah . . . we don't need coffee . . . just listen to me. You know something my darling Vicky? Something I'll never understand about my little girl . . . *(Almost in tears)* . . . how my little girl could do what she did to those children . . . *(Voice raising)* . . . how you could kill those little things . . .

Vicky: *(Stunned . . . quietly)* What are you saying?

Father: Those beautiful things who had their whole life ahead of them . . .

Vicky: *(Backing away)* What are you trying to do? . . .

Father: You don't want to hear it . . . but you **did** it. **You** killed them. What did they ever do to you? I got pictures of them . . . *(Pulling out his wallet and producing small, tatty pictures)* ones you took at the zoo . . . ever since you did it I've carried them with me . . . *(Thrusting them at her)* Look at them . . . your children. Why . . . why . . . why . . . *(Frozen to the spot, Vicky refuses to look at the pictures. Suddenly, like a released spring, she runs off and Father sits, sobbing.)* She's an ordinary person . . . I mean, who'd think she could do something like that. My **own** daughter . . .

(Lights go down slowly.)

End of Act one   Curtain

Act two scene one *(There are three sets for Act two. Up stage and centre is a kitchen set which includes a table with four chairs, a set of cupboards and a fridge and stove.*

Downstage right is Vicky's room in the house. A bed, bedside table and dresser. The picture of Steve McQueen is prominent.

Downstage left, is a new room at the hospital. A modern bed and chair.

The lights come up on the hospital room. Vicky is in bed and June is sitting on the chair.)

June: How you feeling?

Vicky: All right I s'pose.

June: They said you came in late last night.

Vicky: I dunno.

June: They found you on a bridge over the Parkway.

Vicky: Yeah?

June: No coat . . . nothing. I just thought I'd say hello. I should be going.

Vicky: D'you have a cigarette?

June: Only filters.

Vicky: They're fine . . . *(She sits up and lights one)* How's it going . . . in here?

June: Nothing's changed. They days are long.

Vicky: And the nights.

June: They give me a pill to help me sleep.

Vicky: Trouble is the day is still there when you wake up.

June: What's it like outside?

Vicky: I don't know . . . I never left.

June: But . . .

Vicky: It wasn't real . . . a dream . . . that's what it's all about . . . bloody awful dreams. In here you can forget it all . . . but out there they won't let you . . . they want to ram it right down your throat until it chokes . . . Do people talk to you much?

June: No.

Vicky: They will.

June: I don't really care.

Vicky: Nor me . . . it only matters when you have someone to care for.

June: And you don't?

Vicky: No . . . *(Pause)* . . . I must look a terrible mess. My hair . . . no makeup . . .

June: Who'd notice in here? Is . . . there anything I can do . . . to help?

Vicky: *(Long pause, looking at her)* No . . . thanks anyway. I'll be okay now . . . Thorpe phoned my boss and said I'll be in tomorrow . . . you see, I'm scared. If I don't get out of here . . .

June: You could stay forever.

Vicky: Yeah . . . it makes it all very easy . . . being here.

(The lights go down and come up on the kitchen set. There are signs posted at various points: "Please leave kitchen clean": "Rent due on Fridays": "No alcoholic beverages": "No radios or visitors after midnight". Ben Heath is standing at the stove preparing some hot milk. His back is to the audience. He hums to himself, waiting for the milk to heat up, and then produces a mickey of scotch from his pocket and pours some into the glass. As Vicky enters he quickly and nervously puts the mickey in his pocket.)

Ben: My God you scared me Mrs. Adams . . . I thought it was the old bitch spying again. *(Pulling out the mickey)* I find, when I can't sleep, a little hot milk and scotch does wonders. *(Vicky*

smiles and crosses to plug in the kettle) There's water in it . . . Mrs. Kroyt made herself some tea a while ago. Working nights this week?

Vicky: And next week . . .

Ben: I find this is the best time to use the kitchen. When everyone's asleep . . . but she almost caught me last week. I really think I must look for a place with fewer restrictions. It's like being in the army . . . can't do this and can't do that. Mrs. Kroyt says you were away for a couple of days.

Vicky: *(Pausing)* Yeah . . . my mum was sick . . . operation. So I went and looked after her for a few days. North Bay . . .

Ben: Long way this time of the year. D'you go by train?

Vicky: Yeah.

Ben: Nothing serious I hope?

Vicky: W-e-l-l . . .

Ben: Personal I expect . . . I don't mean to pry.

Vicky: Oh . . . it wasn't that bad . . . hemorrhoids.

Ben: That's bad. I remember my father suffered from that . . . would you care for a little scotch in your coffee? Helps improve that instant stuff.

Vicky: Thanks.

Ben: It gives me a good feeling to defy the system right in her kitchen. Cheers.

Vicky: Cheers. How's the selling going?

Ben: So so . . . I mean, they say the Bible's the number one best seller . . . but it sure as hell isn't in the top ten in my territory.

Vicky: Maybe it's seasonal . . . like Easter and Christmas and things like that.

Ben: Could be . . . but everyone seems to have a family Bible . . . all very old . . . I tell you, the bottom's really fallen out of that market. I was

offered a line of plastic Jesus' and Marys . . . should have taken it. They're coming back in, so they say.

Vicky: It must be difficult to know who wants what?

Ben: In my business, trends are . . . well, difficult to predict. Medals were big until they changed the calendar in Rome and we got stuck with a lot of good lines. Mind you, in smaller towns, it takes a while for people to accept this sort of thing. You just don't pull a saint from under them and expect them to go for it . . . especially if they've just bought a fourteen karat St. Christopher as a present for someone.

Vicky: I s'pose . . . (Silence) . . . how come you live in a place like this?

Ben: Same reason as you. It's cheap and clean. Where would I go? An apartment that costs a fortune? No . . . it'd be a waste. You get to the stage where everything is too much effort . . . and suddenly you're forty five and a stranger . . .

Vicky: I'm surprised you're not married and . . .

Ben: I was . . . she died eight years ago . . . I guess I've just vegetated. I was selling cars then . . . did quite well.

Vicky: Why d'you switch to Bibles?

Ben: Well . . . how about a little more scotch?

Vicky: Okay . . . (Silence as he pours)

Ben: Why ruin a new friendship?

Vicky: How would that happen?

Ben: (Silence) You see . . . I never know where the truth begins and the lie stops. I lie so much even I believe it. Then I tell you . . . and I'm back to zero. It's difficult when there's nothing to hide behind.

Vicky: I know.

Ben: No. You couldn't possibly. You're too young. Oh, I'm sure you've had some pain in your life. I mean, you don't live with your husband. That must have produced some pain.

Vicky: We're divorced.

Ben: But you'll recover . . . bounce back . . . but me . . .

(He suddenly becomes very vulnerable. He is a man whose strengths always leave him when he needs them most . . . a man who lay down and gave up on life and is now content to exist.)

Ben: I'm too old . . . it doesn't matter anymore. I go out each week to some part of the territory . . . Timmins . . . Kenora . . . wherever . . . and I become another Ben Heath . . . a man who sells Bibles . . . a man with some dignity. I'm Mister Heath from Toronto and they give me a good welcome and we talk about the world and they like to hear what I have to say . . . but they don't buy very often. It doesn't matter though. I enjoy living on an expense account. It's not very much . . . but it allows me to go to my motel room at night and drink some scotch and watch the local TV . . . it's nothing much . . . but it's better than what I'm used to. You see, I stole some money . . . fraud they called it . . . from the company I was selling cars for. I got five years and served three. I'm still on parole. My wife didn't die . . . she left me.

(He shares the remainder of the bottle)

Ben: I was caught . . . humiliated in front of my friends . . . and in prison I lost my pride and dignity. When I came out my so called 'friends' didn't want to know me . . . we were divorced . . . and I can't afford to climb back up. I'm not sure that I want to. I once earned twenty thousand dollars in one year . . . imagine that! Now I'm selling Bibles. Not because I'm trying to atone or want some sort of salvation . . . it was the only job going. So you see Mrs. Adams . . . you've only brushed the surface of pain. You haven't met degradation. I might tell you . . . it's lonely . . .

(Vicky goes to say something . . . then thinks better of it. A silence falls as the lights go down on two confused, lonely people, trapped in their own worlds.)

Blackout

Scene two   *(Lights come up on Vicky's room in the house. Vicky is sitting with her Father.)*

Father: I just wanted to apologise . . .

Vicky: So you've apologised . . .

Father: You have to understand . . . I'd had a little too much to . . .

Vicky: I understand only too well. I shouldn't have come in the first place.

Father: I wanted to make up for things . . . for the shitty way I'd treated you . . . at the hospital . . . when you were a kid . . . I meant well . . .

Vicky: You have a funny way of showing it. I've bin trying to understand you all my life and now I know I'm better off without you. The problem is, you've never known **me**. I was just a snivelling kid to you . . . someone who got in the way and helped around the house. I probably only got born because you got pissed one night . . . you even got pissed at my wedding. Made that crazy speech . . .

Father: It was a big occasion . . . I was feeling sad that your mum wasn't there to see it . . . I thought that maybe . . . you'd be very happy for the first time in your life . . .

Vicky: Well it didn't happen, did it?

Father: No . . .

Vicky: D'you know what burns me up though? I'm s'posed to understand you . . . but you don't try to understand me . . . well, screw it. I'm doing all right . . . I've learned some lessons in my life . . . and one is I'm better off by myself. Not relying on anyone . . .

Father: *(Preparing to leave)* Yer job going all right?

Vicky: Fine . . .

Father: Making enough?

Vicky: I manage.

Father: If you need any . . . I can always . . .

(There is a knock at the door which Vicky answers. Ben is standing there.)

Ben: Hi Vicky . . . oh, I'm sorry . . . I didn't know . . .

Father: I'm just leaving.

Ben: I'll come back in a few minutes.

Vicky: Ten minutes . . .

Ben: Yes . . . I'm sorry . . . *(He smiles uneasily at Vicky, then at Father, and leaves.)*

Father: Who was **that**?

Vicky: He has a room upstairs.

Father: Well . . . it sounded like the confessional . . . I thought if he says "I'm sorry" once more he'll wind up on his knees . . .

Vicky: He's a very nice man.

Father: What's he do?

Vicky: He sells . . . he's in the car business. Does very good.

Father: Then why's he living here?

Vicky: Why d'you always look for the worst in people?

Father: All I did was ask a question for Chris-sakes . . . trying to interested . . . I was saying before he came . . . if you need any bread . . .

Vicky: No thanks . . .

Father: I was also gonna say . . . Flo and me are thinking of getting married . . .

Vicky: Come on . . . *(Mimicing)* "What's a bit of paper" you always said. So now you want it . . . wanna be all respectable.

Father: I felt it was the only fair thing . . . we get along good . . . we know each other's habits . . . It's not **me** . . . it's just that most women like to be secure. Anyway . . . I'd like you to come to the weddin' . . . I'd like us to start again.

Vicky: *(Laughing)* What do I call her?

Father: Who?

Vicky: Mum? . . . Flo? . . .

Father: I don't see that it's funny . . . you'll call her Flo . . . we're going to City Hall . . .

Vicky: It's terrible there. That's where Gord and me got married.

Father: I know . . . there's nowhere else to go . . . an' after we'll have a few drinks with some friends and then . . .

Vicky: *(Unable to control her laughter)* An' then you'll go on your honeymoon . . . **you** . . . on a honeymoon.

Father: I don't think you're . . .

Vicky: *(Still laughing)* You'll be all coy in yer striped pyjamas . . . the young lover . . . oh, my God, I can see it . . . you blushing . . . taking yer Geritol in the bathroom . . . boy, she really must have worked on you to get you to agree to that.

Father: *(Waiting for her to stop laughing)* After you left the other day . . . she came in . . . she'd seen you on the street, only she didn't know it was you then . . . and when I told her what had happened . . . well, that was it . . . she was gonna leave me. So I said I'd come here and see you . . . and try an' apologise . . . and that we'd get married . . . I didn't wanna lose her . . . *(Silence)*

Vicky: I've never seen you care about anything before.

Father: Well . . . there you are . . . so, think about it. It'll be in a couple of months . . . let me know. We'd like you there . . . give me a call. *(Exits)*

Vicky: Yeah . . . I'll give you a call . . .
(She lights a cigarette and goes and checks her hair and quickly makes sure everything is tidy. There is a knock at the door and she lets Ben in. He stands in the doorway.)

Ben: I didn't mean to interrupt you earlier . . .

Vicky: It was no problem . . . it was my father.

Ben: How's your mother doing?

Vicky: My what . . . oh, she's fine . . . much better. So how was your week . . . come on in for God's sake. Mrs. Kroyt'll have you reported for loitering with intent.

Ben: *(Entering)* Strange woman . . . Mrs. Kroyt.

Vicky: A nosey bitch . . .

Ben: I was wondering . . . I had a good week and I bought a mickey . . . and I thought we could . . .

(Vicky goes to her purse and produces a mickey of scotch, laughing.)

Ben: You too?

Vicky: I was gonna ask you for a drink . . . I mean, I've had lots of yours in my coffee . . . and then I chickened out. I thought you might be too busy or something.

Ben: Me busy? I wanted someone to celebrate with. I've been given an additional territory . . . south western Ontario . . . a very good selling area. They say New Testaments do better there than anywhere else in Ontario. It's funny how reading habits vary. Anyway . . . we could get some pizza sent in . . . with two mickeys.

Vicky: Here?

Ben: Well . . . we could go to the kitchen . . . but if . . .

Vicky: An' have to share it with someone . . . no way. Let's have a drink.

(She pours two shots into some cups, giving one to Ben.)

Vicky: Here's to the best Bible salesman in Ontario.

Blackout

D36

Scene three

(Lights up on the kitchen set. Some of the roomers are moving quietly around and Mrs. Kroyt sits at the table, reading a newspaper, but watching everyone at the same time. Vicky enters carrying a grocery bag and proceeds to put her things in her own section of the cupboard. The roomers tend to ignore each other.)

Mrs. Kroyt: *(Coldly to Vicky)* Mrs. Adams . . . that picture on your wall . . . the film star . . . it'll have to come down.

Vicky: Why?

Mrs. Kroyt: We have picture hooks if you need them . . . but scotch tape peels off the paint . . . and I found a cigarette burning on your dresser . . .

Vicky: My room's private.

Mrs. Kroyt: . . . which 'll have to be fixed.

Vicky: There's no reason for you to go in.

Mrs. Kroyt: I smelled burning . . . and I have the right to inspect . . . we'll charge the cost of repair to your rent.

Vicky: *(Angry)* You stay out of my room you prying bitch . . .

Mrs. Kroyt: I don't have to put up with . . .

Vicky: You just stay out of my room . . . just 'cause you've got nothing better to do all day than sit around spying on people . . . I pay good money to be private.

Mrs. Kroyt: You could have burned us all down . . .

Vicky: It would have done you good you old fart . . .

Mrs. Kroyt: Mrs. Adams . . . any more from you and I'll have to ask you to leave . . . I also happen to entertain your visitors while they sit around waiting for you. If you don't like this place you can go . . . a week from today . . .

Vicky: *(Leaving in a huff)* You just stay outa my room. Don't you have no respect for people's privacy?

Mrs. Kroyt: *(To the other roomers who stay out of it)* I've never been so insulted in my life . . . that's the thanks you get for providing a good, clean place to live . . . *(To roomer)* . . . and make sure the sink's left clean . . .

(Lights down on kitchen set and come up on two chairs down at front, centre stage. Vicky and Ben are sitting there.)

Vicky: What's your wife doing now?

Ben: She's remarried . . . has the kids of course. D'you have kids?

Vicky: *(Pause)* No.

Ben: It makes it easier.

Vicky: *(Looking out)* I used to come over to the Islands when I was a kid . . . sneak on the ferry an' have a ball all day for nothin' . . . an' I once snuck on the big boat that goes over to the yacht club . . . and sit and watch all the rich people with their yachts and picnics and blazers. I mean, it'd be ninety and these men would stand on the deck with their shirts and ties on . . . sweatin' and pretending it wasn't even hot.

Ben: They still do it.

Vicky: You're kidding . . . an' I got caught once . . . and this man with a red face and tie on says "What d'you think you're doing miss?" An' I said I was goin' out on my father's boat an' he said "What name may I ask?" "You may" I said . . . "H.M.S. Stuffed Shirt" . . . *(Laughing)* . . . an' they sent me back over on the next boat an' didn't like it 'cause I ate my peanut butter and jam . . . You know . . . this is the first time . . . you won't believe this . . . but this is the first time I've bin out with someone . . . a man . . . since I was seventeen.

Ben: Come on . . . what about your husband?

Vicky: It wasn't like this . . . we used to go to pool halls or maybe a movie now an' again. It's like the first time I've ever bin to the Islands. I see them all differently. I mean, they're nice. Pretty . . . all those geese and ducks and boats. Must be nice to have money.

Ben: It is . . .

Vicky: Oh, I didn't mean to . . .

Ben: That's all right . . .

Vicky: D'you ever see your kids?

Ben: About three times a year. They live in Montreal. I save up and take a couple of hotel rooms downtown. I couldn't have them see . . . they think I'm better than . . .

Vicky: Do they know about? . . .

Ben: Yes . . . I used to have a boat and sail it around here . . . I used to see people sitting on the pier watching the boats . . .

Vicky: Gord used to watch planes at the airport.

Ben: Same thing I suppose . . . now I watch people with their boats.

Vicky: It's sad, eh? The way lives get screwed up.

Ben: Yes . . . you never talk about you.

Vicky: There's nothin' to talk about . . .

Ben: Things didn't work out with your husband?

Vicky: *(Wanting to let go and talk, but afraid to)* Ah . . . we got along okay . . . I mean, it wasn't perfect . . . he used to hit me now and again an' . . . an' we decided to split . . . he got married again. *(Laughing to herself)* I used to think he was all I had . . . and that life would get better. But it didn't . . . it doesn't work that way. 'Sfunny . . . I used to love him even if he did knock me around. Did you ever hit your wife?

Ben: No . . . she'd have walked out . . .

Vicky: She did anyway . . .

Ben: Yes . . . but that was different.

Vicky: Yeah . . . I used to say . . . that if a wife hasn't bin knocked around by her husband . . . well, she doesn't know the real power of a man

. . . like Gord, he was my husband, and my father . . . Gord always came home to me . . . an' I figured I had the answer to making things work . . .

Ben: D'you still think that?

Vicky: Nah . . . I was dumb and stupid . . . living there scared shitless, worrying what sort of mood he'd be in when he got home . . . I jus' didn't know any better . . . *(Looking out)* . . . hey, look at the city . . . it's big, eh? I remember when that squirt of a building over there was the tallest in the Empire . . . *(Relaxing)* My Dad was all for the Empire and the Queen . . . I I could care less . . . I mean, she's not real is she?

Ben: I've never thought about it.

Vicky: I remember I wanted a Corgi dog 'cause the Queen had one . . . but my Dad wouldn't let me. Said it'd pee all over the carpet. When I told him the Queen had one he said that was different. Royal dogs don't pee he said . . . an' I believed him *(Leaning against him, relaxed and happy.)* When you leaving to go to Chatham?

Ben: Monday morning . . . they've rented me a car. I pick it up on the way out. Maybe next Friday, before I turn it in, we could go for a drive.

Vicky: I'd like that.

Ben: You know . . . this weekend is the first time I've felt human since I got out.

Vicky: I know what you mean . . . it's funny, eh? Someone to talk to can make you feel good. If someone had said I'd spend a whole afternoon riding around the harbour on a ferry boat . . . I'd have said they were crazy . . .

Ben: *(Laughing)* Yeah . . .

Blackout

D40

Scene four (*Lights up on Vicky's room in the house. Low key. Vicky and Ben are in bed together, in each other's arms. It is a very relaxed, quiet moment.*

Vicky: You don't think I'm too . . . skinny? That I was . . . you know, too small . . . my breasts?

Ben: And I was worried that you'd think I was too fat . . . and too old. You know what I mean?

Vicky: That it wouldn't be any good?

Ben: Yeah . . .

Vicky: I wasn't worried about that. I just knew . . . (*Sitting up and looking at him*) . . . an' you're not fat and you're not **old** . . . boy, you worry a lot.

Ben: It was too important . . . for it to go wrong. I mean . . . we were both nervous . . .

Vicky: Yeah . . . it's bin a long time for me.

Ben: And me . . .

Vicky: (*Teasing*) Sure . . . all those girls in Timmins . . .

Ben: You don't know Timmins . . .

Vicky: (*Putting on an act*) Come to my motel room and see my Bibles . . . I will read to you from the first book of Saint Ben and you will be saved . . . (*Laughing*) . . . I bet you've had a lot of laughs . . . (*Cuddling into him again*) It feels good to be held tight . . . warm . . . and smell that aftershave. (*She starts to giggle*)

Ben: What's so funny?

Vicky: I was just thinking . . . if Mrs. Kroyt could see us now . . . I mean, there's no sign that says we can't . . . I think Mister Kroyt did himself a good turn by leaving the evils of this world. Dumb bitch. I bet she's never had it.

Ben: You think so?

Vicky: S-u-r-e . . .

Ben: You really say what you think.

Vicky: Sometimes . . . depends who I'm talking to. Other times . . . so it's gonna be a whole week of work waitin' for you to get back.

Ben: I'll be back Friday.

Vicky: That's good . . . you know something? I haven't felt . . . so . . . I dunno, so good . . . for years. I mean . . . that it all happened . . . well, natural. It gives me goosebumps . . .

Ben: That's good.

Vicky: Yeah . . . I think so too . . .

Ben: I could phone you during the week.

Vicky: *(Pleased)* Hey . . . that'd be good . . . but won't it cost a lot.

Ben: I'm on expenses . . . I'll eat cheaply and get a cheap room . . . and with the money I save . . . we could go out next Friday in the car, like I said, and have dinner somewhere . . . do it in style . . . you know, some wine . . . really live it up.

Vicky: Yeah . . . let's do it . . . live it up . . . an' all those things . . .

(She half sits up and kisses him, letting the sheets fall, and pulls him to her.)

Ben: Vicky . . .

Vicky: What?

Ben: Nothing . . . I just like to say it.

Vicky: You talk too much . . . *(Kissing him again.)*

Ben: I don't think I . . .

Vicky: You wanna bet . . .

Blackout.

(Lights up on the kitchen set. Three or four roomers are in the kitchen cleaning up or putting away groceries. Mrs. Kroyt enters, followed by Ruth. By her clothing we can see that she's done well since she left the hospital.)

Mrs. Kroyt: She's usually home by this time if she's working days . . . mind you, she keeps pretty well to herself so it's hard to say when she'll be in.

Ruth: I'll wait for a while.

Mrs. Kroyt: If you don't mind waiting in here . . . I couldn't let you into her room you understand but I could make you some tea . . .

Ruth: Thanks . . .

Mrs. Kroyt: She's a lovely person . . . as I say, very quiet and keeps to herself . . . we try to attract the genteel sort of person here . . . I mean, we have our name to think about. People like yourself for example . . . but no young people. Trouble . . . that's all they are. Parties, alcholic beverages and things like that . . . what did you say your name was again?

Ruth: Ruth.

Mrs. Kroyt: Ruth . . . you must be a good friend of Mrs. Adams.

Ruth: Yeah . . . we know each other pretty good.

Mrs. Kroyt: She shows respect . . . that's what I like . . . keeps a tidy room . . . considerate of others. People aren't like they used to be are they?

Ruth: I don't know.

Mrs. Kroyt: They take too much for granted . . . things have been made too easy for them. All this welfare . . . and strikes. There's something that'll send this country right down the drain . . . how d'you take it?

Ruth: Milk and sugar please.

Mrs. Kroyt: Right down the drain . . . no one wants to work for a living anymore . . . and crime. That's another thing . . . strong or weak?

Ruth: Medium.

Mrs. Kroyt: These tea bags are for one cup only . . . very sensible. Soon the street won't be safe to walk on at night. Someone like Mrs. Adams has to be very careful . . . especially when she comes home late from work. And we're right next to the park and some terrible things happen in there at night. It's not safe anymore. A girl walking through there at night . . . well, could be assulted.

Ruth: Vicky can look after herself.

Mrs. Kroyt: Vicky? Oh, Mrs. Adams you mean . . .

Ruth: We used to say . . . if anyone tries to rape you. Kick 'em in the balls fast . . .

Mrs. Kroyt: *(A little shocked)* Oh . . . yes . . . I suppose . . . Sugar?

Ruth: One please.

Mrs. Kroyt: *(Passing tea)* There we are . . . *(As Ruth takes out a cigarette)* . . . you smoke?

Ruth: As a matter of fact . . . yes. *(Before Mrs. Kroyt can say anything)* I know . . . it's not good for me . . . but I like it.

Mrs. Kroyt: I see you're married . . .

Ruth: Well . . .

Mrs. Kroyt: Does your husband smoke?

Ruth: No. Not any more.

Mrs. Kroyt: He gave it up?

Ruth: *(Smiling)* Yes . . . he gave it up.

Mrs. Kroyt: Very wise . . . he's much better off for it, I'm sure.

Ruth: Yeah . . . he doesn't cough anymore.

Mrs. Kroyt: That's good . . . my late husband used to smoke. Just occasionally . . . then he gave it up. When he was twenty-five. Didn't drink either . . . he said the evils of this world weren't for him. But he's in a better place now . . . I've been a widow for thirty years this month.

The fifteenth. Very sudden it was. He got a chill shovelling snow and a week later he was gone . . . thirty years alone is a long time.

Ruth: Yes.

Mrs. Kroyt: With no children to keep me company . . .

Ruth: He didn't think . . .

Mrs. Kroyt: . . . but I've managed. It's so sad to see people like Mrs. Adams divorced . . . I think young people rush into marriage these days too young. It needs maturity . . . but I don't like to see people like her alone . . . how's the tea?

Ruth: Fine . . .

Mrs. Kroyt: I don't know what's keeping her . . . did she know you were coming?

Ruth: No. It was a surprise visit.

Mrs. Kroyt: Nice . . . maybe she's gone shopping, being Friday . . . that's your car outside?

Ruth: Yes.

Mrs. Kroyt: Very nice . . . what is it?

Ruth: A Buick . . . convertible.

Mrs. Kroyt: Very nice . . .

Ruth: Yes . . .

(The lights go down on the kitchen set and come up on Vicky's room in the house. We find Vicky, in a slip, taking a new dress from a box. She holds it up to herself and then puts it on, excited and pleased with what she has bought.)

(There is a knock at the door.)

Vicky: Hang on . . .

(She makes sure the dress is looking good, hides the box under the bed, quickly tidies the dresser, putting a whole bottle of scotch in the drawer, and goes to answer the door. She deflates as we find Mrs. Kroyt standing there.)

Vicky: I was just gonna bring the rent down.

Mrs. Kroyt: I'd like to have a word with you.

Vicky: What?

Mrs. Kroyt: Inside . . . (*Walking in without waiting for a sign from Vicky.*) I'm going to have to ask you to go.

Vicky: Go?

Mrs. Kroyt: Leave . . . vacate . . . whatever you want to call it . . . by tomorrow.

Vicky: (*Stunned*) Why? What have I done?

Mrs. Kroyt: I've had complaints . . . there are people in this house who'd feel happier if you didn't live here . . . that's all.

Vicky: What sort of complaints? I'm not noisy. I get my garbage out and never go over my time in the bathroom . . .

Mrs. Kroyt: Lookit . . . you're making it very difficult. I don't want to spell it out . . . just be gone by tomorrow.

Vicky: You bloody well spell it out.

Mrs. Kroyt: Don't shout at me . . . I just don't want someone around who killed their kids. All right? That suit you? Now just be out of here by this time tomorrow. I won't even charge you for the extra day . . . okay?

(*She leaves and Vicky stands, rooted to the spot, shattered, wanting to cry but tears won't come. She unconsciously feels the new dress as her head begins to pound . . . then suddenly she rushes out.*)

Blackout.

(*Lights up on the kitchen set.*

Most of the roomers are standing around with Mrs. Kroyt sitting at the table, the centre of attention. Ben is there, having just returned from his trip, wearing his suit and top coat and holding his sample case. Vicky rushes in, stopping suddenly. She looks at the people, one by one, and they are unable to hold her gaze as her anger, frustration and shattered emotions build up inside of her. Her voice is seething. The roomers start to leave.)

Vicky: Whatsa matter? You all struck dumb or something? You never seen a murderer before? Eh? Well . . . take a good look so you can tell the folks . . . **look at me . . .!**

(*She starts to sob, looking across at Ben, pleading with her eyes for some sort of help, support.*

But Ben stands there, unable to move. Unable to even look at her as the rest of the roomers start to leave. Mrs. Kroyt sits there, her eyes fixed on Vicky whose face is covered in tears, waiting for Ben to make a gesture. Anything that will say "It's all right . . . I understand". But Ben doesn't understand and just wants to get away from what, for him, is a torturous moment of betrayal. Even he knows that but can do nothing about it. Mrs. Kroyt leaves and Vicky and Ben are left facing each other. Quickly, Ben picks up his sample case and leaves, not looking at her.

Vicky's call should echo to the rafters, sending a chill up the spines of the audience. It is a plaintive, pathetic call . . . pleading . . .)

Vicky: B-e-n . . .

(*But Ben doesn't hear and Vicky is left, a lonely figure as the tears stream uncontrollably and the lights go down slowly, crossfading until Vicky is held in a single spot . . . her crying stops but she is empty . . . her voice is controlled and flat.*)

Vicky: They don't understand out there . . . it's only . . . after you've bin across . . . and come back . . . that you can understand . . .

D45

D46

(The therapist enters and stands behind Vicky, holding her shoulders . . . helping her to relax.)

Therapist: You knew it wouldn't be easy . . . it never is. But you've still got a job . . . and lots of time.

Vicky: Yeah . . .

Therapist: And what about . . .

Vicky: Ben?

Therapist: Yes . . . Ben.

Vicky: *(After a pause and without emotion)* I wanted to ask him . . . how it went in Chatham . . . but he wasn't listening . . . he didn't even notice my new dress . . . *(Long pause)* . . . I killed my children didn't I?

Therapist: Yes.

Vicky: It wasn't a dream?

Therapist: No . . . and that's important.

Vicky: It'll always be there . . .

Therapist: Yes.

Vicky: *(Forcing a laugh)* Like . . . I gotta face it . . . and not be dumb about it?

Therapist: You have.

Vicky: What?

Therapist: Faced it . . . and the world's still standing.

Vicky: Yeah . . .

Therapist: And that's what it's all about.

Vicky: *(Pleased)* Yeah . . . and that's pretty good, eh? I mean . . . *(Little laugh)* . . . that's pretty good . . .

Blackout.   End of Play.

The Vice
President

Joseph Schull

E2

Joseph Schull grew up in Moose Jaw, Saskatchewan, and moved later to Montreal. He now lives in Rosemere, Quebec.

Schull began as a free-lance writer after service with the Canadian navy in the Second World War as an Intelligence and Information Officer. After the war he was commissioned by the government to write the official history of Canadian naval operations, and the result was 'The Far Distant Ships'.

It was the first of several books dealing with Canadian history, of which the best-known are the biography 'Laurier: the First Canadian', 'The Salt Water Men', 'The Battle for the Rock', 'Ships of the Great Days' and the latest book 'Rebellion', which is a moving account of the 1837 uprising in Lower Canada. He is engaged currently on a biography of Edward Blake.

Over the past twenty years he has written hundreds of plays for radio and television, presented not only by the CBC but in the United States, England and in other European countries as well as Australia and New Zealand. Many of these were historical documentaries on Canadian history, and later appeared in book form. Of his other dramatic offerings, his radio play 'The Jinker' later became the novel of the same name.

Drawings by **Karen Liggins**

'The Vice-President' is the latest of his plays for the stage. He is at some pains to emphasize that it was not inspired by the October, 1970, crisis in Quebec. It had been drafted in television form and completed in radio form at least two years earlier; though for various reasons the presentation on radio was long delayed.

'The Vice-President' deals with a problem which could be seen shaping in Quebec long before the October crisis, and is not changed yet in its real dimensions. It is neither a political analysis of French-English relations, nor a plea for either side. It is an attempt to paint in human terms the problem of the uprooted man, returned to abandoned loyalties and forced to search for himself.

All rights, including performing rights to 'The Vice-President' are reserved by the author himself. Requests for rights or information should be addressed to: Joseph Schull, 544 Grande Côte, Rosemere, P.Q. Postal code: J7A 1M7.

Cast of Characters

Katherine Mackay — Executive secretary,
around thirty
Jean-Pierre Allard — in his early forties
Lise — Allard's wife, late thirties
André — Allard's brother, seventeen
Mitchell — Company president, in his sixties
Reilly — Company executive, in his forties
Borojik — Another executive, about forty
Walker — Another executive, in his fifties
Allard's Mother — In her sixties
Allard's Father — Late sixties
Francois — Allard's brother, about fifty
Curé — Priest of the parish, in his sixties

Minor characters:
A sign painter, two or three other company executives, police sergeant, constable, plant guard,
and six youths between the ages of about sixteen and twenty-one.

An executive office of Imperial Ajax (Canada) Ltd, headquarters Montreal. Furniture is fresh and new; the large desk is perfectly clear except for one card in the middle of the shining surface. The office of Katherine Mackay, the secretary, opens off. She comes in from it; she has nothing to do; she's waiting. Moves over to where a sign painter is finishing some lettering on the glass-panelled door; Jean Pierre Allard — Vice-President. Then she straightens, readying herself for a meeting; someone is coming down the corridor.

Allard walks in with a vaguely truculent brisk-ness. He is in his early forties, dark, tall, quick-moving, an outdoors man, bronzed and hard, not too happy in his city clothes though they're expensive and well cut. Stops at the threshold, takes in the size of the room.

Allard: Sacrément! If I yelled here there wouldn't be an echo back till quitting time.

Katherine: Mr. Allard —?

Allard: That's me.

(Moves over: watches the sign painter going on with his work)

Painter: Only be half a minute now — near done.

Allard: Are you? *(Points)* Vice-President of what?

Painter: Dunno. That's all they gimme.

Allard: *(Points again)* Jean-Pierre. Should have a hyphen between 'em. You haven't got one.

Painter: *(Sourly)* Been doin' these French names for years. Never bothered with that.

Allard: *(Cuts him off: curtly)* **And** an accent over that first e in Président. We bother with 'em now. Do it.

(Man starts sulkily to unpack his paints and brushes again. Allard waves him out)

Later — tomorrow morning. I can live with it for half a day.

(Man goes out. Allard turns to the desk. Kather-

ine has been watching it all, a shade quizzical. He picks up the card as he reaches the desk)

One little white card in the middle of all that desk. Looks lonely. Your hiring card?

Katherine: Yes. Thought you'd like the details.

Allard: *(Studying it)* Katherine Mackay — born Edinburgh — out here seventeen years. Thirty-one, and admits it. Bilingual — *(Looks over)* — that mean the works? — talk, write, read — take dictation?

Katherine: Yes.

Allard: You must have been hard to dig up at Imperial Ajax — never knew there were any. Will you tell me why a good Scotch lassie ever bothered to learn French?

Katherine: I live in Montreal — and I like a decent pay cheque. It comes easier this way.

Allard: Fair enough. You look bright, Katherine Mackay.

Katherine: *(Not overwhelmed)* Thank you, sir.

Allard: So perhaps you'll tell me what the devil I'm here for.

Katherine: I thought that's what you were demonstrating — with the sign man.

Allard: That? I was just getting rid of a little excess acid. I must have a larger function.

Katherine Of course.

Allard: Well?

Katherine: Wouldn't it come better from the President — even if I knew?

Allard: The president and I aren't going to get along — I could see that at lunch. You and I might.

Katherine: *(Breath)* All right — I've only had this job for a day — I suppose I can go back to the pool if I have to. You're part of the new look, Mr. Allard. Imperial Ajax — brackets —

Canada, Limited, has decided that a French name up near the top of the letterhead might look well in Quebec. And then, besides that, of course — *(Stops)*

Allard: *(Grimly)* Well? Come on — don't stop now. You've heard more than that in the powder rooms —

Katherine: *(Taking the plunge)* All right. You're slated for the Matteville plant when it's built — naturally.

Allard: *(Flares)* Naturally! Sure — of course! I was born in Matteville and worked for twenty years to get out of the place, so now I'll be dumped back there and buried there naturally!

Katherine: Since you've invited me to talk about what's none of my business, may I ask what's the gripe? It's going to be a big plant and half the other VP's would love the job.

Allard: Then let 'em have it! What do I know about management — payrolls — unions — God knows what? I'm an engineer!

Katherine: I was going to say — naturally. Maybe I hadn't better.

Allard: *(More intensely)* I was in New York for the company — London — Australia — Peru. It didn't make a damn bit of difference whether I was a French Canadian or a Finn — I knew my stuff. I was going places. Matteville, hell! — I would have had London some day if I'd wanted it — or Paris — my pick of the world. But oh no — I'm back as a bloody symbol. — some kind of performing bear!

Katherine: *(Mildly)* Read any of the home papers while you were on your travels?

Allard: *(Flatly)* No.

Katherine: It must have been an effort not to. Did you try hard? You know what's been going on, Mr. Allard. The quiet revolution's not all that quiet.

Allard: Politics! Politics be damned! It's another of the things I thought I'd got away from.

E5

E6

Katherine: Been on the run from quite a lot, haven't you? (Pause) And now I've said too much — am I fired yet?

Allard: No.

Katherine: (Assumes slight formality) Any dictation to give me, Mr. Allard?

Allard: Yes. (Dictates) Memo to Miss Katherine Mackay: Watch it, Scotty.

Katherine: Very good, sir. Memo received and noted.

Allard: P.S. I'm married. Don't get any ideas.

Katherine: I'm engaged. To a Pole. (Deliberately) A difficult bastard too.

Allard: (Touch of a grin: moves to her: puts a hand on her shoulder) You know — we might get along.

(Lise comes in, a little diffident and uncertain. She is in her middle thirties: carries a parcel or two: might just have come from shopping. Stops at sight of the two: always a little uncertain. Allard turns to her.)

Ah — tracked me down —

Lise: (Little smiles: light French accent) It was not so hard. The doctor is in the same building.

Allard: What's he say about the headaches?

Lise: (Slight hint of evasion) Nothing serious — a little strain. I will be all right when we're settled.

Allard: Good. (Turns to make introductions) Lise — Katherine Mackay — my wife.

Katherine: (Smiles: acknowledges: turns toward her office) If there's nothing more —

Allard: Won't be for the rest of the week. I'm settling into an apartment. You show up Monday.

Katherine: Good.

(Smiles for both of them: goes: Lise looks at Allard: touch of constraint)

Allard: (Gestures round: grimly) Bit different from a construction hut in Peru —

Lise: (Nods) You have met the President.

Allard: Head on. It's going to be a sweet friendship. They've taken a hundred cards and run 'em through the computers and they've come up with me — Allard, Jean-Pierre — born, Matteville, Quebec — native son, speaks the language — senior enough to look right behind a desk — stupid enough, they hope, to think it's important —

Lise: And you are not stupid, and it is not important —

Allard: A job like this? — to come back as a home-grown stooge?

Lise: (Little breath) Even to come back at all — that is the real trouble. (Moves) I can go back to the hotel, if you —

Allard: (Moving with her) No, no — there's nothing to do here.

Lise: I called papa — and your mother. If we could go down only for the weekend —

Allard: (Dismisses it impatiently) We'll be moving into the apartment — and I've got to get going here. Maybe in another week —

Lise: (Accepts it bleakly) Yes.

(They stop: surprised. Andre has appeared in the doorway, a seventeen-year old in jeans: long hair: not exactly a hippie, but an uninhibited student. He has a slip of paper in his hand)

Allard: (Blank for a moment: then a start of recognition) André — !

André: (Indicates his slip) Maman called, Jean-Pierre — gave me the address. I must rush over and embrace you —

Allard: (Puts arms round him warmly) Well for God's sake do it! Lise — do you remember this? — it used to be a nice, clean schoolboy —

Lise: *(Laughing warmth: taking him into her arms)* I remember very well! Oh — André, how you have changed — will you have dinner with us tonight — tell us all about Matteville —?

André: Tomorrow night, maybe. And I don't see much of Matteville — only on weekends. Going down soon, Jean-Pierre?

Allard: *(Evasive breath)* When I get on my feet here. There's so damn much to —

André: Yes. Me, I had to fight doormen and elevator operators to get in at all.

Allard: *(Chuckles)* I'll bet. Come on — you'll have a drink with us anyway — or do you drink yet?

André: *(Looks at his wrist watch)* Oh yes — I have a date at six o'clock —

Allard: Bring her.

André: Another time, maybe. Anyway, we'll have an hour.

Allard: *(Warm and affectionate)* And ten years to cover — we'd better get going.

André: *(Looks at him directly: there is warmth, yet there is also an edge of something sardonic and vaguely hostile)* You are looking fine, Jean-Pierre — just right. *(Looks round the office)* And they have given you a fine cage.

Allard's office, a month later. Allard, Mitchell the President, and other executives, filing in, settling around the table. They take their places, look to Mitchell at the head. He is in his sixties, gruff, brusque: a one-time out-doors man transplanted to the executive suite. He opens the meeting simply with a glance and a nod to Allard.

Mitchell: Your meeting, Allard —

Allard: Well, gentlemen, we all know why I'm here, and nobody sees any sense in it. Some of you wanted this nice big corner office, and as far as I'm concerned you're welcome. But my function, if I have any, is to improve the Corporate Image, and I've been getting the gears for a month from Public Relations. So I've called this meeting with the President's kind permission —

Mitchell: *(Irritably)* Get on with it, Allard — get on with it —

Allard: Thank you Mr. Mitchell. I've called this meeting to tell you all what's wrong with you — in relation to Quebec, that is. *(Over slight, half-amused stir)* Gentlemen — relax. There's not a single thing. We like you just as you are. You live up in Westmount or out in the high-priced English suburbs, and you play golf with each other and drink Martinis with each other, and talk and think like each other, and you don't mix with foreigners. Why should you? Nobody expects it, nobody wants it — least of all the French. Sticky and difficult and stand-offish, the whole lot of them, aren't they? Quaint.

Reilly: *(Forties: impatiently)* Oh, come off it, Jean-Pierre! That's ancient bull and you know it.

Allard: Lot of your best friends French, Pat?

Reilly: I haven't counted 'em lately. I don't think that way. But when you were here in the old days we drank enough beer together.

Allard: Sure. And when I was in New York or London or Rio and you showed up on your trips it was the same still. Only now I'm back, Pat — in a bigger office than yours. And I'm not just old Jean-Pierre, a guy you work with. I'm Mr.

Mitchell's professional French Canadian.

Mitchell: (Growls) It wasn't my idea to send for you, Allard. And I could still live without you.

Allard: Fine. Let's fire me. Or chase me back to Peru, where I knew what I was doing.

Mitchell: (Gathers himself: grimly) All right — you want a gloves-off session — you can have it. Imperial Ajax is a world-wide corporation. We've got a lot on our mind. Our men move round. We don't pay much attention to local politics —

Allard: I wouldn't say that — not after South America.

Mitchell: (Impatiently) All right — all right — I'm talking Quebec now! We've been fifty years in Quebec and we've made money — made it — we didn't steal it — and eighty percent of the money has stayed right here. We came for cheap labor — sure — and labor's not cheap any more. All right — we rode along with that — we pay well — we get along with the unions — nobody's sweated in our plants. We're a good, sound, honest, well-run business and we've done a lot for Quebec. But all of a sudden we stink — we stink because we're not French. French, hell! How could we be? How many lawyers and doctors and priests and notaries can you use in —;

Allard: (Weary anger) Oh for God's sake — haven't they buried that one —?

Mitchell: (Answering flare) I'm talking about twenty years ago! — when we were shaping up the men at the top today. We had a business to run — we took the best we could get. (Gestures round) Look at this lot here — the brains and guts of the place — an Irishman, an Englishman, a Yank a Dutchman — God knows what you are, Borojik — I can't even pronounce your name right —

Borojik: (Forties: mildly amused) You do pretty well when you try, sir. And I am Polish, if it is of interest —

Mitchell: It's not. I don't give a damn what you are. All that matters to me is, you know figures.

Allard: He does, eh? All right, Borojik — how many French Canadians have been turned out of technical schools and engineering schools and business administration schools and research laboratories in the last twenty years? — how many of 'em are studying round the world now — or back here with their degrees, hungry to go to work? (Pause) Nobody knows. Nobody but us foreigners.

Walker: (Fifties: cold: clipped) We don't know anything about 'foreigners' in personnel. Any French Canadian that comes to me gets the best shake I can give him.

Allard: That's right. The same old chance to bash his head against the same old stone walls. And you don't go out looking for 'em — oh no — not policy!

Mitchell: Your slip's showing, boy. You've been away five years. That's all changed now.

Allard: You can't see it from the thirty-second floor. A French name on the letterheads — French courses for executives! (Laugh) That must be tough after a hard day — sitting in school again. Nobody'd get me to do it if I was in your shoes — I'd know I was twenty years late. Twenty years late with everything, gentlemen — that's about the picture.

Walker: (Coolly) There's just one thing that doesn't seem to fit, Allard — you've done pretty well.

Allard: Don't count me in all this. I'm a freak — out of it — the farther out the better. But you're not. You're still living in quaint old Quebec, gentlemen, with the pea-soup and the ox carts and the folk songs and the hooked rugs. And the hooked rug's been pulled right out from under you. Quaint old Quebec's gone.

Mitchell: (Grunts) Pity it didn't take the politicians with it — and the bomb throwers.

Allard: I haven't heard a bang since I've been back — not one. And the politicians are milling round as usual — heading the way they're pushed. What's really powering this generation, Mr. Mitchell, is a whole new crop of economists and engineers and planners and technicians and

E10

scientists and merchandisers and builders. They don't make much noise, they never break a law, and they only use politics the way you do — when they need it. They think like you, they're as tough as you already, and in ten years they'll know as much. They don't give a damn for the past. They don't give a damn if you speak French or not — they'd really rather you didn't. They're not your enemies, gentlemen — just your competitors. All they want is what you've got — your jobs, your money and your business. And they're on their home ground. You're the foreigners now, and you're running scared. I don't blame you.

Mitchell: *(Dourly, after pause)* Any more constructive suggestions?

Allard: Not one.

Mitchell: All right. I'm hungry. Meeting adjourned.

Cast: *(Stir of rising)*

Reilly: *(Comes over to Allard)* Kee-ripes! All that after one month home?

Allard: *(Laughs)* Relax, Pat. You'll be out on pension before the revolution hits. How about a beer?

Reilly: Martinis, and you'll buy, you bloody rabble-rouser. I'm feeling poor already.

(Allard's office. Katherine at the typewriter Borojik comes in.)

Katherine: *(Looking up: pleased welcome)* Hel-lo — ! That was a smoky meeting this morning.

Borojik: *(Indicating)* He made most of it. Mind if I take his chair?

Katherine: You might find time to come over and kiss me first.

Borojik: *(Doing so)* Excellent. Excellent. A little leads to more —

Katherine: Not in office hours. Go over there and sit down. *(Pause)* You look nice there. You belong there.

Borojik: *(Dryly)* So I have often thought. Met his wife?

Katherine: Once. Haven't even talked to her on the phone since. She's certainly no office-haunter.

Borojik: Well, she had better be beautiful and satisfying and watchful and jealous. I'd like to keep something out of this mess.

Katherine: Keep worrying, please — it's wonderful for my morale. I'll probably hate his insides in another month.

Borojik: Why? Is he too cocky?

Katherine: That doesn't bother me much — it's part of his shell. But there's either nothing under it, or two men fighting each other and I don't know which I'd — *(Stops)*

(Allard comes in)

Allard: *(Breezily)* Well! That's what you get for taking three-hour lunches — somebody else in my chair. Not fired yet am I?

Katherine: Not that I've heard, he just dropped in for a chat.

Allard: *(Breath of enlightenment)* A Pole — I should have known. *(Comes over)* Congratulations, Borojik — she'll have you in kilts yet.

Borojik: Thank you. So I suspect.

Allard: Just don't marry her till spring, will you? I need her for a couple of months.

Borojik: Not planning to stay long?

Allard: Did it sound like it at the meeting?

Borojik: Very interesting. I looked up those statistics, by the way. Impressive — but not — quite so impressive as you made them sound.

Allard: *(Waves it off restlessly)* Talk — talk. I want out of here.

Borojik: *(Dryly)* I wish you every success.

Allard: Ah. This desk look good to you? Were you aiming for it?

Borojik: Well — there'd been a rumour or two of a Vice-President's hat. Then, of course — politics —

Allard: Sorry, old man — for both of us.

Borojik: *(Shrugs)* I have had worse jolts.

Allard: Across the water?

Borojik: *(Nods)* Where politics is really tough. *(Preparing to go)* Well — you are busy —

Allard: Busy! That's a laugh. Haven't done a day's work since I left Peru. *(Luxurious yawn)* Oh take me back to my peons! *(Abrupt dismissal)* Go on off with your man, Scotty — take what's left of the day — do some Christmas shopping.

Katherine: Sure you mean it?

Allard: Am I sure I mean it! Get that, Borojik, you bachelor — this is how they operate. The suggestion is I'm plastered.

Katherine: Well, it was a long, long lunch.

Allard: *(Breath)* Yeah. Pat Reilly and I trying to get easy together. And it won't come — it just

damn well won't. *(Moves a little off: pause: fretfully: looking out broodingly)* Snow. God how I hate snow — always did — even looking down on it from the thirty-second floor. And now Christmas — and I've still got the family to face — and a couple of hours tonight with the kid brother — *(Looks over: dryly)* My source, Borojik — most of that stuff at the meeting came from him.

Borojik: Ah. So he is the economist —

Allard: Economist! Seventeen years old — second year in college — living in some backstreet dump with the other long hairs. Three times since Lise and I got back he's condescended to come round to the apartment and spend an evening with us, — usually the wrong evening. He'll probably turn up tonight because he was asked to dinner last night. Just didn't show at all — and God, it was a relief!

Borojik: Really? Why?

Allard: *(Breath)* Try to figure 'em out, these kids today! It's a crime to be over forty — it's a crime to have been away — you open your mouth to say something, and that damned grin stops you. He knows everything — he's got everything pegged — and he can't be bothered to tell you what he makes of it. You don't count that much.

Borojik: *(Laughs)* Seventeen — it is the age for all that.

Allard: *(Thoughtfully)* Not in Matteville. He must be hard on mother and the old man.

Borojik: Does he go back there often?

Allard: Every weekend. And next week, Lise and me. The big family reunion — that ought to be something. Something I'd miss if I could, to tell you the truth — but Lise wouldn't have that. Christmas is Christmas — families should be together.

Katherine: I think she's right.

Allard: You do, eh? How about you two? Loners in this country? — no relatives?

E13

Katherine: I'm going to try a turkey in my apartment — the first one I've ever cooked. He may end up eating cornflakes.

Allard: I've got a better idea. Come on home with me.

Katherine: To Matteville?

Allard: Why not? Big old French Canadian farmhouse — midnight mass — reveillon — thousands of relatives — you'd get the full treatment —

Katherine: I'm afraid you're looking for buffers, Mr. Allard. We'd be very much in the way.

Allard: Not a bit of it. Dances too, Borojik — you could try out your new kilts — *(Moves: abrupt, restless playfulness)* Come on, Scotty — up on your feet, you starched old Presbyterian — let's show him a square dance —

Katherine: *(Laughs: trying to escape him as he swings her round)* No — not on the sacred thirty-second floor — it's office hours — and it's not Christmas yet — and my man's watching —

Allard: *(Swinging her)* Good — give him something to watch — *(X)* — up with those heels and swing that bustle now — round on my arm, and *(Stops)*

(Mitchell comes in)

Allard: *(Slightly breathless: ironic formality)* Well! Mr. Mitchell. Welcome to a small pre-Christmas celebration.

Mitchell: *(Grimly)* Fun and games, eh? See what you make of this one. I've just had a call from Matteville —

Allard: Well?

Mitchell: Five hundred sticks of dynamite — complete with blasting caps — stolen from the construction workshed.

Allard: *(A quick breath)* No!

Mitchell: Been down there since you got back?

Allard: No.

Mitchell: Fine. You better take off right now. *(Sardonic)* Get you home for Christmas.

Allard: *(Hotly)* If your damn fool contractors left dynamite lying around, that's their headache! Or it's a police job —

Mitchell: Sure — sure — but it's our headache too.

Allard: I've nothing to do with the works down there — or the personnel either. It's Reilly's pigeon — or Walker's.

Mitchell: They'll be there, all right. But we'd like our French Canadian expert around too — just in case. *(Slight pause: hard irony)* And if everything's as sweet and simple as you made it sound this morning — what are you worrying about?

(*Office. Later. Allard stands at the window, looking out gloomily. Katherine comes in from her office.*)

Katherine: Anything you want me for?

Allard: No. Lise is coming round with the car. Oh — one thing. Maybe you'd better dig me up a Quebec road map. New highways — new building — I don't even know the way.

Katherine: (*Turns for it*) I've one in my desk —

(*He stands as before while she goes and gets the map. Brings it to him. He takes it absently.*)

Allard: Thanks. (*Broodingly*) Back into it. The whole bit. Tears, hugs, kisses — why did you go away? And this thing on top of it. And Lise.

Katherine: (*Stiffens: dislikes the subject*) How are her headaches now?

Allard: (*Breath*) I guess I'm the biggest. And the one cure for it — you'd never get her to take. Not Lise. You marry a man for life — even if it kills you.

Katherine: (*Looks at her watch*) I'm meeting Paul — I'm late — I'd better be off. (*Going*) Good luck —

Allard: (*After her*) Scotty — (*She turns*) How high does he really rate?

Katherine: (*Coolly*) Quite high enough.

Allard: It's hell being married to a Pole — everyone says so.

Katherine: May I refer you to an office memo you dictated the first day you came. And here's your wife —

(*Lise comes in: Katherine nods to her and goes out.*)

Good evening, Mrs. Allard —

(*Lise looks after her, vaguely sensing an atmosphere: turns to Allard*)

Lise: I packed things for a week. Did I keep you waiting?

Allard: (*Vaguely*) No hurry. I suppose we could have offered André a lift down —

Lise: He probably has classes tomorrow.

Allard: Or one of his damned meetings. Did he call you?

Lise: (*Faintly dry*) About his — 'damned meetings'? Haven't you heard enough?

Allard: (*Irritably*) I'm talking about last night. Just lets you cook a dinner and sit and wait — no apologies — nothing.

Lise: It is not so very important. Why do you worry about it?

Allard: (*Shortly*) I don't. I've a dozen other worries — (*Pause*) Too bad, this mess, just before Christmas —

Lise: Yes.

Allard: Might really be better if you didn't come, Lise.

Lise: How long do you think we can go on putting it off — both of us?

Allard: (*Pause: fretful brooding*) Damned kids, that's what it is — a bunch of sick young fools!

Lise: Sick?

Allard: Sick — sick! Batting their heads against walls — going crazy with it. I know the feeling.

Lise: You have been away a long time. Are you sure you know anything now?

Allard: (*Shortly*) If you want the truth — no. Not even what you're thinking.

Lise: (*Slight, answering sharpness*) And I have too much time to think. No children to distract me.

Allard: Would you have liked a baby up at that camp in the Andes? No milk — rotten food — flies — filth —

E16

Lise: No. No life for children, is it, this life of ours? Even in a big apartment in Montreal —

Allard: Well?

Lise: Still no. What would we make of our children if we had them? Who are we?

Allard: (Weary shortness) Oh — not that again. We've had it out too often. (Moves for the door) Take us about three hours to get there. I'll stop off at the plant. You can take the car and go on to the house.

Lise: (Strained quiet) Jean-Pierre —

Allard: (Turns back to her) Well?

Lise: When you have found these thieves and the dynamite — what then?

Allard: I don't know. Except that it won't be Matteville. The company think they're going to keep me there. I've got other ideas.

Lise: (Deliberate effort) And I have had enough of camping around the world. I have had enough of strangers — enough of life with a stranger.

Allard: (Coldly) Have you, Lise? How long have I been a stranger?

Lise: (Slight, hysterical catch) A little more every day — every month — every year! And now — (Break: gathers herself: quietly) Whatever happens, this is the end for us. You know that.

(Plant gate. High wire fence. A shed inside and suggestion of a complex of big industrial buildings beyond. Night. Some of the areas are floodlighted. Allard: comes up to the gate; Guard stops him.)

Guard: Hold it, mister — gotta have a pass tonight.

Allard: Locking the stable door, eh? I'm Allard from Montreal —
(Reilly comes over from the shed)

Reilly: (To Guard) It's all right, Fraser. (To Allard: touch of constraint) Hello, Jean-Pierre — you made it in good time. Come on over to the shed —

Allard: (Moving with him) What's the word?

Reilly: Well, they chiselled open the lock — walked in and took the stuff — and drove off in a truck. That's about all we've got.

Allard: Did they do it in broad daylight?

Reilly: Oh no — it was Wednesday night — somewhere round midnight, we think.

Allard: And nobody calls Mitchell till yesterday afternoon. How come?

Reilly: Yeah. How come. There'll be some guts to clean about that, all right. The story is, it was just one of those things. Nobody needed powder yesterday morning, so nobody went near the shed.

Allard: No morning check?

Reilly: No morning check. It was two thirty in the afternoon when somebody noticed the lock — just by accident, then — a man going home off shift.

Allard: (Grunts) Great — great. Don't they have watchmen round here?

Reilly: One. At midnight, night before last, he'd have been half a block away — on his rounds through the main building.

Allard: Saw nothing — heard nothing — no ideas at all?

E17

Reilly: If he has, he's not giving out — not to me.

Allard: Where's he from?

Reilly: Round here.

Allard: You mean he's French.

Reilly: That's what I mean.

Allard: Police been and gone?

Reilly: Yes.

Allard: Where's Walker?

Reilly: Nosing round in the office — he's — ah —

Walker: *(Coming in: coolly)* Ah, Allard — glad you got here. Been round to your family yet?

Allard: No. My wife dropped me off on the way in. Why?

Walker: Just wondered. I suppose you're anxious to see them.

Allard: It can wait, if there's anything to do here.

Reilly: Maybe Allard can get something out of that watchman. Shall I go see if he's —

Walker: *(Cuts him off: smoothly)* No. *(To Allard)* Pat and I were going back to the hotel. We can drop you off at your house.

Allard: *(Sensing something: stiffening)* All right. Fine. Or if I'm one too many on this party I can walk. I didn't invite myself.

Walker: *(Moving off: still cool and veiled)* No trouble — car's over by the gate. You're down off the mill road, aren't you?

Allard: *(Moving with him)* That's right.

Walker: Father and mother still alive and well?

Allard: Yes.

Walker: And then you've an older brother who's a notary here?

Allard: That's right.

Walker: And a younger brother at college in Montreal. Come home many weekends?

Allard: Most of them.

Walker: Name's André, isn't it? Been seeing much of him lately?

Allard: *(Edgy laugh)* Look — what is this? Are you running a check on me?

Walker: Oh no. Not necessary. We've all that stuff in the files. Saves trouble.

Allard: Does it?

Walker: That's what the real job is, you know — save trouble. Who wants newspaper stories — trials — jail sentences — stirring up the country for what? — some kids' prank.

Allard: How do you know it was kids?

Walker: Oh — we think so. That's the way we're playing it — for a start, anyway. Now if that powder was to find its way back to the plant — or turn up anywhere else —

Allard: What?

Walker: By tonight, say — or even tomorrow night — I'm sure we could keep the lid on — forget the whole thing. Tell André.

Allard: André! He was in Montreal on Wednesday night. He was — *(Stops)*

Walker: Well?

Allard: He — was supposed to have dinner with us —

Walker: Didn't make it?

Allard: No. *(Steadily)* Are you telling me it matters, Walker?

Walker: Of course not. I'm not telling you a thing. But the boy has friends round here and he could pass the word. *(Slight pause: direct significance)* For that matter, so could you.

E18

E19

(Big kitchen of a comfortable French Canadian farmhouse. The stir of a family gathering — Mother and Father in their sixties. Allard and Lise are with them.

Mother: *(Warm, reproachful laugh)* A month, Jean-Pierre — a whole month you are back — and it is only now you come to us —

Allard: *(Trying for a little playfulness)* You don't know how they work you, these English, mother — I am at it day and night.

Father: *(Genially)* Making plenty of money — that is a fine big car. And Lise is dressed like — Hollywood.

Lise: *(Laughs)* I hope not, beau-pére. Is he such an expert, maman, on Hollywood fashions?

Mother: TV — TV — he is always sitting in front of it! When he is not looking at hockey players it is legs in mini-skirts.

Father: Mini-skirts? — hah! For that it is better at Mass on Sunday mornings.

Mother: Papa, you are an old goat — and a blasphemer too!

Father: Pah! What is a sin now? — who knows? Meat on Friday — no penance in Lent — everywhere you go the Pill on the bathroom shelf —

Mother: No — !

Father: And the way they have changed the Mass! I tell you, Jean-Pierre I sit there and watch the altar and I don't know what goes on. So I look at legs instead.

Mother: Raymond! His stupid jokes. *(Sigh)* But everything is changed, Jean-Pierre — everything. You will not know us here. Even my little André —

Allard: *(Shade intent)* Changed too, maman —?

Mother: Have you not seen it yourself? I do not know what he learns at that college. But each week he comes home more a stranger.

Allard: *(Effortful briskness)* Oh nonsense! We'll have a good old-fashioned Christmas.

Father: *(Meaning)* Will we? And what comes first, Jean-Pierre? You are here about the plant?

Allard: Oh yes — I'll have to be round there a bit.

Father: And around the shed where the dynamite used to be. I thought that would bring you down.

Mother: *(Rising: sigh)* Wickedness — wickedness! Always more wickedness — *(Turning: slight fade)* Come, Lise — since you have no babies to show me, we will see your clothes — *(Lise and Mother go out)*

Father: *(More quietly: looking after them)* She is pale that one. Lise is all right, Jean-Pierre?

Allard: She's — upset, I think. Coming back here and all —

Father: Yes — yes.

Allard: *(Effort)* Papa — about that dynamite — what do you think? Have you heard any talk around?

Father: Me? *(Rueful chuckle)* When I go down to the store it is not a store — it is a damned great supermarket — with no place to sit and talk. And even when we do get together, some of us old ones, it is like the last leaves in November. We talk about cows, sure — and how was the hay this year — and the next election — all like we used to. But we don't even listen to each other — it is just noise. We don't know anything any more, Jean-Pierre — we don't understand. *(Gloomy hesitancy)* Even if I did have maybe a notion or two —

Allard: (As he pauses) Well — ?

Father: It is all they are — notions. Maybe make trouble for someone —

Allard: No — that's not what we want — they might be a help —

E21

Father: *(Slight pause: breath)* I have lived here always. They will bury me out on the hill there with my friends. Better I keep my little thoughts from — strangers.

Allard: *(Pause: the word strikes home: Allard rises: tightening a little)* All right — maybe Francois, then. Notaries always know what's going on.

Father: *(Chuckles dryly)* Oh yes — Francois, sure — he is expecting you. *(On fade)* But it will be the same as always with you two — maybe worse.

(Notary's office — a room in Francois' home.)

Francois: *(Late forties: slight, hard little chuckle)* Me, Jean-Pierre? Why should I know anything about your company's little problems?

Allard: Because you know the problems for fifty miles around here — and you've helped make some of 'em worse.

Francois: Indeed? I see we like each other as well as ever. A pity — after all these years.

Allard: Look — Francois —

Francois: **Like,** I said. Somewhere under it, I suppose, there is still love. We are, after all, brothers. Do you know, I got little goosepimples of affection when you walked into the office — Jean-Pierre was home for Christmas. But he is not home for Christmas. He is home to find some dynamite.

Allard: Before it blows somebody up.

Francois: Yes. We would not want that, would we? I wish you luck, Jean-Pierre.

Allard: Anything else to offer?

Francois: Only a suggestion, maybe. Have you thought of closing the plant?

Allard: *(Hard, bitter irony)* My God! So nothing's got through the crust — you haven't changed. Do you know what that plant is going to mean to the town?

Francois: Yes, Jean-Pierre, I do. It will mean another invasion — another conquest. Have you taken a walk around that construction site?

Allard: No.

Francois: You should. Five hundred men at work there, and the picture is clear already. Americans, Italians, Germans — Englishmen, Irishmen, Scotchmen — **they** are giving the orders —

Allard: They're giving **some** of the orders. A dozen imported experts you can't get anywhere else. What about the rest of the picture? — do

E23

you want the figures on that? Ninety percent of that work force was hired from right round here.

Francois: To do what the bosses tell them, the foreign bosses. It is not enough, Jean-Pierre, it never will be — till you come here on our terms — till the men are our own men — till the orders are given in French, by French Canadians!

Allard: And where are they? Find me the men right now.

Francois: (Breath) They will come. There is much that is more important — much to be done first.

Allard: And meanwhile the world stands still. We keep our French virginity. Vive Québec Libre!

Francois: Yes. That is the point with me — it always has been. Freedom first — money, perhaps, later —

Allard: And politics all the time.

Francois: If that is what you wish to call it. I am what I was born to be — I intend to keep what I have. I will not change — you cannot bribe me with plants. I work, agitate, make speeches, fight elections —

Allard: And lose them —

Francois: What has that ever mattered? Yes, look at me, Jean-Pierre — I know what you see. A little backwoods notary with six kids — twenty years in this office — eight years older than you — hair turning grey already — and I have nothing, I have been nowhere. But I am alive on my own soil — a man in my own skin. I would not change places with you.

Allard: (Pause: more gently) I always had the best of it — I knew that — even before the company took me over. More schools — more chances — more of papa's money — it always seemed to be something new for me. Was that the trouble, Francois? — did you resent that?

Francois: Why should I? What the company did for you was not my concern — and the money you had from papa you have paid back three times over (Breath) No, Jean-Pierre — no. Sadness, maybe — maybe a kind of disgust — but never any resentment. You wanted it all so desperately, and now you have it. You are back, you are a success, and you are English.

Allard: (Rises: harsh, resigned sigh) All right. We won't start on that again — there's no time —

Francois: (Steadily) I did not steal your dynamite, Jean-Pierre. I do not know who did.

Allard: And you won't even make a guess?

Francois: (Dryly) To be passed back to your company, and then on to the police? It is going to be uncomfortable enough — and even dangerous enough — merely to have you for a brother.

Allard: Dangerous?

Francois: Where are your eyes and ears, Jean-Pierre? — what have you learned on your travels? Do you think there is only danger somewhere else? — Algiers? — Cuba? — Africa? — have you thought about Montreal? (Pause: watching his face) So you have thought about it. Yes. Dangerous men — dangerous ideas. The threads run everywhere now — they are here too.

Allard: (Slight pause: absorbs it: quietly) Has it occurred to you you've two brothers? (Pause) Seen much of André lately?

Francois: (Stiffens) André? No — he is only home on weekends —

Allard: Sure of that?

Francois: Of course I'm sure! I — (Pause: helplessly) I am as sure of that as I am of anything else with these — (Stops)

Allard: (Pressing) These what? (Pause: roughly) Come on — what do you mean? — what are you talking about? I need your help, damn it — and maybe he'll need it too!

Francois: (Slight, shaken laugh) My help? In these times — with the people who make these times? I should like some help myself.

E25

(The office of the Curé of the Village.)

Curé: *(Elderly: dry: tired)* Help? No doubt he would, Jean-Pierre. Francois is like myself — yearning for the old simplicities. And there are none left.

Allard: There are the old idiocies, father. He is still preaching them.

Curé: *(Coldly)* That is a point of view. I am not prepared to discuss it.

Allard: Will you discuss this dynamite, then? It is a matter of urgency, father —

Curé: *(Heavily)* And another matter on which I cannot help you.

Allard: *(Touch of sharpness)* Do you understand what I'm here for? I want to **save** trouble, not make it. Five hundred sticks of dynamite, father, with the blasting caps to explode them — they're somewhere here in this parish — **your** parish —

Curé: So you think. They may be a hundred miles from here — or more. But you are about to tell me my duty. The priest knows everything, the priest gets wind of everything — the priest can use his influence — *(Short exclamation)* Influence! *(Pause: tiredly)* I remember you out there, a boy on the altar. How long ago?

Allard: It's — a long time.

Curé: And then — later. The bright young protégé of your English company. Why not? — you were a lad bound to get on. But now — you have been married for twenty years?

Allard: Twenty-one.

Curé: You have no family?

Allard: No.

Curé: Are you still a Catholic?

Allard: I — don't go to mass very often.

Curé: But you still think like an altar boy. The church and the priest — they are always there, the rock. You come to them when you need them. *(Pause: intensely)* Have you thought of the church at all in twenty years? Open your eyes, Jean-Pierre — where is that rock now? Who turns to it? The old men? — I taught them the Latin mass, flogged them to fast and pray, scorched them with hellfire. And now the mass is in French, fasting is done away with, the fires of hell are out. The old women? — I was the shape that towered over their beds — they wore themselves out with children because of me — do they thank me for it now? How do I speak to the young — even if the young listened — with this babble of quarrelling priests, councils, synods — bishops at bishops' throats — the Holy Father himself at war with a Pill — and losing? Look at me — old — a dried husk — but for thirty years I slept with the thought of women — the white bodies of women — torturing me in the nights, following me through the days — twisting me into the shape of the man of God. And now — maybe it is the wrong shape. Maybe the priest is better with a wife — children — a home. Sometimes I almost see them, here in this stone-cold vestry — it is one of the thoughts I live with — one of the many thoughts, and not the worst. *(Breath)* No, Jean-Pierre — no. I have no help for you. I am the old voice in the new wilderness. I hear nothing, I am not heard. I grope my way with the rest.

(Kitchen. Father sitting alone. Allard comes in.)

Father: Ah! So we will have you here for supper. That is something, at least.

Allard: *(Coming in: tired: dour)* Sure I'm welcome?

Father: *(Gently)* Always, always. That has not changed, Jean-Pierre.

Allard: *(Looking round)* All alone?

Father: Yes. Supper is going to be late. Maman has gone with Lise to visit her father.

Allard: Ah.

Father: *(Carefully)* And Lise will be staying there —

Allard: Staying?

Father: She said she thought she better — for a little while anyway. He is getting old and lonely since her mother died. *(Slight pause)* Pretty near two years now, and he took it hard —

Allard: *(Vaguely)* Yes — yes. I was sorry we couldn't get back — I know Lise wanted to be with him. But it was a long trip — and I was up to my neck in problems —

Father: *(Gently)* I know.

Allard: Anyone call from the plant?

Father: Nobody. There were no calls.

Allard: I've just come from the curé.

Father: And —?

Allard: Nothing — nothing at all. Worse than nothing.

Father: He is always in a black mood now at Christmas time. But you will see — they will fill up the church as usual at midnight mass.

Allard: Why?

Father: God knows. It is a time to be together —

Allard: Hmph. *(Brooding pause)* That damned Francois —

Father: *(Chuckles)* Hah. That is like old times. So you did go to him, then?

Allard: And I might as well not have bothered.

Father: Oh, it is good for brothers to be together. Even though it hurts, Jean-Pierre.

Allard: Hurts?

Father: He is not so bad as he seems, that little man. He is not even so little. In one corner of my heart, you know, I am very proud of Francois. I am even like Francois.

Allard: Papa, will you not realize that this thing is serious?

Father: *(Quietly direct)* Do you not think I am scared? Eleven pipes I have smoked this afternoon, just sitting here waiting. I am burnt out like a chimney, and — when he does come — I am glad your mother was not here to see him.

Allard: *(Rising quickly)* André —?

Father: Out in the barn there now — *(Slight fade: slight meaning)* changing tires on the truck.

E28

(The barn. André, dishevelled, is hastily changing tires on a truck. Allard comes in.)

Allard: *(Constrained casualness)* Well — things are improving. We didn't use to think of snow tires till the snow was a foot deep —

André: *(Absorbed in hasty work: turning: small start)* Oh. Hi, Jean-Pierre. Pretty near finished now — just this one to go on —

Allard: *(Observing: slight surprise)* Changing the front tires too?

André: Whole lot — I had a good set of spares — might as well. *(Working)* Been round seeing the town?

Allard: A bit of it. When did you get in?

André: Oh — maybe an hour ago.

Allard: Bus?

André: Hitch-hike. Fridays it's pretty good on that highway — lots of cars for the week-end.

Allard: Had a notion to call you last night when Lise and I came down — but I was still a little bit sore.

Andrè: Sore —?

Allard: No-show for dinner on Wednesday night — no call — nothing. It was a bit rough on Lise — she'd spent half the day cooking.

André: Yeah — I know — sorry.

Allard: That all?

André: *(Snaps edgily)* I said I was sorry, dammit! I'll tell Lise.

Allard: Do that. She's pretty fond of you, you know.

André: I know.

Allard: So am I, for that matter — when I can figure you out. *(Moves casually: lifting)* These the tires you took off? — shall I put 'em up on the rack —?

André: *(Shade quickly)* No — they are no good — I'm going to throw them away —

Allard: *(Inspecting)* Can't see much wrong with this one —

André: *(Angrily)* It's no good, I tell you — there's a crack on the inside. Leave it alone —!

Allard: All right, sonny — all right — no cause for a battle. Edgy today, aren't we? — seems to run in the family. *(Pause)* I was over to see Francois —

André: *(Slight laugh)* Like always?

Allard: Like always — maybe a bit worse.

André: No changing him now. He is an old record — playing the same tune.

Allard: Many around here listen?

André: He can still fill a hall if it is little enough. Grey heads — bald heads —

Allard: How about the no-haircuts? Does he make any sense to the kids?

André: Oh — they like Francois all right — but he is old stuff to them now. They've got other ideas.

Allard: Like what?

André: *(Touch of impatience)* Ask me some other time — I'll give you a lecture.

Allard: You've given me a couple already, kid, and they're a bit scary.

André: I was just singing for my supper — showing off for Lise.

Allard: That's what I thought, then. Maybe I should have listened a bit harder. All these meetings you go to — these people you mix with — Fronts — Alliances — Protest Groups — Action Groups — God knows what else. How much else? How much do they mean to you? How deep are you into 'em?

André: That depends.

E30

Allard: On what?

André: (A shrug) What they've got — where they're headed — what they can do for me. I listen to anybody — it don't say I always buy. A hundred thousand ideas floating round — you sort out the ones you like.

Allard: Big job. Must be confusing sometimes. And you're seventeen years old. A bit young for — action. Action Groups — I guess they're the ones that count, eh? Any of them round here?

André: Why?

Allard: Know why I'm down in Matteville, don't you?

André: Who doesn't? Word gets around fast.

Allard: How did it get to you?

André: Oh — little birds. And papa had it all, of course.

Allard: Not quite all. I stopped at the plant last night on the way in. Two of my friends there, down from Montreal — but they weren't as friendly as usual. They gave me a bit of a chill. Any idea why?

André: No.

Allard: One of 'em mentioned your name. Had it in the files, he said, which was a damn lie. He got it here and he got it for some reason. Could you make a guess what it is?

André: (Husky quiet) I could make maybe a dozen. Go on, Jean-Pierre — ask me your other questions. They won't help much.

Allard: All right. Where were you Wednesday night?

André: With a girl.

Allard: (Dryly) What? — no meeting?

André: That's where I picked her up. We got talking —

Allard: Just forgot you were coming to us for dinner?

André: Just — didn't. I know it was rude, but — there never seemed to be a phone booth when I thought of it —

Allard: Where in hell were you?

André: Around. A boîte or two for a drink and then home. I mean — I walked her to her place — and I didn't sleep with her either.

Allard: Fine. Full marks for that — and then?

André: Home.

Allard: What time?

André: I didn't look at my watch.

Allard: And the next day?

André: Classes. Two in the morning, one in the afternoon, and — (Stops)

Allard: Well —?

André: (Hesitantly) There was a phone call — ! —

Allard: Phone call? What phone call —? (Pause) Come on, boy — I'm not asking this for fun. Who was it? What was the call about?

André: (Hesitates: then decides: hard quiet) No. This is where the answers stop. Sorry, Jean-Pierre — and I'm sorry for you. Why did you ever let them bring you back? It is not a question of fixing letterheads now — or of French names on doors. This is the real thing. And it's not so good, is it — even with a big fat pay-check!

Allard: (Grim quiet) No, it's not so good. So you came down this afternoon, did you? I wonder who'd pick you up in the shape you're in. Mud all over your pants — circles under your eyes — a six-inch rip in your coat there. When did you wash last? Where've you been sleeping, boy — these last two nights? (Pause)(Intensely) Look — André — all I want is to get that powder back — and get you out of a mess!

André: (Dry, weary, tense: looking off) I know. And bring us Merry Christmas and Peace on Earth. You are a bit late for it now — (Car pulling up outside: Reilly comes in)

Reilly: (Coming in) Ah, Jean-Pierre — saw the barn door open, so I drove round. I suppose this would be André —

Allard: Right. André — Pat Reilly. Got any news to give us?

Reilly: Oh, a little. Thought we might talk it over. Changing tires, André?

André: (Huskily) Snow tires — I — it is getting bad on the roads —

Reilly: Oh, not yet, really — but I could have used a pair. I've been skidding around in fields all afternoon.

Allard: Fields?

Reilly: Barnyards — pastures — logging trails — you name it. Thirty police out looking, and they dig up some queer places. You'd never guess what they found.

Allard: Wouldn't I?

Reilly: An old root cellar — hadn't been used for years. Man by the name of Filion owned it, they said. Know him?

André: (Huskily) There are lots of Filions round here —

Reilly: I guess so. Handy place for some purposes. Big stretch of woods right behind it. Easy to come in from the road, easy to get out through the wood — if you had to take off on foot.

Allard: (Cold quiet) All right, Reilly — what is it? (Reilly turns. Another car has driven up outside)

Reilly: (Indicates car) Want to have a look, André —? (André edges out the door. Walker, a police sergeant and a constable come in as he disappears. Sergeant is carrying a package. They are quite aware of André's going but make no move to stop him)

Allard: So what have we got now? — a convention?

Walker: Looks a bit like a tire shop. Mind if we take a sample? (Indicates one that André has taken off) This one do, Sergeant? (The Sergeant nods: gives the tire to the constable: constable goes out with it: Walker wipes his gloves) Pah — they still stink of that root cellar — a million old turnips —

Allard: (Angrily) Quit the games, Walker! What the hell are you here for?

Walker: Reilly didn't tell you?

Allard: (Acidly) Maybe he left it for you. You enjoy it. What do you think you've found?

Walker: Nothing. That's really the point. The stuff had been and gone. Heavy boxes, we think — they'd been dragged in and piled up on the floor of that cellar. And then they'd been dragged out — there were only the marks to go by. (Puts hand in his pocket: takes out something) And this stuff — there were a few bits of this around. (Hands it to Allard) What do you make of it?

Allard: (Inspects it: heavily) Packing.

Reilly: From a box of powder, Allard. They brought·the dynamite into the cellar and opened one box — to make sure of what they had. That's how we figure it. Then they closed it up, piled the others on top of it —

Walker: — and somebody looked outside — somebody smarter than the others — and he started to think.

Allard: Well?

Walker: There was snow — it had started up round midnight — wet snow. Stopped again around two — about the time they'd be looking out — what did they see? Tire tracks in from the road — to that old cellar — where no one had been for years. Couldn't have that, could they? — so they moved the stuff again.

Allard: That night?

E33

Walker: We don't think so. Maybe the next day — maybe the next night. It was nearly twenty-four hours before the search began in earnest. That right Sergeant? — this is Detective-Sergeant Menard —

Sergeant: That's right. That's how we think it was, sir.

Allard: Scrapes in a mud floor and half a dozen shreds of packing. You haven't got much to go on.

Reilly: Not much — but there's a bit more. *(Turns: carefully casual)* Where's young André got to —?

Allard: André? *(Turns: startled)* He was right here — he must be up at the house — *(Starts out)*

Reilly: *(Stops him)* Don't bother. Maybe he had things to do. We'll find him when we want him.

Allard: *(Shaken)* But — *(Hard angry quiet)* What are you playing at, Reilly? You're setting him up for something —

Reilly: Sergeant —

(Sergeant opens his package lays it carefully out on floor)

Allard: What's that?

Reilly: Plaster cast — of the truck tires — the ones running in from the road. Do I have to tell you I don't like what I'm doing?

Allard: Just tell me what, that's all. You, Walker —

Walker: Well, they picked up those tracks there and followed them back — to the road that passes your house.

Allard: After twenty-four hours of traffic and another snowfall?

Walker: It was just flurries yesterday — blowy and cold. They don't do much to tracks. And there was hardly any traffic the way he went. He stuck to the side roads.

Allard: He —?

Reilly: It wasn't easy, but it wasn't so tough, either. Anyway, they think they're right.

Allard: Suppose they are. What the hell does it prove?

(Catch: looks at Walker: remembering) Oh — *(Constable comes in with a new cast)*

Walker: *(Nods)* That's right. *(Indicates other cast)* This one's from the tire here —

(Sergeant sets it down carefully beside the first one)

Sergeant: *(As he, Reilly and Walker kneel down, intently comparing the two casts)* Steady — move 'em a bit — tread's worn, but *(Pauses)* Matches. A good match — see?

Reilly: *(Heavily)* Want to have a look, Jean-Pierre? That was the truck, all right.

(Porch, door of farmhouse. Winter night. Allard comes up breathless, knocks loudly.)

Allard: Lise — Lise! *(Louder)* Lise! — come down and open this door!

(Door opens: porch light goes on)

Lise: Jean-Pierre — it is past midnight — why are you —

Allard: Never mind that — get him out here! *(Pause angrily)* Don't stand there — you've not been sleeping — I've got to talk to André —

Lise: Why should André be here?

Allard: Because he's a damned young fool! Come on — he made through the woods for the creek — and came up through your father's fields. I could see his track from the road.

Lise: He is not here.

Allard: You're a bad liar. Do I have to push my way in?

Lise: Stop it! Father is asleep and he's sick. I will not talk to you now.

Allard: I said the boy. And I'm going to see him, Lise — I — *(Stops: looks off: a thought at what he sees)* Why's that barn door open?

Lise: He is not there either.

Allard: No! He's off in your father's car. There was a car there, all right. Where's he gone, Lise — where? — I've been hunting him for five hours — do you know the trouble he's in?

Lise: He does not want you to find him — that is enough for me.

Allard: *(He takes her by the shoulders pleading)* Lise —!

Lise: No. *(Steadily)* I am back with my own, Jean-Pierre.

(The door closes in his face)

(The office. Next morning. Katherine is at her desk, typing. Looks up as Allard comes in, unshaven and dishevelled.)

Katherine: Well! Welcome back. Everything settled at Matteville?

Allard: *(Curt: exhausted)* Everything settled. Finished off last night.

Katherine: Was it — messy? You look awful. I could find you a razor if —

Allard: *(Cuts her off)* It was messy. And never mind how I look and I don't want a razor. Got your notebook there?

Katherine: Yes —

Allard: *(Dictates: curtly)* John J. Mitchell, President; Sir: I submit my resignation as of today —

Katherine: *(Startled)* Your resignation —!

Allard: No comments, please. *(Resumes dictation)* I feel for obvious reasons that my usefulness to the company has ended. Yours very truly —

Mitchell: *(At doorway: coming in: sarcasm)* That's nice — stiff and tidy. And maybe a little yellow. *(Slight pause: nearer)* I followed you in and eavesdropped. Do you want an apology for that?

Allard: No. It'll save you reading the letter.

Mitchell: Oh, go ahead and type it, Miss Mackay — we'd better have it for the record. Can you find another machine — someplace else?

Katherine: *(Gathering up to go: upset)* Yes — certainly — *(She goes into her own office and closes door)*

Mitchell: Well — it's the end of twenty-three years with Imperial Ajax.

Allard: Twenty-four.

Mitchell: I guess so. I'm a bit hazy about the early part — wasn't around here then. But old man Heath used to brag about you till I sometimes wanted to puke. Still does, for that matter — he's getting soft in the head. But he's still Chairman of the Board, and he gives the orders. It's the one reason you're here. I'd like you to get that straight — it wasn't my idea.

Allard: So you've said — half a dozen times before.

Mitchell: I guess so. Starting to repeat myself too. Why not? — I've been President as long as Heath was, and made as many mistakes. How did he come to take a fancy to you?

Allard: I don't know.

Mitchell: How did he ever come to find you at all? — you weren't even out of school, were you?

Allard: (Husky: impatient) I was working a summer on construction — he came to visit the job —

Mitchell: That's right — now I remember. He just took a walk round the works with you in tow, and that did it. How come? What the hell did you talk about?

Allard: (Shortly) Nothing — I don't remember —

Mitchell: Well — anyway — that's how careers are made. Lifted you out of that French college and pushed you into McGill. And then on to Harvard. And then it was M.I.T. — compliments of Imperial Ajax — and back to the good jobs. The real jobs — the ones that led straight up. And then, let's see — where did Mrs. Allard come into the picture? — you married early, didn't you — and a married man needs money.

Allard: (Angrily) You know when I was married — and all the rest of it too! The company's treated me well — I've never complained —

Mitchell: Complained? — my God! There's always been a marker on you — push Allard along. Heath's pet — Heath's favorite project. He'd taken a native and made him a company man — civilized him. And it paid off. You turned out fine — just fine. Except for the soft centre.

(Katherine comes in with letter)

Katherine: (Stiffly) Your letter, Mr. Allard.

Allard: Thanks.

(She goes out: Allard signs letter)

Allard: (Handing it over) There you are. That does it.

Mitchell: Thanks.

Allard: You've had the word from Reilly?

Mitchell: Oh yes — Walker too. So you've a brother mixed up in the business?

Allard: He drove the truck that night.

Mitchell: Did he tell you so?

Allard: I've not seen him since they made the check on the tires. Spent the night looking for him.

Mitchell: When did he take off?

Allard: When Reilly set him up for it. Showed him what they were onto. Now he's the little pigeon that will lead them straight to the others, and the others won't like it. They might do something about it, if I don't find him first.

Mitchell: Here?

Allard: He could be in Montreal — he's got a pad here someplace.

Mitchell: Found it yet?

Allard: I will. The address is up at the apartment. I haven't been there yet.

Mitchell: Well, it's something to do, anyway. Keep you out of Matteville. Not the place for you with the heat on, is it? (Slight pause) I suppose you know you were slated to run that plant?

Allard: I know. And I know why. I should have quit when I came back.

Mitchell: But you didn't. The money's pretty good. And it wasn't so tough bawling out elevator operators and sign painters and a few backward Vice Presidents. You were strutting round here with a five-ton chip on your shoulder, and it was okay. But when it comes to the real job — no — not you.

Allard: *(Breath)* Not me. Not Heath's boy — I turned out too well. *(Turns away: abruptly)* Tell Miss Mackay to clear out my desk, will you? *(Moving for door)* I'm in a bit of a hurry —

Mitchell: *(After him: voice slightly raised)* Allard — *(Allard turns back)* Try 2812 Ste-Adelaide — Mrs. Marie Lacoste.

Allard: *(Blankly)* What?

Mitchell: Sounds familiar? We did a little checking at this end too — that's the address. A pad, maybe, but not so bad as some — you should have gone round to see it. One of those beat-up mansions crawling with students — the woman runs the place and gives some of 'em breakfast. Want to hear her story?

Allard: *(Tensely)* Well —?

Mitchell: On Wednesday night she was watching the late movie, with her door open and one eye on the stairs — she doesn't like visiting ladies. She saw the boy come in and go up to his room — it was before the movie finished, so it was before one o'clock. Seven-thirty next morning he was down for breakfast. So he had six and a half hours — maybe a little more — to climb out of a window, drive down to Matteville, do the job and get back. Close — but it's just possible —

Allard: No! — the stuff was stolen somewhere around midnight — Reilly was sure of that!

Mitchell: Everyone's sure of that. So if the kid was anywhere near the place — what did he use for wings?

Allard: *(Quick, indrawn breath: pause)*

Mitchell: Change anything?

Allard: *(Vaguely: absorbing it)* No — no. He knows something — he's mixed up in it some-

how —

Mitchell: And it'll be no trick to find him — nobody needs your help. The tough part's after that.

Allard: After —?

Mitchell: *(Impatiently)* We want the powder, dammit — and maybe he'll lead us to it. Maybe he won't. But whatever happens we won't be out of the woods. Do I have to draw you a picture?

Allard: No —

Mitchell: Used to be a nice town. I used to fish round there. The big-shot from Montreal — hiring guides — throwing round ten-dollar tips — I made a lot of friends — I was fond of the place. But I shove in twenty millions of the company's money and it's all changed. Dirty looks — dirty talk — politics — petitions — dynamite. Why? What the hell do they want down there? — what's eating their guts? I want a man who can tell me — I want a man who can feel it — right in his own guts! *(Slight pause)* Well?

Allard: *(Huskily)* No.

Mitchell: *(Gathers himself: grimly)* All right. I'm three months late already — can't waste any more time *(Moves to door: opens it: calls)* Miss Mackay —

Katherine: *(Coming)* Yes —?

Mitchell: I want you to stick around here — I'm sending Borojik in. Speak French, don't you?

Katherine: Yes —

Mitchell: How are your nerves?

Katherine: Nerves?

Mitchell: You don't scare easy — get jumpy in strange surroundings?

Katherine: No — I don't think so —

Mitchell: Good. It's short notice, but I'm sending you down to Matteville.

Katherine: *(Startled)* Matteville?

Mitchell: Borojik's taking over and he'll need a secretary. *(Starts to move off)* I'll have him here in a minute — *(Turns at door: hard: sarcastic)* Oh yes — Allard's in a hurry. He wants you to clear out his desk.

(Mitchell goes out)

Katherine: *(After considerable pause)* Do you? *(Pause)* Or would you like me to make some coffee?

Allard: Come here — *(Pause)* Closer —

Katherine: This is close enough —

Allard: *(Slight pause: breath)* Yes. Yes, I guess it is. I'm a bit shaky this morning, but — *(Moves for her: abrupt, shaken intensity)* God Almighty, why couldn't it have been you? No ghosts — no strings — alive in the real world —!

Katherine: *(Sharply: struggling with him)* Stop that! *(Freeing herself)* So you're on the run from everything now — even your wife.

Allard: *(Breath: turning away)* No marks for that. It was a pretty easy guess.

Katherine: *(Shaken)* I shouldn't have made it — I've no right to — it's none of my business anyway! I was upset with you grabbing at me — and looking the way you do — and —

Allard: Well?

Katherine: Maybe it's because I'm Scottish. I hate waste. You're throwing yourself away.

Allard: Oh no. Lots of jobs in the world. I'll find one — *(Borojik enters)* Ah — come on in, Borojik. Just on my way out.

Borojik: *(Coming in: deliberately)* Anything you'd like to tell me before you go?

Allard: Can't think of a thing. She knows as much as I do about the job, such as it was.

Borojik: *(Quietly)* All right. Go home and pack a bag, Katherine — we're to be down there by

tonight.

Katherine: But —

Borojik: *(Cuts her off)* Let's not discuss it now, shall we? Just — go.

(She goes out)

Allard: What's she supposed to do down there? — type out police reports?

Borojik: There'll be a lot of other reports, according to Mitchell. And he wants them to start now. *(Quietly)* It makes no sense, of course. I'll be worse than useless.

Allard: Why? Good-looking, affable Pole — speaks beautiful French, better French than mine — I suppose you're even a Catholic —

Borojik: *(Hardening)* When will you shut that mouth and start to think? — or is that what you're afraid of? *(Pause)* Weren't in the war, were you? — you've never seen a bomb go off?

Allard: No.

Borojik: But you've seen plenty of dynamite. You know what that can do.

Allard: *(Also hard)* Then get it before it does. You're on the spot now — and God knows you're welcome!

Borojik: *(Turns away: harsh, contemptuous exclamation)* Fifteen years I've been in this country now — coast to coast — north and south. They shifted me round a lot — wanted me to see the lot. I must have been half asleep — anaesthetized — drunk with the fresh air. I was a Pole with a thousand years behind me — wars, pestilence, invasions — pogroms, massacres, ghettos — the wrecks of a dozen people crammed together, rubbing each others' sores. You sucked in hate with your mother's milk — it manured the ground you walked on. And then — here! My God! *(Dry laugh)* The French and the English didn't like each other! I listened to all the racket and I couldn't even get interested — I couldn't take it seriously — it was a dismal kids' squabble. Fat — stuffed — with everything they need in the world — space, freedom, ideas —

E39

machines, men, knowledge — ten times enough — for all of them, and ten times as much ahead. They **couldn't** kick it away — they'd **have** to grow up and take it! Now — I don't know. Maybe that's how the thousand years begin — with the fools nursing the quarrels and the good men ducking out.

Allard: *(Coldly)* Maybe. I wouldn't know.

Borojik: What are you telling yourself you're going to do? look for your brother?

Allard: For a start — yes.

Borojik: And you know damn well he won't be in Montreal. Or you should know. *(Slight pause)* They found that car, by the way.

Allard: *(Starts)* What car?

Borojik: The one he took last night. You know all about that. It was ditched by the side of a road — he could see it was no good to him. How'd you come up yourself?

Allard: By car.

Borojik: Stopped anywhere?

Allard: There were a couple of road-blocks out —

Borojik: There were about twenty. And there still are. Nothing gets out of Matteville to Montreal.

Allard: *(Huskily)* Because they think it was planned here?

Borojik: Because it could have been. By some of the hard-nosed boys. But they don't think so — they think it's a local job. So they've bottled up the Matteville area, and they're combing it out now.

Allard: Is — the boy still on the loose?

Borojik: So far as I know. *(Slight pause)* Cold, by now, I imagine — and hungry, and scared — circling round in the woods — hiding in old barns —

Allard: *(Shaken: bitter)* Set out like — bait. How many men after him?

Borojik: Maybe fifty or so. They're doing it as quietly as they can, so as not to stir things up. But they'll get more if they need them, and — *(Deliberately)* — tomorrow it may be dogs.

Allard: Yes. That'll be nice — dogs. And tomorrow Christmas Eve. *(Harsh, shaken laugh)* Merry Christmas, Borojik — a real old English — *(Stops as phone rings: gestures curtly to Borojik)* Your phone now. You answer.

Borojik: *(Answering)* Borojik. Yes, he's still here — do you want to — *(Pause: stiffens)* Where? *(Pause)* Was the boy there when they — *(Pause)* Right. Right. I'll be on my way in an hour. *(Hangs up: tonelessly)* Mitchell. They know where the stuff is.

Allard: *(Quickly)* Have they got all of it back?

Borojik: He didn't say they had any. He said they know where it is. In an old mill.

Allard: *(Catch)* Dagenais's!

Borojik: What?

Allard: Stone grist mill — two miles out from town — in thick bush. Hasn't been used for maybe fifty years. *(Thinking)* Creek doesn't freeze up there till the real cold — they could have got in by boat. Was the boy there when they —

Borojik: *(Cuts him off: shortly)* There wasn't anyone there. But the party's on for tonight — or so they think. *(Preparing to go)* Well?

Allard: I — *(Huskily: a little helpless gesture)* What the hell can I **do**?

Borojik: *(Stonily)* If you have to ask me — you can't do a damn thing.

(Night. Wall section and angle of a stone mill looming in bush. Door low in the wall. The ground seems to slope down; there's a river bank below. Along the wall the remains of a decaying work-shed; flashlights flickering in it and dim forms in the dark. This is the command post for an ambush. From it comes the occasional mechanical murmur of a walkie-talkie, over the low voices of men. Borojik and Allard have been a little off; they move in closer to the group.)

Allard: *(Low: surly)* I don't know why **I'm** here.

Borojik: *(Tense: irritable)* Don't you? Then bugger off — *(The sergeant is bending over his walkie-talkie in the darkness of the hut: Walker and Reilly beside him: the reports come through the speaker)*

WT: Station 3 — all quiet

WT: Station 4 — Nothing to report, sergeant —

Sergeant: Station 5 — come in, station 5 — over —

WT: Station 5 — all set up — nothing to report yet

Sergeant: All stations — no more negative reports. Only if you sight 'em now — *(Snaps at the murmers behind him)* And no talking.

Walker: *(Irritably)* They must be on the move now — Christ! I'm freezing —

Sergeant: *(Sharper)* You too, Mr. Walker. Better get back with the rest —
(Walker moves back from the sergeant to join Borojik and Allard and Reilly)

Walker: Borojik —?

Borojik: Here —

Walker: *(Slight laugh: soft excitement)* Quite a command post, eh? — he knows his job, that cop. He's got fifty men in the woods and along the river — there won't be a rabbit get through. *(Slight, unpleasant meaning)* You still here, Allard?

Allard: *(Dourly)* Still here.

Borojik: *(Touch of sharpness)* I brought him, Walker — and he'll stay as long as he likes.

Walker: Why not? Just thought it might be painful for him if —

Allard: *(Cuts him off)* I'll worry about that.

Walker: Place seem familiar to you?

Allard: The mill? It might if I could see it. It was a couple of hundred years old when I was born.

Walker: *(Irony)* Very clever choice — very. They figured to get in by water and out by water — no tracks. But they didn't make much of a job of hiding their boat. When one of the men found it the game was up — led us straight to the mill. *(Chuckle)* They're amateurs, all right —

Borojik: *(Dour scepticism)* They must be — if they're coming back when they know you've found the boat.

Walker: They don't know. We left it right where it was. And there's a pea-green watchman playing sick at the plant — they're busy grilling him now. Scared stiff — wanting to be let off duty —

Borojik: Why?

Walker: Because he's had a warning — he knows there's something up. They want that powder to hit the plant tonight.

Allard: You think. Where did they find the boat?

Walker: Oh — about a mile from the place where we found the car — the one your brother took. *(Slight pause)* Sorry about this, Allard — sorry for everything. But we've got a job to do.

Allard: And my God how you love it.

Borojik: *(Stirs: moodily impatient)* Shut up, Allard! Isn't this bad enough? *(Fretfully)* Eleven-twenty-five already — I still don't believe they'll —
(Stops: the sergeant's walkie-talkie has started up)

WT: *(Soft excitement)* Station 3 — boat passing, sergeant — it's them —

Sergeant: Station 2 — come in station 2 —

WT: Station 2 — we can see 'em now — they're slowing — there's a bit of ice ahead —

Walker: *(Grim elation)* Freeze-up coming to-night — they waited too long —

Borojik: Shut up !

Sergeant: Quiet back there, please —

WT: *(Touch of more excitement)* Station 2 — they're leaving the boat, sergeant — can't get it any further —

Sergeant: Don't have to — they're damn near here. Come in, Station 1 — sighted 'em yet —?

WT: Station 1 — Nothing here yet — they might have gone off through — no — wait — here they come — turning up for the mill — stopping — some kind of conference or something — no — they're putting on hoods — three — four — six men altogether —

Sergeant: Any weapons?

WT: No sign of 'em — on the move again — making for the path — over to Station 5 —

Sergeant: Come in, Station 5 —

WT: Station 5. Can't see 'em yet, but we can hear 'em — bush crackling — trail twists like hell, but — *(Excitement)* Now! — here they come — they're making for the mill door —

Walker: *(Excitement)* That'll be the one down there —

Sergeant: *(Tensely)* Quiet! *(Into WT: softly)* Mill party close on the door —

WT: Acknowledge. Mill party closing on the door —

Borojik: *(A soft catch: points down toward door in mill wall: there is a blur of moving figures separating one by one from the darkness)*

Walker: *(Soft chuckle)* Rats in the trap, by God — rats in the trap —

Sergeant: *(Watching: counting figures to himself as they appear)* Three — four — five — six. *(Pause: into WT)* Mill party, move in — *(To policeman near him)* Gimme that loud hailer —

Voice: *(Off: sudden and loud)* Lights —! *(The side of the wall and the door are suddenly illuminated in a blaze of spotlights. The six hooded figures turn: startled and dazzled: a panicky cry or two.)*

Allard: *(Pity and anguish: the cry is jerked out of him)* ANDRE —!

Sergeant: *(Voice hard and metallic: through loud hailer)* Stand still — this is the police. *(Another stir of panic : a man turns wildly to run: bumps into a tree: staggers back)*

Borojik: The damned lights are blinding 'em —

Sergeant: *(Loud hailer)* Not a move. We're all round you. Stand up — hands on your heads — line up facing the lights — *(Sharper)* Facing 'em, I said — stand still! *(Pause)* Mill party close and take 'em —

(Police begin to emerge from woods: move toward the men)

Walker: *(Jubilantly)* And get those hoods off the bastards — let's have a look at their faces!

Sergeant: *(Turns on him: furiously)* Shut up, you goddamn English vulture! *(Formally into loud hailer)* Remove the prisoners' hoods. *(Policemen move to do so. One after one the young faces stand revealed, looking up at the lights. One by one Allard expects André. He gives a soft gasp as the sixth one stands revealed. Borojik stands watching him)*

Allard: Not there —

Borojik: Good.

Allard: But — *(Breath: anguish)* Oh my God — look at 'em!

Borojik: *(Nods: quietly)* Know what you're here for now?

(Francois's home-office. Night. He is opening the door to Allard. Allard comes in; tired, cold, certain of what he will find.)

Allard: *(Tired quiet)* Hello, Francois. Not gone to bed yet?

Francois: Come in, Jean-Pierre — I have been expecting you.

Allard: Yes — I should have thought of it before. Maybe I did — I'm a bit confused right now. Where is he?

Francois: Just in the bedroom there — sleeping. He's been sleeping most of the day.

Allard: Needed it, I imagine. Came to you when he ditched the car last night — was that it?

Francois: It was five o'clock in the morning — he had taken a long way round.

Allard: *(Breath)* God — he's had three days of it! — ducking, hiding, lying around in the cold —

Francois: He is young. He will get over that.

Allard: Oh yes. He'll get over that, all right, but — *(Stops)* *(André comes in from another room)*

André: Hello, Jean-Pierre.

Allard: *(Moved: restraining it)* Hello, kid. *(Pause)* We got six — terrorists — tonight.

André: *(Repeats the word with a touch of scorn)* Terrorists! *(Dully: unsurprised)* So that is that.

Allard: All from around here — three from your class in school. Oldest twenty, the youngest fifteen.

André: *(Brooding quiet)* Hmph. Three months they are talking about it — them and a dozen others. The plant is wide open — we can easy steal some dynamite — and blow a hole in the fence! Not in the plant, mind you — some of their fathers work there. *(Angry mimicry)* This is symbolic destruction — this is the great message — this will scare out the foreigners and leave us rich and free! It is no good arguing with the stupid meatheads — they just keep yelling louder. And then they go out and do it — because Papa leaves the barn door open — it's a chance to swipe our truck!

Allard: When did you find out?

André: That was the phone call. They had the stuff in the root house and the truck back in the barn, and they knew they were in trouble already. Only, so was I. So I have to come down and try to get 'em out of it — we lug it off through the woods, pinch a boat on the creek and move the stuff to the mill. That was a night, I tell you! I want 'em to leave it rot there — forget they ever saw it — but oh no — the heroes still got lungs — they are going through with it. Not me. I come home to change my tires and to hell with them all — but — then it is your friend — Reilly. It is all up with them now — I have to get back and tell them — but — when you are running round like a rabbit it is hard to do — even to make a phone call. Did Lise get through to that watchman?

Allard: *(Startled)* Lise? She was the one who called him?

André: So that worked. It was the only thing that did. Started off in the car and had to ditch it — the roads are full of police. I duck back to the woods — it is five miles round to the mill — I am half dead when I get there and when I do — nobody — the place is empty. I don't know where they went —

Allard: I do. It's all in their statements now. They were cold and wet and hungry and out of grub. So they went back down the river, hid the boat on the bank, and went off across the highway to an all-night hamburger joint — one of their uncles runs it —

André: René's place — I never thought of that. He don't like trouble much, but he wouldn't have turned 'em in —

Allard: No. But by the time he'd filled 'em up it was nearly dawn — no getting back to the mill. So they had to wait for the next night, and they spent the day in his cellar.

E44

André: *(Contempt)* Making speeches to each other — trying on those hoods. Sounds like 'em, all right — that's the way they work. Anyway, I don't know it — I see they're gone from the mill. I think they have got smart — I think maybe it's off. Maybe I wanted to think it — I don't know. Anyway, this is the finish — nothing more I can do — I am done in. So I come back here and — sleep.

Allard: *(Softly)* My — God! And you couldn't have come to me?

André: What for? Where were you? Anyway — they were my friends, God damn 'em — *(Pause)* And now they will go to jail — it is six more of us — wasted — *(Bitterly)* Fools! — like apes with a watch — smash what you can't understand, what you don't know how to use. They don't know where to turn — they got nothing left to hold onto. They are afraid of the English, they are afraid of Italians and Germans — they are afraid of machines and ideas and computers and education — they are afraid of everything in the world! Me, I am not afraid. I am going to use it all. I am going to live in the world and live — French.

Allard: *(Bleakly)* Great — where?

André: Anywhere. Right here. For me, Jean-Pierre, it is going to be different from you. Sure I will talk English — Sure I will work with the English — but they will damn well have to push over — they will have to make room for me — the way I am. *(Pause)* You think that's a crazy dream?

Allard: Maybe. And maybe I'd like a piece of it.

André: You? The big English Vice-President — the hand-made company man? You are forty-two, Jean-Pierre, and you are dead already. Better go back to Peru.

Allard: *(Absorbs it: breath: quietly)* Yeah. Well — I suppose the police will be coming round for your story, but they know most of it now. Better go back and sleep.

(Allard goes out)

Francois: *(To André: gentle reproach)* You hurt him like that because you are hurt yourself — little boy. But he is aching as much as you now — with the old pain.

(Church steps. Night. Clear, moonlight, a slight powdering of snow on the ground. Mass is over, a Christmas carol sounds from the belfry, the last few of the people are coming out, Borojik among them. As he comes to the bottom of the steps, Allard is coming toward him)

Allard: *(Quiet: subdued)* Stayed to the end, did you?

Borojik: *(Slight start of surprise)* I didn't see you in there.

Allard: I wasn't. I was out here. So you are one of the flock?

Borojik: *(Shrugs)* Christmas time, anyway. I like midnight mass. *(Slight constraint)* I took a look round for you, but —

Allard: Not tonight. There'd be six families in there not looking at anybody, and another hundred or so with their eyes on me. I walked round the town instead. *(Pause)* What have you done with the Scot? — did you leave her back at the hotel?

Borojik: She — didn't come down, after all. Maybe she won't be coming. But she sent a message for you.

Allard: Message?

Borojik: She's got the two halves of a letter of resignation, torn up in her in–basket. *(Pause)* Mitchell's not stupid, you know.

Allard: No. He just wants a man who can — feel this place in his guts — whatever that means. And then do something about it — work miracles. Tie up the past with the present and make them like it. Turn out English Frenchmen and French Englishmen. Creating a new species — that's about the size of the job.

Borojik: *(Dryly)* The picture's a bit — large-screen — isn't it? You'd only be running a plant.

Allard: Would I? I'll let you talk to my brother — both my brothers. *(They listen for a moment as the bells drift into another carol)*

Allard: *(Listening)* That's one I always liked.

Canned now, I suppose — canned in the U.S. Used to be old Ti Langlois pulling a bellrope. No more sleighs and sleigh-bells — cars now, and asphalt parking lots —

Borojik: But the old spire in the moonlight — still there.

Allard: Umm. *(Pause)* There was a stone church before that, and a frame one before that, and the first one was logs — burnt by the Indians. My great-great-grandfather went up with it, and the great-great-grandfathers of a lot of others round here. This was good earth before the damned parking lots and supermarkets and split-levels and plants came along — there was bones and blood and history in it. **Our** bones, **our** blood, **our** history —

Borojik: I know —

Allard: *(Shortly)* You don't know. Nobody knows but us. Why should it mean a thing? — don't ask me. All I know is, it's a life's work to get rid of it — and God help you if you succeed. You work and run and drive yourself, and you keep your eye on the job — you think Imperial Ajax. You don't ask yourself questions because you don't dare face the answers. You talk English like the English, you talk American like the Americans — and you end up — nothing.

Borojik: *(Gently)* If that's the way you want it. Things change sometimes —

Allard: Yeah. *(Breath)* How about buying me a drink, down at the hotel?

Borojik: *(A little surprised)* Of course — if you like —

Allard: I know. A couple of thousand years ago I asked you home for a reveillon — you and the Scot. Wouldn't work out tonight — it was bad enough all day.

Borojik: *(Nods)* Well — shall we —

Allard: *(Abrupt quiet)* Wait —

(He is looking off: sees someone coming. Borojik sees too: puts a hand on Allard's shoulder: turns away)

Borojik: Good night, Allard. Good luck.

(He walks out. Lise comes in, moves deliberately to Allard)

Allard: Hello, Lise. Been over at the presbytère?

Lise: Yes.

(She stands: waiting: the pause grows a little long)

Allard: Well — where to now?

Lise: Home — to my husband's bed. Wherever that may be.

Allard: *(Slight, constrained laugh)* You've been having a talk with the curé. It was — pretty predictable advice.

Lise: He said I owe it to the child.

Allard: Child?

Lise: Those — headaches, Jean-Pierre — did you really believe I went to the doctor for them?

Allard: No —

Lise: Headaches I have always had — I suppose I always will. And I know well enough why. But this — there will be a child. He is three months on the way. *(As he absorbs it)* And now you are angry again.

Allard: *(Vaguely)* Angry? I think I guessed it. *(Pause)* 'He' —?

Lise: I hope so. The first a son — it is better. For us — probably the only one.

Allard: *(Nods)* Another of those night thoughts. I've been sweating it out with the rest.

Lise: The rest?

Allard: *(Moved)* He could have been one of them. Those six kids in the lights last night — how many more like that? — how many? — is that what's waiting for **him**? And he'd be better than me at that — he'd feel **something**! *(Desperately)* I'm smashed, Lise — empty — I haven't got anything left!

Lise: No, Jean-Pierre — no — we will go away —

Allard: *(Raises his eyes to her; steadily)* As what? *(It stops her: he turns a little away)* How do you live with the man in your own skin? How do you start to look for him? He's here, Lise, if he's anywhere, doing this bloody job — Mitchell's job. *(Short, grim little exclamation)* What's eating their guts, he wants to know. Maybe he'll find out yet.

Curtain